Java Program Design

Principles, Polymorphism, and Patterns

Edward Sciore

Apress®

Java Program Design: Principles, Polymorphism, and Patterns

Edward Sciore
Newton, MA, USA

ISBN-13 (pbk): 978-1-4842-4142-4   ISBN-13 (electronic): 978-1-4842-4143-1
https://doi.org/10.1007/978-1-4842-4143-1

Library of Congress Control Number: 2018965461

Managing Director, Apress Media LLC: Welmoed Spahr
Acquisitions Editor: Jonathan Gennick
Development Editor: Laura Berendson
Coordinating Editor: Jill Balzano

Cover image designed by Freepik (www.freepik.com)

Distributed to the book trade worldwide by Springer Science+Business Media New York, 233 Spring Street, 6th Floor, New York, NY 10013. Phone 1-800-SPRINGER, fax (201) 348-4505, e-mail orders-ny@springer-sbm.com, or visit www.springeronline.com. Apress Media, LLC is a California LLC and the sole member (owner) is Springer Science + Business Media Finance Inc (SSBM Finance Inc). SSBM Finance Inc is a **Delaware** corporation.

For information on translations, please e-mail rights@apress.com, or visit www.apress.com/rights-permissions.

Apress titles may be purchased in bulk for academic, corporate, or promotional use. eBook versions and licenses are also available for most titles. For more information, reference our Print and eBook Bulk Sales web page at www.apress.com/bulk-sales.

Any source code or other supplementary material referenced by the author in this book is available to readers on GitHub via the book's product page, located at www.apress.com/9781484241424. For more detailed information, please visit www.apress.com/source-code.

Printed on acid-free paper

Table of Contents

About the Author

Edward Sciore is a recently retired Associate Professor at Boston College, who gleefully taught computer science to college students for over 35 years. This book is the result of his experiences teaching courses on Java programming, object-oriented design, and software engineering. Edward is author of *Understanding Oracle APEX 5 Application Development* (Apress, 2015) and *Database Design and Implementation* (Wiley, 2008).

About the Technical Reviewer

 **Alexandru Jecan** is a senior software engineer, consultant, author, trainer and speaker currently residing in Munich, Germany. He earned a degree in computer science from the Technical University of Cluj-Napoca, Romania. Alexandru is the author of the "Java 9 Modularity Revealed" book and is currently writing another book on Eclipse MicroProfile - all for Apress. He speaks at tech conferences and user groups, both in Europe and the United States, on different topics related to software development and software technologies. He is also involved in the Java community. In his spare time, Alexandru likes to spend time with his wonderful wife. Whenever he gets some free time, he likes to read and to develop tools for the GitHub Marketplace. He also likes to play sports like soccer and tennis and to go skiing in the mountains. You can follow Alexandru on Twitter at @alexandrujecan, read his tech blog at www.alexandrujecan.com, or email him at alexandrujecan@gmail.com. If you would like to join Alexandru in his endeavor to build world class tools that enhance work productivity, feel free to contact him. He'll be glad to discuss with you.

Acknowledgments

My interest in object-oriented programming began in the mid-1980s, and steadily increased over the years as the discipline developed and matured. I am indebted to those who helped introduce the "big ideas" along the way, as well as those who filled in the gaps. I view this book as a consolidation of the current state of the discipline, and hope it will help others appreciate the power and potential of the object-oriented approach to programming.

My editor at Apress, Jonathan Gennick, has been unconditionally supportive during the entire process. I think of him as a friend that I have never met. Perhaps some day....

My daughter, Leah Schneider, wanted to know more about object orientation for her job, so I had her preview an early draft of the book. Her enthusiasm for each chapter was gratifying. I appreciate the time she put in and the comments she made. She is wonderful. She is also a stickler for good grammar and mercilessly hounded me about my inappropriate overuse of commas. She was, of course, correct, and I did my best to tighten things up, except perhaps for this sentence, where I couldn't help myself.

Finally, I need to acknowledge my wife, Amy Schneider, who supported me far more than she realizes—through discussions, proofreading, explaining comma usage, and by simply being there. Thanks for everything.

Introduction

This book is concerned with the following topic: *How to use the object-oriented programming facilities of Java effectively*. There are several reasons why you might find this book useful.

Perhaps you are one of the many Java programmers who don't know a lot about object orientation. You can use classes and write simple ones, and may even have written an interface or a subclass. But you don't really get the point of it. You don't see (let alone appreciate) the power and expressiveness of an object-oriented program design. This book will give you that understanding and appreciation.

Or perhaps you are comfortable with object-oriented concepts and appreciate the usefulness of polymorphism. You might have even dabbled with design patterns. They seem like a good idea, and everyone talks about them, but you don't really understand how to use them in your own programs. This book will show you the underlying intent of the patterns, how their techniques can become a seamless addition to your programming toolbox, and how you can adapt their solutions to fit the needs of a given situation.

The Java library has a vast number of classes. You are probably comfortable with some of these classes, such as `String`, `ArrayList`, and `HashMap`, but you may have encountered other classes whose intent seems obscure. For example, perhaps you were told that you should always combine a `BufferedReader` with a `FileReader` when reading from a text file, but you never understood why things have to be so complicated. And what about all the other `Reader` subclasses—when should they be used? This book can help you make sense of the Java library. Many of its classes are organized around design patterns, and understanding the pattern helps to understand why the classes are the way they are and how they should be used.

Design patterns were introduced by Gamma, Held, Johnson, and Vlissides in their seminal 1994 book. The Java language has several features that support the use of these patterns. For example, the `Iterable` and `Iterator` interfaces support the iterator pattern, the `Observable` class and `Observer` interface support the observer pattern, and the `Stream` and `Consumer` interfaces support the visitor pattern. In addition, the availability of lambda expressions in Java makes it possible to reformulate several design patterns more simply and organically. I view this book as a *modern* treatment of design patterns because it presents them from the standpoint of modern Java. My goal is to show how design patterns arise naturally from the principles of object-oriented design. Although this book does not cover all design patterns, I am confident that it will give you the tools you need to more deeply understand other patterns you may read about.

This book illustrates object-oriented concepts by taking examples from the Java class library. Many of the library classes are well designed, and it is instructive to examine their designs and implementations. Some library classes have questionable designs, and it is equally instructive to examine their defects and consider alternatives.

The book also has an extensive running example, which is the design of a simplified banking program. The first version of the program appears in Chapter 1, and consists of a single, non–object-oriented class. New versions are created throughout the book, as each new concept is introduced. By the end of Chapter 11, the example will have expanded to encompass five programs, containing 53 classes and interfaces. I hope that you will enjoy following its development as you read the book, and appreciate how the different design concepts can interact to produce an elegant, nontrivial architecture.

Needless to say, these examples constitute a lot of code. To save space and enhance readability, not all of the code appears in the book. When a class is being discussed, only the portion of the class relevant to the discussion is shown. Import declarations are always omitted.

A good way to examine the example code is to use a Java editor or IDE. Complete working versions of all files mentioned in the text are available from the Apress website, and I encourage you to download them. Included with the files is a README file that explains the scope of the code and how to install it. Each package also has a README file that explains the purpose of its source files. While writing this book, I found it useful (and often necessary) to have the code in an IDE on my computer so that I could consult it and execute it. I expect that the source code files will be equally useful to you as you read the book.

CHAPTER 1

Modular Software Design

When a beginning programmer writes a program, there is one goal: the program must work correctly. However, correctness is only a part of what makes a program good. Another, equally important part is that the program be maintainable.

Perhaps you have experienced the frustration of installing a new version of some software, only to discover that its performance has degraded and one of the features you depend on no longer works. Such situations occur when a new feature changes the existing software in ways that other features did not expect.

Good software is intentionally designed so that these unexpected interactions cannot occur. This chapter discusses the characteristics of well-designed software and introduces several rules that facilitate its development.

Designing for Change

Software development typically follows an iterative approach. You create a version, let users try it, and receive change requests to be addressed in the next version. These change requests may include bug fixes, revisions of misunderstandings of how the software should work, and feature enhancements.

© Edward Sciore 2019

E. Sciore, *Java Program Design*, https://doi.org/10.1007/978-1-4842-4143-1_1

There are two common development methodologies. In the *waterfall* methodology, you begin by creating a design for the program, iteratively revising the design until users are happy. Then you write the entire program, hoping that the first version will be satisfactory. It rarely is. Even if you manage to implement the design perfectly, users will undoubtedly discover new features that they hadn't realized they wanted.

In the *agile* methodology, program design and implementation occur in tandem. You start by implementing a bare-bones version of the program. Each subsequent version implements a small number of additional features. The idea is that each version contains "just enough" code to make the chosen subset of features work.

Both methodologies have their own benefits. But regardless of which methodology is used, a program will go through several versions during its development. Waterfall development typically has fewer iterations, but the scope of each version change is unpredictable. Agile development plans for frequent iterations with small, predictable changes.

The bottom line is that programs always change. If a program doesn't work the way users expect then it will need to be fixed. If a program does work the way users expect then they will want it to be enhanced. It is therefore important to design your programs so that requested changes can be made easily, with minimal modification to the existing code.

Suppose that you need to modify a line of code in a program. You will also need to modify the other lines of code that are impacted by this modification, then the lines that are impacted by those modifications, and so on. As this proliferation increases, the modification becomes more difficult, time-consuming, and error prone. Therefore, your goal should be to design the program such that a change to any part of it will affect only a small portion of the overall code.

This idea can be expressed in the following design principle. Because this principle is the driving force behind nearly all the design techniques in this book, I call it the *fundamental design principle*.

The Fundamental Principle of Software Design

A program should be designed so that any change to it
will affect only a small, predictable portion of the code.

For a simple illustration of the fundamental design principle, consider
the concept of variable scope. The *scope* of a variable is the region of
the program where that variable can be legally referenced. In Java, a
variable's scope is determined by where it is declared. If the variable is
declared outside of a class then it can be referenced from any of the class's
methods. It is said to have *global* scope. If the variable is declared within a
method then it can be referenced only from within the code block where it
is declared, and is said to have *local* scope.

Consider the class ScopeDemo in Listing 1-1. There are four variables:
x, z, and two versions of y. These variables have different scopes.
Variable x has the largest scope; it can be referenced from anywhere in
the class. Variable y in method f can only be accessed from within that
method, and similarly for variable y in g. Variable z can only be accessed
from within f's for-loop.

Listing 1-1. The ScopeDemo Class

```java
public class ScopeDemo {
    private int x = 1;

    public void f() {
        int y = 2;
        for (int z=3; z<10; z++) {
            System.out.println(x+y+z);
        }
        ...
    }
```

```
public void g() {
    int y = 7;
    ...
}
}
```

Why should a programmer care about variable scoping? Why not just define all variables globally? The answer comes from the fundamental design principle. Any change to the definition or intended use of a variable could potentially impact each line of code within its scope. Suppose that I decide to modify ScopeDemo so that the variable y in method f has a different name. Because of y's scope, I know that I only need to look at method f, even though a variable named y is also mentioned in method g. On the other hand, if I decide to rename variable x then I am forced to look at the entire class.

In general, the smaller the scope of a variable, the fewer the lines of code that can be affected by a change. Consequently, the fundamental design principle implies that each variable should have the smallest possible scope.

Object-Oriented Basics

Objects are the fundamental building blocks of Java programs. Each object belongs to a *class*, which defines the object's capabilities in terms of its public variables and methods. This section introduces some object-oriented concepts and terminology necessary for the rest of the chapter.

APIs and Dependencies

The public variables and methods of a class are called its *Application Program Interface* (or API). The designer of a class is expected to document the meaning of each item in its API. Java has the Javadoc tool specifically for this purpose. The Java 9 class library has an extensive collection of Javadoc pages, available at the URL https://docs.oracle.com/javase/9/docs/api. If you want to learn how a class from the Java library works then this is the first place to look.

Suppose the code for a class X holds an object of class Y and uses it to call one of Y's methods. Then X is called a *client* of Y. Listing 1-2 shows a simple example, in which StringClient is a client of String.

Listing 1-2. The StringClient Class

```java
public class StringClient {
    public static void main(String[] args) {
        String s = "abc";
        System.out.println(s.length());
    }
}
```

A class's API is a contract between the class and its clients. The code for StringClient implies that the class String must have a method length that satisfies its documented behavior. However, the StringClient code has no idea of or control over how String computes that length. This is a good thing, because it allows the Java library to change the implementation of the length method as long as the method continues to satisfy the contract.

If X is a client of Y then Y is said to be a *dependency* of X. The idea is that X depends on Y to not change the behavior of its methods. If the API for class Y does change then the code for X may need to be changed as well.

Modularity

Treating an API as a contract simplifies the way that large programs get written. A large program is organized into multiple classes. Each class is implemented independently of the other classes, under the assumption that each method it calls will eventually be implemented and do what it is expected to do. When all classes are written and debugged, they can be combined to create the final program.

This design strategy has several benefits. Each class will have a limited scope and thus will be easier to program and debug. Moreover, the classes can be written simultaneously by multiple people, resulting in the program getting completed more quickly.

We say that such programs are *modular*. Modularity is a necessity; good programs are always modular. However, modularity is not enough. There are also important issues related to the design of each class and the connections between the classes. The design rules later in this chapter will address these issues.

Class Diagrams

A *class diagram* depicts the functionality of each class in a program and the dependencies between these classes. A class diagram has a rectangle for each class. The rectangles have three sections: the top section contains the name of the class, the middle section contains variable declarations, and the bottom section contains method declarations. If class Y is a dependency of class X then the rectangle for X will have an arrow to the rectangle for Y. The arrow can be read "uses," as in "StringClient uses String." Figure 1-1 shows a class diagram for the code of Listing 1-2.

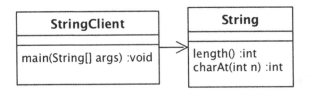

Figure 1-1. *A class diagram for Listing 1-2*

Class diagrams belong to a standard notational system known as UML (for *Universal Modeling Language*). UML class diagrams can have many more features than described here. Each variable and method can specify its visibility (such as *public* or *private*) and variables can have default values. In addition, the UML notion of dependency is broader and more nuanced. The definition of dependency given here is actually a special kind of UML dependency called an *association*. Although these additional modeling features enable UML class diagrams to more accurately specify a design, they add a complexity that will not be needed in this book and will be ignored.

Class diagrams have different uses during the different phases of a program's development. During the implementation phase, a class diagram documents the variables and methods used in the implementation of each class. It is most useful when it is as detailed as possible, showing all the public and private variables and methods of each class.

During the design phase, a class diagram is a communication tool. Designers use class diagrams to quickly convey the functionality of each class and its role in the overall architecture of the program. Irrelevant classes, variables, methods and arrows may be omitted in order to highlight a critical design decision. Typically, only public variables and methods are placed in these class diagrams. Figure 1-1 is an example of a design-level class diagram: the private variable of type `StringClient` is omitted, as are the unreferenced methods in `String`. Given that this book is about design, it uses design-level class diagrams exclusively. Most of the classes we model will have no public variables, which means that the middle section of each class rectangle will usually be empty.

Static vs. Nonstatic

A *static* variable is a variable that "belongs" to a class. It is shared among all objects of the class. If one object changes the value of a static variable then all objects see that change. On the other hand, a *nonstatic* variable "belongs" to an object of the class. Each object has its own instance of the variable, whose value is assigned independently of the other instances.

For example, consider the class StaticTest in Listing 1-3. A StaticTest object has two variables: a static variable x and a nonstatic variable y. Each time a new StaticTest object is created, it will create a new instance of y and overwrite the previous value of x.

Listing 1-3. The StaticTest Class

```java
public class StaticTest {
    private static int x;
    private int y;

    public StaticTest(int val) {
        x = val;
        y = val;
    }

    public void print() {
        System.out.println(x + " " + y);
    }

    public static int getX() {
        return x;
    }

    public static void main(String[] args) {
        StaticTest s1 = new StaticTest(1);
        s1.print();  //prints "1 1"
```

```
    StaticTest s2 = new StaticTest(2);
    s2.print();  //prints "2 2"
    s1.print();  //prints "2 1"
  }
}
```

Methods can also be static or nonstatic. A static method (such as getX in StaticTest) is not associated with an object. A client can call a static method by using the class name as a prefix. Alternatively, it can call a static method the conventional way, prefixed by a variable of that class.

For example, the two calls to getX in the following code are equivalent. To my mind, the first call to getX is to be preferred because it clearly indicates to the reader that the method is static.

```
StaticTest s1 = new StaticTest(1);
int y = StaticTest.getX();
int z = s1.getX();
```

Because a static method has no associated object, it is not allowed to reference nonstatic variables. For example, the print method in StaticTest would not make sense as a static method because there is no unique variable y that it would be able to reference.

A Banking Demo

Listing 1-4 gives the code for a simple program to manage a fictional bank. This program will be used as a running example throughout the book. The code in Listing 1-4 consists of a single class, named BankProgram, and is version 1 of the demo.

The class BankProgram holds a map that stores the balances of several accounts held by a bank. Each element in the map is a key-value pair. The key is an integer that denotes the account number and its value is the balance of that account, in cents.

Listing 1-4. Version 1 of the Banking Demo

```
public class BankProgram {
   private HashMap<Integer,Integer> accounts
                                  = new HashMap<>();
   private double rate  = 0.01;
   private int nextacct = 0;
   private int current  = -1;
   private Scanner scanner;
   private boolean done = false;

   public static void main(String[] args) {
      BankProgram program = new BankProgram();
      program.run();
   }

   public void run() {
      scanner = new Scanner(System.in);
      while (!done) {
         System.out.print("Enter command (0=quit, 1=new,
                           2=select, 3=deposit, 4=loan,
                           5=show, 6=interest): ");
         int cmd = scanner.nextInt();
         processCommand(cmd);
      }
      scanner.close();
   }

   private void processCommand(int cmd) {
      if      (cmd == 0) quit();
      else if (cmd == 1) newAccount();
      else if (cmd == 2) select();
      else if (cmd == 3) deposit();
```

```
        else if (cmd == 4) authorizeLoan();
        else if (cmd == 5) showAll();
        else if (cmd == 6) addInterest();
        else
            System.out.println("illegal command");
    }
    ... //code for the seven command methods appears here
}
```

The program's run method performs a loop that repeatedly reads commands from the console and executes them. There are seven commands, each of which has a corresponding method.

The quit method sets the global variable done to true, which causes the loop to terminate.

```
private void quit() {
    done = true;
    System.out.println("Goodbye!");
}
```

The global variable current keeps track of the current account. The newAccount method allocates a new account number, makes it current, and assigns it to the map with an initial balance of 0.

```
private void newAccount() {
    current = nextacct++;
    accounts.put(current, 0);
    System.out.println("Your new account number is "
                        + current);
}
```

The select method makes an existing account current. It also prints the account balance.

```
private void select() {
    System.out.print("Enter account#: ");
    current = scanner.nextInt();
    int balance = accounts.get(current);
    System.out.println("The balance of account " + current
                    + " is " + balance);
}
```

The deposit method increases the balance of the current account by a specified number of cents.

```
private void deposit() {
    System.out.print("Enter deposit amount: ");
    int amt = scanner.nextInt();
    int balance = accounts.get(current);
    accounts.put(current, balance+amt);
}
```

The method authorizeLoan determines whether the current account has enough money to be used as collateral for a loan. The criterion is that the account must contain at least half of the loan amount.

```
private void authorizeLoan() {
    System.out.print("Enter loan amount: ");
    int loanamt = scanner.nextInt();
    int balance = accounts.get(current);
    if (balance >= loanamt / 2)
        System.out.println("Your loan is approved");
    else
        System.out.println("Your loan is denied");
}
```

The showAll method prints the balance of every account.

```
private void showAll() {
   Set<Integer> accts = accounts.keySet();
   System.out.println("The bank has " + accts.size()
                  + " accounts.");
   for (int i : accts)
      System.out.println("\tBank account " + i
                  + ": balance=" + accounts.get(i));
}
```

Finally, the addInterest method increases the balance of each account by a fixed interest rate.

```
private void addInterest() {
   Set<Integer> accts = accounts.keySet();
   for (int i : accts) {
      int balance = accounts.get(i);
      int newbalance = (int) (balance * (1 + rate));
      accounts.put(i, newbalance);
   }
}
```

The Single Responsibility Rule

The BankProgram code is correct. But is it any good? Note that the program has multiple areas of responsibility—for example, one responsibility is to handle I/O processing and another responsibility is to manage account information—and both responsibilities are handled by a single class.

Multipurpose classes violate the fundamental design principle. The issue is that each area of responsibility will have different reasons for changing. If these responsibilities are implemented by a single class then the entire class will have to be modified whenever a change occurs to one aspect of it. On the other hand, if each responsibility is assigned to a different class then fewer parts of the program need be modified when a change occurs.

This observation leads to a design rule known as the Single Responsibility rule.

The Single Responsibility Rule

A class should have a single purpose, and
all its methods should be related to that purpose.

A program that satisfies the Single Responsibility rule will be organized into classes, with each class having its own unique responsibility.

Version 2 of the banking demo is an example of such a design. It contains three classes: The class Bank is responsible for the banking information; the class BankClient is responsible for I/O processing; and the class BankProgram is responsible for putting everything together. The class diagram for this design appears in Figure 1-2.

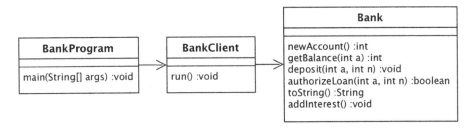

Figure 1-2. *Version 2 of the banking demo*

The code for Bank appears in Listing 1-5. It contains the three variables of version 1 that are relevant to the bank, namely the map of accounts, the interest rate, and the value of the next account number. The six methods in its API correspond to the command methods of version 1 (except for quit).

Their code consists of the code of those methods, with the input/output code stripped out. For example, the code for the newAccount method adds a new account to the map but does not print its information to the console. Instead, it returns the account number to BankClient, which is responsible for printing the information.

Listing 1-5. The Version 2 Bank Class

```
public class Bank {
    private HashMap<Integer,Integer> accounts
                                 = new HashMap<>();
    private double rate = 0.01;
    private int nextacct = 0;

    public int newAccount() {
        int acctnum = nextacct++;
        accounts.put(acctnum, 0);
        return acctnum;
    }

    public int getBalance(int acctnum) {
        return accounts.get(acctnum);
    }

    public void deposit(int acctnum, int amt) {
        int balance = accounts.get(acctnum);
        accounts.put(acctnum, balance+amt);
    }

    public boolean authorizeLoan(int acctnum, int loanamt) {
        int balance = accounts.get(acctnum);
        return balance >= loanamt / 2;
    }
```

```java
    public String toString() {
        Set<Integer> accts = accounts.keySet();
        String result = "The bank has " + accts.size()
                        + " accounts.";
        for (int i : accts)
            result += "\n\tBank account " + i
                    + ": balance=" + accounts.get(i);
        return result;
    }

    public void addInterest() {
        Set<Integer> accts = accounts.keySet();
        for (int i : accts) {
            int balance = accounts.get(i);
            int newbalance = (int) (balance * (1 + rate));
            accounts.put(i, newbalance);
        }
    }
}
```

Similarly, the deposit method is not responsible for asking the user for the deposit amount. Instead, it expects the caller of the method (i.e., BankClient) to pass the amount as an argument.

The authorizeLoan method eliminates both input and output code from the corresponding version 1 method. It expects the loan amount to be passed in as an argument and it returns the decision as a boolean.

The getBalance method corresponds to the select method of version 1. That method is primarily concerned with choosing a current account, which is the responsibility of BankClient. Its only bank-specific code involves obtaining the balance of the selected account. The Bank class therefore has a getBalance method for select to call.

The showAll method in version 1 prints the information of each account. The bank-specific portion of this method is to collect this information into a string, which is the responsibility of Bank's toString method.

The addInterest method in version 1 has no input/output component whatsoever. Consequently, it is identical to the corresponding method in Bank.

The code for BankClient appears in Listing 1-6. It contains the three global variables from version 1 that are related to input/output, namely the current account, the scanner, and the am-I-done flag; it also has an additional variable that holds a reference to the Bank object. BankClient has the public method run and the private method processCommand; these methods are the same as in version 1. The code for the individual command methods is similar; the difference is that all bank-specific code is replaced by a call to the appropriate method of Bank. These statements are written in bold in the listing.

Listing 1-6. The Version 2 BankClient Class

```
public class BankClient {
    private int current = -1;
    private Scanner scanner = new Scanner(System.in);
    private boolean done = false;
    private Bank bank = new Bank();

    public void run() {
        ... // unchanged from version 1
    }

    private void processCommand(int cmd) {
        ... // unchanged from version 1
    }

    private void quit() {
        ... // unchanged from version 1
    }
```

```java
private void newAccount() {
   current = bank.newAccount();
   System.out.println("Your new account number is "
                      + current);
}

private void select() {
   System.out.print("Enter acct#: ");
   current = scanner.nextInt();
   int balance = bank.getBalance(current);
   System.out.println("The balance of account "
                      + current + " is " + balance);
}

private void deposit() {
   System.out.print("Enter deposit amt: ");
   int amt = scanner.nextInt();
   bank.deposit(current, amt);
}

private void authorizeLoan() {
   System.out.print("Enter loan amt: ");
   int loanamt = scanner.nextInt();
   if (bank.authorizeLoan(current, loanamt))
      System.out.println("Your loan is approved");
   else
      System.out.println("Your loan is denied");
}

private void showAll() {
   System.out.println(bank.toString());
}
```

```
   private void addInterest() {
      bank.addInterest();
   }
}
```

The class `BankProgram` contains the `main` method, which parallels the main method of version 1. Its code appears in Listing 1-7.

Listing 1-7. The Version 2 BankProgram Class

```
public class BankProgram {
   public static void main(String[] args) {
      BankClient client = new BankClient();
      client.run();
   }
}
```

Note that version 2 of the banking demo is more easily modifiable than version 1. It is now possible to change the implementation of `Bank` without worrying about breaking the code for `BankClient`. Similarly, it is also possible to change the way that `BankClient` does its input/output, without affecting `Bank` or `BankProgram`.

Refactoring

One interesting feature of the version 2 demo is that it contains nearly the same code as in version 1. In fact, when I wrote version 2 I began by redistributing the existing code between its three classes. This is an example of what is called *refactoring*.

In general, to refactor a program means to make syntactic changes to it without changing the way it works. Examples of refactoring include: renaming a class, method, or variable; changing the implementation of a variable from one data type to another; and splitting a class into two. If you use the Eclipse IDE then you will notice that it has a Refactor menu, which can automatically perform some of the simpler forms of refactoring for you.

Unit Testing

Earlier in this chapter I stated that one of the advantages to a modular program is that each class can be implemented and tested separately. This begs the question: How can you test a class separate from the rest of the program?

The answer is to write a *driver* program for each class. The driver program calls the various methods of the class, passing them sample input and checking that the return values are correct. The idea is that the driver should test all possible ways that the methods can be used. Each way is called a *use case*.

As an example, consider the class BankTest, which appears in Listing 1-8. This class calls some of the Bank methods and tests whether they return expected values. This code only tests a couple of use cases and is far less comprehensive than it ought to be, but the point should be clear.

Listing 1-8. The BankTest Class

```
public class BankTest {
    private static Bank bank = new Bank();
    private static int acct = bank.newAccount();

    public static void main(String[] args) {
        verifyBalance("initial amount", 0);
        bank.deposit(acct, 10);
        verifyBalance("after deposit", 10);
        verifyLoan("authorize bad loan", 22, false);
        verifyLoan("authorize good loan", 20, true);
    }
```

```
private static void verifyBalance(String msg,
                                     int expectedVal) {
    int bal = bank.getBalance(acct);
    boolean ok = (bal == expectedVal);
    String result = ok ? "Good! " : "Bad! ";
    System.out.println(msg + ": " + result);
}

private static void verifyLoan(String msg,
                 int loanAmt, boolean expectedVal) {
    boolean answer = bank.authorizeLoan(acct, loanAmt);
    boolean ok = (answer == expectedVal);
    String result = ok ? "Good! " : "Bad! ";
    System.out.println(msg + ": " + result);
}
}
```

Testing the BankClient class is more difficult, for two reasons. The first is that the class calls a method from another class (namely, Bank). The second is that the class reads input from the console. Let's address each issue in turn.

How can you test a class that calls methods from another class? If that other class is also in development then the driver program will not able to make use of it. In general, a driver program should not use another class unless that class is known to be completely correct; otherwise if the test fails, you don't know which class caused the problem.

The standard approach is to write a trivial implementation of the referenced class, called a *mock* class. Typically, the methods of the mock class print useful diagnostics and return default values. For example, Listing 1-9 shows part of a mock class for Bank.

Listing 1-9. A Mock Implementation of Bank

```java
public class Bank {
   public int newAccount() {
      System.out.println("newAccount called, returning 10");
      return 10;
   }

   public int getBalance(int acctnum) {
      System.out.println("getBalance(" + acctnum
                      + ") called, returning 50");
      return 50;
   }

   public void deposit(int acctnum, int amt) {
      System.out.println("deposit(" + acctnum + ", "
                      + amt + ") called");
   }

   public boolean authorizeLoan(int acctnum,
                              int loanamt) {
      System.out.println("authorizeLoan(" + acctnum
                      + ", " + loanamt
                      + ") called, returning true");
      return true;
   }
   ...
}
```

The best way to test a class that takes input from the console is to redirect its input to come from a file. By placing a comprehensive set of input values into a file, you can easily rerun the driver program with the assurance that the input will be the same each time. You can specify this redirection in several ways, depending on how you execute the program. From Eclipse, for example, you specify redirection in the program's Run Configurations menu.

The class BankProgram makes a pretty good driver program for BankClient. You simply need to create an input file that tests the various commands sufficiently.

Class Design

A program that satisfies the Single Responsibility rule will have a class for each identified responsibility. But how do you know if you have identified all the responsibilities?

The short answer is that you don't. Sometimes, what seems to be a single responsibility can be broken down further. The need for a separate class may become apparent only when additional requirements are added to the program.

For example, consider version 2 of the banking demo. The class Bank stores its account information in a map, where the map's key holds the account numbers and its value holds the associated balances. Suppose now that the bank also wants to store additional information for each account. In particular, assume that the bank wants to know whether the owner of each account is foreign or domestic. How should the program change?

After some quiet reflection, you will realize that the program needs an explicit concept of a bank account. This concept can be implemented as a class; call it BankAccount. The bank's map can then associate a BankAccount object with each account number. These changes form version 3 of the banking demo. Its class diagram appears in Figure 1-3, with new methods in bold.

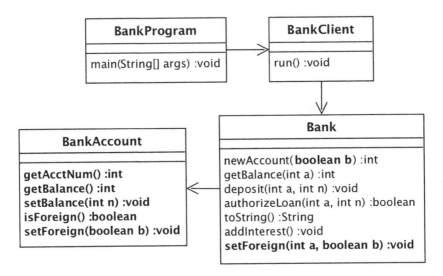

Figure 1-3. *Version 3 of the banking demo*

Listing 1-10 gives the code for the new BankAccount class. It has three global variables, which hold the account number, the balance, and a flag indicating whether the account is foreign. It has methods to retrieve the values of the three variables and to set the value of the balance and isforeign variables.

Listing 1-10. The Version 3 BankAccount Class

```
public class BankAccount {
    private int acctnum;
    private int balance = 0;
    private boolean isforeign = false;

    public BankAccount(int a) {
        acctnum = a;
    }
}
```

```
public int getAcctNum() {
   return acctnum;
}

public int getBalance() {
   return balance;
}

public void setBalance(int amt) {
   balance = amt;
}

public boolean isForeign() {
   return isforeign;
}

public void setForeign(boolean b) {
   isforeign = b;
}
}
```

Listing 1-11 gives the revised code for Bank. Changes are in bold. The class now holds a map of BankAccount objects instead of a map of integers and has code for the new method setForeign.

Listing 1-11. The Version 3 Bank Class

```
public class Bank {
   private HashMap<Integer,BankAccount> accounts
                              = new HashMap<>();
   private double rate = 0.01;
   private int nextacct = 0;
```

```
public int newAccount(boolean isforeign) {
   int acctnum = nextacct++;
   BankAccount ba = new BankAccount(acctnum);
   ba.setForeign(isforeign);
   accounts.put(acctnum, ba);
   return acctnum;
}

public int getBalance(int acctnum) {
   BankAccount ba = accounts.get(acctnum);
   return ba.getBalance();
}

public void deposit(int acctnum, int amt) {
   BankAccount ba = accounts.get(acctnum);
   int balance = ba.getBalance();
   ba.setBalance(balance+amt);
}

public void setForeign(int acctnum,
                       boolean isforeign) {
   BankAccount ba = accounts.get(acctnum);
   ba.setForeign(isforeign);
}

public boolean authorizeLoan(int acctnum, int loanamt) {
   BankAccount ba = accounts.get(acctnum);
   int balance = ba.getBalance();
   return balance >= loanamt / 2;
}

public String toString() {
   String result = "The bank has " + accounts.size()
                   + " accounts.";
```

```
    for (BankAccount ba : accounts.values())
        result += "\n\tBank account "
            + ba.getAcctNum() + ": balance="
            + ba.getBalance() + ", is "
            + (ba.isForeign() ? "foreign" : "domestic");
    return result;
    }

public void addInterest() {
    for (BankAccount ba : accounts.values()) {
        int balance = ba.getBalance();
        balance += (int) (balance * rate);
        ba.setBalance(balance);
    }
  }
}
```

As a result of these changes, obtaining information from an account has become a two-step process: A method first retrieves a BankAccount object from the map; it then calls the desired method on that object. Another difference is that the methods toString and addInterest no longer get each account value individually from the map keys. They instead use the map's values method to retrieve the accounts into a list, which can then be examined.

The BankClient class must be modified to take advantage of Bank's additional functionality. In particular, it now has a new command (command 7) to allow the user to specify whether the account is foreign or domestic, and it modifies the newAccount method to ask for the account's ownership status. The relevant code appears in Listing 1-12.

Listing 1-12. The Version 3 BankClient Class

```
public class BankClient {

    ...

    public void run() {
        while (!done) {
            System.out.print("Enter command (0=quit, 1=new,
                    2=select, 3=deposit, 4=loan,
                    5=show, 6=interest, 7=setforeign): ");
            int cmd = scanner.nextInt();
            processCommand(cmd);
        }
    }

    private void processCommand(int cmd) {
        if      (cmd == 0) quit();
        else if (cmd == 1) newAccount();
        else if (cmd == 2) select();
        else if (cmd == 3) deposit();
        else if (cmd == 4) authorizeLoan();
        else if (cmd == 5) showAll();
        else if (cmd == 6) addInterest();
        else if (cmd == 7) setForeign();
        else
            System.out.println("illegal command");
    }

    private void newAccount() {
        boolean isforeign = requestForeign();
        current = bank.newAccount(isforeign);
        System.out.println("Your new account number is "
                            + current);
    }

    ...
```

```
    private void setForeign() {
       bank.setForeign(current, requestForeign());
    }

    private boolean requestForeign() {
       System.out.print("Enter 1 for foreign,
                          2 for domestic: ");
       int val = scanner.nextInt();
       return (val == 1);
    }
}
```

This relatively minor change to BankClient points out the advantage of modularity. Even though the Bank class changed how it implemented its methods, its contract with BankClient did not change. The only change resulted from the added functionality.

Encapsulation

Let's look more closely at the code for BankAccount in Listing 1-10. Its methods consist of accessors and mutators (otherwise known as "getters" and "setters"). Why use methods? Why not just use public variables, as shown in Listing 1-13? With this class, a client could simply access BankAccount's variables directly instead of having to call its methods.

Listing 1-13. An Alternative BankAccount Class

```
public class BankAccount {
    public int acctnum;
    public int balance = 0;
    public boolean isforeign = false;
```

```
public BankAccount(int a) {
    acctnum = a;
  }
}
```

Although this alternative BankAccount class is far more compact, its design is far less desirable. Here are three reasons to prefer methods over public variables.

The first reason is that methods are able to limit the power of clients. A public variable is equivalent to both an accessor and a mutator method, and having both methods can often be inappropriate. For example, clients of the alternative BankAccount class would have the power to change the account number, which is not a good idea.

The second reason is that methods provide more flexibility than variables. Suppose that at some point after deploying the program, the bank detects the following problem: The interest it adds to the accounts each month is calculated to a fraction of a penny, but that fractional amount winds up getting deleted from the accounts because the balance is stored in an integer variable.

The bank decides to rectify this mistake by changing the balance variable to be a float instead of an integer. If the alternative BankAccount class were used then that change would be a change to the API, which means that all clients that referenced the variable would also need to be modified. On the other hand, if the version 3 BankAccount class is used, the change to the variable is private, and the bank can simply change the implementation of the method getBalance as follows:

```
public int getBalance() {
    return (int) balance;
  }
```

Note that getBalance no longer returns the actual balance of the account. Instead, it returns the amount of money that can be withdrawn from the account, which is consistent with the earlier API. Since the API of BankAccount has not changed, the clients of the class are not aware of the change to the implementation.

The third reason to prefer methods over public variables is that methods can perform additional actions. For example, perhaps the bank wants to log each change to an account's balance. If BankAccount is implemented using methods, then its setBalance method can be modified so that it writes to a log file. If the balance can be accessed via a public variable then no logging is possible.

The desirability of using public methods instead of public variables is an example of a design rule known as the rule of Encapsulation.

The Rule of Encapsulation

A class's implementation details should be hidden from its clients
as much as possible.

In other words, the less that clients are aware of the implementation of a class, the more easily that class can change without affecting its clients.

Redistributing Responsibility

The classes of the version 3 banking demo are modular and encapsulated. Nevertheless, there is something unsatisfactory about the design of their methods. In particular, the BankAccount methods don't do anything interesting. All the work occurs in Bank.

For example, consider the action of depositing money in an account. The bank's deposit method controls the processing. The BankAccount object manages the getting and setting of the bank balance, but it does so under the strict supervision of the Bank object.

This lack of balance between the two classes hints at a violation of the Single Responsibility rule. The intention of the version 3 banking demo was for the Bank class to manage the map of accounts and for the BankAccount class to manage each individual account. However, that didn't occur—the Bank class is also performing activities related to bank accounts. Consider what it would mean for the BankAccount object to have responsibility for deposits. It would have its own deposit method:

```
public void deposit(int amt) {
   balance += amt;
}
```

And the Bank's deposit method would be modified so that it called the deposit method of BankAccount:

```
public void deposit(int acctnum, int amt) {
   BankAccount ba = accounts.get(acctnum);
   ba.deposit(amt);
}
```

In this version, Bank no longer knows how to do deposits. Instead, it delegates the work to the appropriate BankAccount object.

Which version is a better design? The BankAccount object is a more natural place to handle deposits because it holds the account balance. Instead of having the Bank object tell the BankAccount object what to do, it is better to just let the BankAccount object do the work itself. We express this idea as the following design rule, called the Most Qualified Class rule.

The Most Qualified Class Rule

Work should be assigned to the class that knows best how to do it.

Version 4 of the banking demo revises the classes Bank and BankAccount to satisfy the Most Qualified Class rule. Of these classes, only the API for BankAccount needs to change. Figure 1-4 shows the revised class diagram for this class (with changes from version 3 in bold).

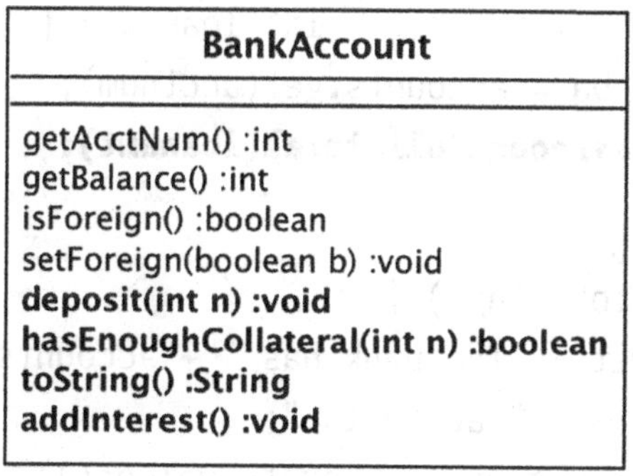

BankAccount
getAcctNum() :int getBalance() :int isForeign() :boolean setForeign(boolean b) :void **deposit(int n) :void** **hasEnoughCollateral(int n) :boolean** **toString() :String** **addInterest() :void**

Figure 1-4. *The version 4 BankAccount class*

The BankAccount class now has methods that correspond to the deposit, toString, and addInterest methods of Bank. The class also has the method hasEnoughCollateral, which (as we shall see) corresponds to Bank's authorizeLoan method. In addition, the class no longer needs the setBalance method.

The code for the classes BankAccount and Bank need to change. The relevant revised code for Bank appears in Listing 1-14, with changes in bold.

Listing 1-14. The Version 4 Bank Class

```
public class Bank {
  ...

  public void deposit(int acctnum, int amt) {
    BankAccount ba = accounts.get(acctnum);
    ba.deposit(amt);
  }

  public boolean authorizeLoan(int acctnum,
                               int loanamt) {
    BankAccount ba = accounts.get(acctnum);
    return ba.hasEnoughCollateral(loanamt);
  }

  public String toString() {
    String result = "The bank has " + accounts.size()
                    + " accounts.";
    for (BankAccount ba : accounts.values())
      result += "\n\t" + ba.toString();
    return result;
  }

  public void addInterest() {
    for (BankAccount ba : accounts.values())
      ba.addInterest();
  }
}
```

As previously discussed, the bank's deposit method is no longer responsible for updating the account balance. Instead, the method calls the corresponding method in BankAccount to perform the update.

The bank's `toString` method is responsible for creating a string representation of all bank accounts. However, it is no longer responsible for formatting each individual account; instead, it calls the `toString` method of each account when needed. The bank's `addInterest` method is similar. The method calls the `addInterest` method of each account, allowing each account to update its own balance.

The bank's `authorizeLoan` method is implemented slightly differently from the others. It calls the bank account's `hasEnoughCollateral` method, passing in the loan amount. The idea is that the decision to authorize a loan should be shared between the Bank and BankAccount classes. The bank account is responsible for comparing the loan amount against its balance. The bank then uses that information as one of its criteria for deciding whether to authorize the loan. In the version 4 code, the collateral information is the only criterion, but in real life the bank would also use criteria such as credit score, employment history, and so on, all of which reside outside of BankAccount. The BankAccount class is responsible only for the "has enough collateral" criterion because that is what it is most qualified to assess.

The four methods added to the BankAccount class appear in Listing 1-15.

Listing 1-15. The Version 4 BankAccount Class

```java
public class BankAccount {
    private double rate = 0.01;
    ...

    public void deposit(int amt) {
        balance += amt;
    }

    public boolean hasEnoughCollateral(int amt) {
        return balance >= amt / 2;
    }
```

```java
    public String toString() {
        return "Bank account " + acctnum + ": balance="
                        + balance + ", is "
                        + (isforeign ? "foreign" : "domestic");
    }

    public void addInterest() {
        balance += (int) (balance * rate);
    }
}
```

Dependency Injection

The Most Qualified Class rule can also be applied to the question of
how to initialize the dependencies of a class. For example consider the
BankClient class, which has dependencies on Scanner and Bank. The
relevant code (taken from Listing 1-6) looks like this:

```java
public class BankClient {
    private Scanner scanner = new Scanner(System.in);
    private Bank bank = new Bank();

    ...
}
```

When the class creates its Scanner object it uses System.in as the
source, indicating that input should come from the console. But why
choose System.in? There are other options. The class could read its input
from a file instead of the console or it could get its input from somewhere
over the Internet. Given that the rest of the BankClient code does not care
what input its scanner is connected to, restricting its use to System.in is
unnecessary and reduces the flexibility of the class.

A similar argument could be made for the bank variable. Suppose that the program gets modified so that it can access multiple banks. The BankClient code does not care which bank it accesses, so how does it decide which bank to use?

The point is that BankClient is not especially qualified to make these decisions and therefore should not be responsible for them. Instead, some other, more qualified class should make the decisions and pass the resulting object references to BankClient. This technique is called *dependency injection*.

Typically, the class that creates an object is most qualified to initialize its dependencies. In such cases an object receives its dependency values via its constructor. This form of dependency injection is called *constructor injection*. Listing 1-16 gives the relevant modifications to BankClient.

Listing 1-16. The Version 4 BankClient Class

```
public class BankClient {
    private int current = -1;
    private Scanner scanner;
    private boolean done = false;
    private Bank bank;

    public BankClient(Scanner scanner, Bank bank) {
        this.scanner = scanner;
        this.bank = bank;
    }
    ...
}
```

The class Bank can be improved similarly. It has one dependency, to its account map, and it also decides the initial value for its nextacct variable. The relevant code (taken from Listing 1-11) looks like this:

```
public class Bank {
    private HashMap<Integer,BankAccount> accounts
                                       = new HashMap<>();
    private int nextacct = 0;
    ...
}
```

The Bank object creates an empty account map, which is unrealistic. In a real program the account map would be constructed by reading a file or accessing a database. As with BankClient, the rest of the Bank code does not care where the account map comes from, and so Bank is not the most qualified class to make that decision. A better design is to use dependency injection to pass the map and the initial value of nextacct to Bank, via its constructor. Listing 1-17 gives the relevant code.

Listing 1-17. The Version 4 Bank Class

```
public class Bank {
    private HashMap<Integer,BankAccount> accounts;
    private int nextacct;

    public Bank(HashMap<Integer,BankAccount> accounts,
                int n) {
        this.accounts = accounts;
        nextacct = n;
    }
    ...
}
```

The version 4 BankProgram class is responsible for creating the Bank and BankClient classes, and thus is also responsible for initializing their dependencies. Its code appears in Listing 1-18.

Listing 1-18. The Version 4 BankProgram Class

```
public class BankProgram {
    public static void main(String[] args) {
        HashMap<Integer,BankAccount> accounts = new HashMap<>();
        Bank bank = new Bank(accounts, 0);
        Scanner scanner = new Scanner(System.in);
        BankClient client = new BankClient(scanner, bank);
        client.run();
    }
}
```

It is interesting to compare versions 3 and 4 of the demo in terms of when objects get created. In version 3 the BankClient object gets created first, followed by its Scanner and Bank objects. The Bank object then creates the account map. In version 4 the objects are created in the reverse order: first the map, then the bank, the scanner, and finally the client. This phenomenon is known as *dependency inversion*— each object is created before the object that depends on it.

Note how BankProgram makes all the decisions about the initial state of the program. Such a class is known as a *configuration class*. A configuration class enables users to reconfigure the behavior of the program by simply modifying the code for that class.

The idea of placing all dependency decisions within a single class is powerful and convenient. In fact, many large programs take this idea one step further. They place all configuration details (i.e., information about the input stream, the name of the stored data file, etc.) into a *configuration file*. The configuration class reads that file and uses it to create the appropriate objects.

The advantage to using a configuration file is that the configuration code never needs to change. Only the configuration file changes. This feature is especially important when the program is being configured by end users who may not know how to program. They modify the configuration file and the program performs the appropriate configurations.

Mediation

The BankClient class in the version 4 banking demo does not know about BankAccount objects. It interacts with accounts solely through methods of the Bank class. The Bank class is called a *mediator*.

Mediation can enhance the modularity of a program. If the Bank class is the only class that can access BankAccount objects then BankAccount is essentially private to Bank. This feature was important when the version 3 BankAccount class was modified to produce version 4; it ensured that the only other class that needed to be modified was Bank. This desirability leads to the following rule, called the rule of Low Coupling.

The Rule of Low Coupling

Try to minimize the number of class dependencies.

This rule is often expressed less formally as "Don't talk to strangers." The idea is that if a concept is strange to a client, or difficult to understand, it is better to mediate access to it.

Another advantage to mediation is that the mediator can keep track of activity on the mediated objects. In the banking demo, Bank must of course mediate the creation of BankAccount objects or its map of accounts will become inaccurate. The Bank class can also use mediation to track the activity of specific accounts. For example, the bank could track deposits into foreign accounts by changing its deposit method to something like this:

```
public void deposit(int acctnum, int amt) {
    BankAccount ba = accounts.get(acctnum);
    if (ba.isForeign())
        writeToLog(acctnum, amt, new Date());
    ba.deposit(amt);
}
```

Design Tradeoffs

The Low Coupling and Single Responsibility rules often conflict with each another. Mediation is a common way to provide low coupling. But a mediator class tends to accumulate methods that are not central to its purpose, which can violate the Single Responsibility rule.

The banking demo provides an example of this conflict. The Bank class has methods getBalance, deposit, and setForeign, even though those methods are the responsibility of BankAccount. But Bank needs to have those methods because it is mediating between BankClient and BankAccount.

Another design possibility is to forget about mediation and let BankClient access BankAccount objects directly. A class diagram of the resulting architecture appears in Figure 1-5. In this design, the variable current in BankClient would be a BankAccount reference instead of an account number. The code for its getBalance, deposit, and setForeign commands can therefore call the corresponding methods of BankAccount directly. Consequently, Bank does not need these methods and has a simpler API. Moreover, the client can pass the reference of the desired bank account to the bank's authorizeLoan method instead of an account number, which improves efficiency.

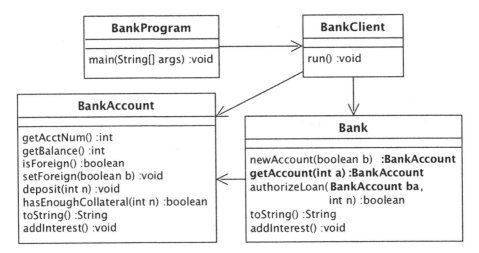

Figure 1-5. *Bank is no longer a mediator*

Would this new design be an improvement over the version 4 banking demo? Neither design is obviously better than the other. Each involves different tradeoffs: Version 4 has lower coupling, whereas the new design has simpler APIs that satisfy the Single Responsibility rule better. For the purposes of this book, I chose to go with version 4 because I felt that it was important for Bank to be able to mediate access to the accounts.

The point is that design rules are only guidelines. Tradeoffs are almost always necessary in any significant program. The best design will probably violate at least one rule somehow. The role of a designer is to recognize the possible designs for a given program and accurately analyze their tradeoffs.

The Design of Java Maps

As a real-life example of some design tradeoffs, consider the Map classes in the Java library. The typical way to implement a map is to store each key-value pair as a node. The nodes are then inserted into a hash table (for a HashMap object) or a search tree (for a TreeMap object). In Java, these nodes have the type Map.Entry.

Clients of a map typically do not interact with Map.Entry objects. Instead, clients call the Map methods get and put. Given a key, the get method locates the entry having that key and returns its associated value; the put method locates the entry having that key and changes its value. If a client wants to examine all entries in the map then it can call the method keySet to get all keys, and then repeatedly call get to find their associated values. Listing 1-19 gives some example code. The first portion of the code puts the entries ["a",1] and ["b",4] into the map and then retrieves the value associated with the key "a". The second portion prints each entry in the map.

Listing 1-19. Typical Uses of a HashMap

```java
HashMap<String,Integer> m = new HashMap<>();
m.put("a", 1);
m.put("b", 4);
int x = m.get("a");

Set<String> keys = m.keySet();
for(String s: keys) {
   int y = m.get(s);
   System.out.println(s + " " + y);
}
```

This design of HashMap corresponds to the class diagram of Figure 1-6. Note that each HashMap object is a mediator for its underlying Map.Entry objects.

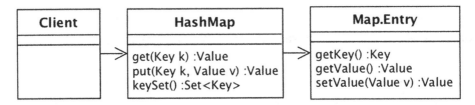

Figure 1-6. *HashMap as a mediator of Map.Entry*

Unfortunately, this mediation can lead to inefficient code. The loop in Listing 1-19 is such an example. The keySet method traverses the entire data structure to acquire all the keys. The get method then has to repeatedly access the data structure again to get the value of each key.

The code would be more efficient if the client code could access the map entries directly. Then it could simply traverse the data structure once, getting each entry and printing its contents. In fact, such a method does exist in HashMap, and is called entrySet. The code in Listing 1-20 is equivalent to Listing 1-19 but is more efficient.

Listing 1-20. Accessing Map Entries Directly

```
HashMap<String,Integer> m = new HashMap<>();
m.put("a", 1);
m.put("b", 4);
int x = m.get("a");

Set<Map.Entry<String,Integer>> entries = m.entrySet();
for (Map.Entry<String,Integer> e : entries) {
    String s = e.getKey();
    int y = e.getValue();
    System.out.println(s + " " + y);
}
```

The existence of the method entrySet changes the class diagram of Figure 1-6. The class HashMap is no longer a mediator of Map.Entry because Map.Entry is now visible to the client. The new class diagram appears in Figure 1-7.

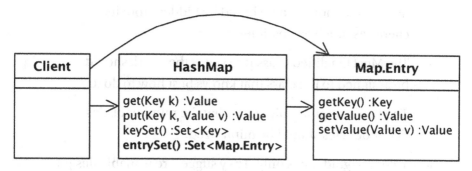

Figure 1-7. *HashMap is no longer a mediator of Map.Entry*

Making the Map.Entry nodes visible to clients increases the complexity of programs that use maps. Clients need to know about two classes instead of just one. Moreover, the API of Map.Entry now cannot be changed without impacting the clients of HashMap. On the other hand, the complexity also makes it possible to write more efficient code.

The designers of HashMap had to take these conflicting needs into consideration. Their solution was to keep the complexity for people who need it but to make it possible to ignore the complex methods if desired.

Summary

Software development must be guided by a concern for program modifiability. The fundamental design principle is that a program should be designed so that any change to it will affect only a small, predictable portion of the code. There are several rules that can help a designer satisfy the fundamental principle.

- The Single Responsibility rule states that a class should have a single purpose, and its methods should all be related to that purpose.

- The Encapsulation rule states that a class's implementation details should be hidden from its clients as much as possible.

- The Most Qualified Class rule states that work should be assigned to the class that knows best how to do it.

- The Low Coupling rule states that the number of class dependencies should be minimized.

These rules are guidelines only. They suggest reasonable design decisions for most situations. As you design your programs, you must always understand the tradeoffs involved with following (or not following) a particular rule.

CHAPTER 2

Polymorphism

Each class in a well-designed program denotes a distinct concept with its own set of responsibilities. Nevertheless, it is possible for two (or more) classes to share some common functionality. For example, the Java classes HashMap and TreeMap are distinct implementations of the concept of a "map," and both support the methods get, put, keySet, and so on. The ability of a program to take advantage of this commonality is known as *polymorphism*.

This chapter explores the use of polymorphism in Java. Java supports polymorphism via the concept of an *interface*. All the techniques in this chapter use interfaces. In fact, polymorphism is so useful that most of the techniques in this book involve interfaces in some way.

It can be argued that polymorphism is the most important design concept in object-oriented programming. A solid understanding of polymorphism (and interfaces) is critical for any good Java programmer.

The Need for Polymorphism

Suppose you have been asked to modify version 4 of the banking demo to support two kinds of bank account: savings accounts and checking accounts. Savings accounts correspond to the bank accounts of version 4. Checking accounts differ from savings accounts in the following three ways:

- When authorizing a loan, a checking account needs a balance of two thirds the loan amount, whereas savings accounts require only one half the loan amount.

© Edward Sciore 2019
E. Sciore, *Java Program Design*, https://doi.org/10.1007/978-1-4842-4143-1_2

- The bank gives periodic interest to savings accounts but not checking accounts.

- The toString method of an account will return "Savings Account" or "Checking Account," as appropriate.

One straightforward (and somewhat naïve) way to implement these two types of accounts would be to modify the code for BankAccount. For example, BankAccount could have a variable that holds the type of the account: a value of 1 denotes a savings account and a value of 2 denotes a checking account. The methods hasEnoughCollateral, toString, and addInterest would use an if-statement to determine which account type to handle. Listing 2-1 shows the basic idea, with relevant code in bold.

Listing 2-1. Using a Variable to Hold the Type of an Account

```java
public class BankAccount {
   ...
   private int type;

   public BankAccount(int acctnum, int type) {
      this.acctnum = acctnum;
      this.type = type;
   }
   ...
   public boolean hasEnoughCollateral(int loanamt) {
      if (type == 1)
         return balance >= loanamt / 2;
      else
         return balance >= 2 * loanamt / 3;
   }
```

```
public String toString() {
   String typename = (type == 1) ?
                            "Savings" : "Checking";
   return typename + " Account " + acctnum
              + ": balance=" + balance + ", is "
              + (isforeign ? "foreign" : "domestic"));
}

public void addInterest() {
   if (type == 1)
      balance += (int)(balance * rate);
}
}
```

Although this code is a straightforward modification to BankAccount, it has two significant problems. First, the if-statements are inefficient. Every time one of the revised methods gets called, it must go through the conditions in its if-statement to determine what code to execute. Moreover, increasing the number of account types will cause these methods to execute more and more slowly.

Second (and more importantly), the code is difficult to modify and thus violates the fundamental design principle. Each time that another account type is added, another condition must be added to each if-statement. This is tedious, time-consuming, and error prone. If you forget to update one of the methods correctly, the resulting bug might be difficult to find.

The way to avoid this if-statement problem is to use a separate class for each type of account. Call these classes SavingsAccount and CheckingAccount. The advantage is that each class can have its own implementation of the methods, so there is no need for an if-statement. Moreover, whenever you need to add another type of bank account you can simply create a new class.

But how then does the Bank class deal with multiple account classes? You don't want the bank to hold a separate map for each type of account because that will just introduce other modifiability problems. For example, suppose that there are several account types that give interest, with each account type having its own map. The code for the addInterest method will need to loop through each map individually, which means that each new account type will require you to add a new loop to the method.

The only good solution is for all account objects, regardless of their class, to be in a single map. Such a map is called *polymorphic*. Java uses interfaces to implement polymorphism. The idea is for version 5 of the banking demo to replace the BankAccount class with a BankAccount interface. That is, the account map will still be defined like this:

```
private HashMap<Integer,BankAccount> accounts;
```

However, BankAccount is now an interface, whose objects can be from either SavingsAccount or CheckingAccount. The next section explains how to implement such a polymorphic map in Java.

Interfaces

A Java *interface* is primarily a named set of method headers. (Interfaces also have other features that will be discussed later in the chapter.) An interface is similar to the API of a class. The difference is that a class's API is inferred from its public methods, whereas an interface specifies the API explicitly without providing any code.

Listing 2-2 shows the code for the version 5 BankAccount interface. It contains a method header for each public method of the version 4 BankAccount class except for addInterest.

Listing 2-2. The Version 5 BankAccount Interface

```
public interface BankAccount {
    public abstract int getAcctNum();
    public abstract int getBalance();
    public abstract boolean isForeign();
    public abstract void setForeign(boolean isforeign);
    public abstract void deposit(int amt);
    public abstract boolean hasEnoughCollateral(int loanamt);
    public abstract String toString();
}
```

The keyword `abstract` indicates that the method declaration contains only the method's header and tells the compiler that its code will be specified elsewhere. The `abstract` and `public` keywords are optional in an interface declaration because interface methods are public and abstract by default. In the rest of the book I will follow common convention and omit the `public abstract` keywords from interface method headers.

The code for an interface's methods is supplied by classes that *implement* the interface. Suppose that I is an interface. A class indicates its intent to implement I by adding the clause `implements I` to its header. If a class implements an interface then it is obligated to implement all methods declared by that interface. The compiler will generate an error if the class does not contain those methods.

In version 5 of the banking demo, the classes `CheckingAccount` and `SavingsAccount` both implement the `BankAccount` interface. Their code appears in Listings 2-3 and 2-4. The code is nearly identical to the version 4 `BankAccount` class of Listing 1-15, so several of the unmodified methods are omitted. Modifications are in bold.

Listing 2-3. The Version 5 SavingsAccount Class

```java
public class SavingsAccount implements BankAccount {
   private double rate = 0.01;
   private int acctnum;
   private int balance = 0;
   private boolean isforeign = false;

   public SavingsAccount(int acctnum) {
      this.acctnum = acctnum;
   }
   ...
   public boolean hasEnoughCollateral(int loanamt) {
      return balance >= loanamt / 2;
   }

   public String toString() {
      return "Savings account " + acctnum
            + ": balance=" + balance
            + ", is " + (isforeign ? "foreign" : "domestic");
   }

   public void addInterest() {
      balance += (int) (balance * rate);
   }
}
```

Listing 2-4. The Version 5 CheckingAccount Class

```java
public class CheckingAccount implements BankAccount {
   // the rate variable is omitted
   private int acctnum;
   private int balance = 0;
   private boolean isforeign = false;
```

```
public CheckingAccount(int acctnum) {
    this.acctnum = acctnum;
}
...
public boolean hasEnoughCollateral(int loanamt) {
    return balance >= 2 * loanamt / 3;
}

public String toString() {
    return "Checking account " + acctnum + ": balance="
                + balance + ", is "
                + (isforeign ? "foreign" : "domestic");
}

// the addInterest method is omitted
}
```

In general, a class may implement any number of interfaces. Its
only obligation is to have code for each method of each interface that it
implements. A class is also free to have methods in addition to the ones
required by its implemented interfaces. For example, SavingsAccount has the
public method addInterest, which is not part of its BankAccount interface.

An interface is denoted in a class diagram by a rectangle, similarly to
a class. The name of the interface goes in the rectangle. To distinguish an
interface from a class, the annotation "<<interface>>" appears above its
name. The interface name and its methods are italicized to emphasize that
they are abstract.

When a class implements an interface, the relationship between the
class and its interface is represented by an arrow having an open head and
a dashed line. The rectangle for the class need not mention the methods
of the interface, because their presence is implied. The class diagram
for the version 5 code appears in Figure 2-1. This diagram asserts that

CheckingAccount and SavingsAccount implement all the methods of
the BankAccount interface, and that SavingsAccount also implements
the method addInterest. Bank has dependencies to BankAccount,
SavingsAccount and CheckingAccount because its code uses variables of
all three types, as will be seen in the next section.

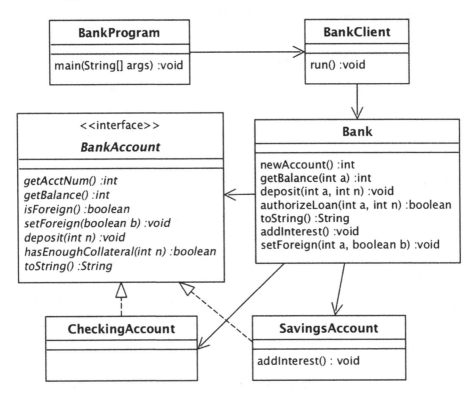

Figure 2-1. *Version 5 of the banking demo*

Reference Types

This section examines how interfaces affect the typing of variables in a Java
program. Each Java variable has a declared type, and this type determines
the kind of value the variable can hold. If a variable holds a basic value
(such as an int or a float) then its type is said to be a *primitive type*. If the
variable holds an object reference then its type is said to be a *reference type*.

Each class and each interface defines a reference type. If a variable is class-typed then it can hold a reference to any object of that class. If a variable is interface-typed then it can hold a reference to any object whose class implements that interface. For example, consider the following two statements:

```
SavingsAccount sa = new SavingsAccount(1);
BankAccount    ba = new SavingsAccount(2);
```

The first statement stores a SavingsAccount reference in the class-typed variable sa. This statement is legal because the class of the object reference is the same as the type of the variable. The second statement stores a SavingsAccount reference in the interface-typed variable ba. This statement is also legal because the class of the object reference implements the type of the variable.

The type of a variable determines which methods the program can invoke on it. A class-typed variable can call only the public methods of that class. An interface-typed variable can call only the methods defined by that interface. Continuing the preceding example, consider these four statements:

```
sa.deposit(100);
sa.addInterest();
ba.deposit(100);
ba.addInterest();  // Illegal!
```

The first two statements are legal because SavingsAccount has the public methods deposit and addInterest. Similarly, the third statement is legal because deposit is declared in BankAccount. The last statement is not legal because addInterest is not part of the BankAccount interface.

This example points out that storing an object reference in an interface-typed variable can "cripple" it. Variables sa and ba both hold similar SavingsAccount references. However, sa can call addInterest whereas ba cannot.

So what is the point of having interface-typed variables? The primary advantage of an interface-typed variable is that it can hold references to objects from different classes. For example, consider the following code:

```
BankAccount ba = new SavingsAccount(1);
ba = new CheckingAccount(2);
```

In the first statement, variable ba holds a SavingsAccount reference. In the second statement, it holds a CheckingAccount reference. Both statements are legal because both classes implement BankAccount. This feature is especially useful when a variable can hold more than one element. For example, consider the following statements.

```
BankAccount[] accts = new BankAccount[2];
accts[0] = new SavingsAccount(1);
accts[1] = new CheckingAccount(2);
```

The variable accts is an array whose elements have the type BankAccount. It is polymorphic because it can store object references from SavingsAccount and CheckingAccount. For example, the following loop deposits 100 into every account of the accts array, regardless of its type.

```
for (int i=0; i<accts.length; i++)
   accts[i].deposit(100);
```

It is now possible to examine the code for the version 5 Bank class. The code appears in Listing 2-5, with changes from version 4 in bold.

Listing 2-5. The Version 5 Bank Class

```
public class Bank {
   private HashMap<Integer,BankAccount> accounts;
   private int nextacct;

   public Bank(HashMap<Integer,BankAccount> accounts) {
      this.accounts = accounts;
      nextacct = n;
   }
```

```java
public int newAccount(int type, boolean isforeign) {
    int acctnum = nextacct++;
    BankAccount ba;
    if (type == 1)
        ba = new SavingsAccount(acctnum);
    else
        ba = new CheckingAccount(acctnum);
    ba.setForeign(isforeign);
    accounts.put(acctnum, ba);
    return acctnum;
}

public int getBalance(int acctnum) {
    BankAccount ba = accounts.get(acctnum);
    return ba.getBalance();
}
...
public void addInterest() {
    for (BankAccount ba : accounts.values())
        if (ba instanceof SavingsAccount) {
            SavingsAccount sa = (SavingsAccount) ba;
            sa.addInterest();
        }
}
}
```

Consider the method newAccount. It now has an additional parameter, which is an integer denoting the account type. The value 1 denotes a savings account and 2 denotes a checking account. The method creates an object of the specified class and stores a reference to it in the variable ba. Because this variable has the type BankAccount, it can hold a reference to either a SavingsAccount or a CheckingAccount object. Consequently, both savings and checking accounts can be stored in the accounts map.

Now consider the method `getBalance`. Since its variable `ba` is interface-typed, the method does not know whether the account it gets from the map is a savings account or a checking account. But it doesn't need to know. The method simply calls `ba.getBalance`, which will execute the code of whichever object `ba` refers to. The omitted methods are similarly polymorphic.

The method `addInterest` is more complex than the other methods. An understanding of this method requires knowing about type safety, which will be discussed next.

Type Safety

The compiler is responsible for assuring that each variable holds a value of the proper type. We say that the compiler assures that the program is *type-safe*. If the compiler cannot guarantee that a value has the proper type then it will refuse to compile that statement. For example, consider the code of Listing 2-6.

Listing 2-6. Testing Type Safety

```
SavingsAccount sa1 = new SavingsAccount(1);
BankAccount ba1 = new CheckingAccount(2);
BankAccount ba2 = sa1;
BankAccount ba3 = new Bank(...);   // Unsafe
SavingsAccount sa2 = ba2;          // Unsafe
```

The first statement stores a reference to a `SavingsAccount` object in a `SavingsAccount` variable. This is clearly type-safe. The second statement stores a reference to a `CheckingAccount` object in a `BankAccount` variable. This is type-safe because `CheckingAccount` implements `BankAccount`. The third statement stores the reference held by `sa1` into a `BankAccount` variable. Since sa1 has the type SavingsAccount, the compiler can infer that its reference must be to a SavingsAccount object and thus can be safely stored in ba2 (because SavingsAccount implements BankAccount).

The fourth statement is clearly not type-safe because Bank does not implement BankAccount. The variable ba2 in the fifth statement has the type BankAccount, so the compiler infers that its object reference could be from either SavingsAccount or CheckingAccount. Since a CheckingAccount reference cannot be stored in a SavingsAccount variable, the statement is not type-safe. The fact that ba2 actually holds a reference to a SavingsAccount object is irrelevant.

Type Casting

The compiler is very conservative in its decisions. If there is any chance whatsoever that a variable can hold a value of the wrong type then it will generate a compiler error. For example, consider the following code:

```
BankAccount ba = new SavingsAccount(1);
SavingsAccount sa = ba;
```

It should be clear that the second statement is type-safe because the two statements, taken together, imply that variable sa will hold a SavingsAccount reference. However, the compiler does not look at the first statement when compiling the second one. It knows only that variable ba is of type BankAccount and thus could be holding a CheckingAccount value. It therefore generates a compiler error.

In cases such as this, you can use a *typecast* to overrule the compiler. For example, the preceding code can be rewritten as follows:

```
BankAccount ba = new SavingsAccount(1);
SavingsAccount sa = (SavingsAccount) ba;
```

The typecast assures the compiler that the code really is type-safe, and that you assume all responsibility for any incorrect behavior. The compiler then obeys your request and compiles the statement. If you are wrong then the program will throw a ClassCastException at runtime.

It is now possible to consider the addInterest method from Listing 2-5. This method iterates through all the accounts but adds interest only to the savings accounts. Since the elements of the variable accounts are of type BankAccount, and BankAccount does not have an addInterest method, some fancy footwork is needed to ensure type-safety.

The method calls the Java instanceof operator. This operator returns true if the object reference on its left side can be cast to the type on its right side. By calling instanceof on each BankAccount object, the method determines which objects are of type SavingsAccount. It then uses a typecast to create an object reference of type SavingsAccount, which can then call the addInterest method.

Both the use of instanceof and the typecast are necessary. Suppose that I omitted the call to instanceof, writing the method like this:

```java
public void addInterest() {
    for (BankAccount ba : accounts.values()) {
        SavingsAccount sa = (SavingsAccount) ba;
        sa.addInterest();
    }
}
```

This code compiles correctly, and if the map contains only savings accounts then this code will run correctly. However, if ba ever refers to a CheckingAccount object then the typecast will throw a ClassCastException at runtime.

Now suppose that I omitted the typecast, writing the method like this:

```
public void addInterest() {
    for (BankAccount ba : accounts.values())
        if (ba instanceof SavingsAccount)
            ba.addInterest();
}
```

This code will not compile because variable ba is of type BankAccount and is therefore not allowed to call the addInterest method. The compiler considers the method call to be unsafe even though it will only be called when ba refers to a SavingsAccount object.

Transparency

The technique of combining a call to instanceof with a typecast gives correct results, but it violates the fundamental design principle. The problem is that the code specifically mentions class names. If the bank adds another account type that also gives interest (such as a "money market account") then you would need to modify the addInterest method to deal with it.

The if-statement problem is rearing its ugly head again. Each time a new kind of account is created, you will need to examine every relevant portion of the program to decide whether that new class needs to be added to the if-statement. For large programs, this is a daunting task that has potential for the creation of many bugs.

The way to eliminate these problems is to add the addInterest method to the BankAccount interface. Then the addInterest method of Bank could call addInterest on each of its accounts without caring which class they belonged to. Such a design is called *transparent* because the class of an object reference is invisible (i.e., transparent) to a client. We express these ideas in the following rule, called the rule of Transparency:

The Rule of Transparency

A client should be able to use an interface without needing
to know the classes that implement that interface.

The version 6 banking demo revises version 5 so that BankAccount
is transparent. This transparency requires changes to the code for
BankAccount, CheckingAccount, and Bank. The BankAccount interface
needs an additional method header for addInterest:

```
public interface BankAccount {
   ...
   void addInterest();
}
```

CheckingAccount must implement the additional method
addInterest. Doing so turns out to be very easy. The addInterest method
simply needs to do nothing:

```
public class CheckingAccount implements BankAccount {
   ...
   public void addInterest() {
      // do nothing
   }
}
```

And Bank has a new, transparent implementation of addInterest:

```
public class Bank {
   ...
   public void addInterest() {
      for (BankAccount ba : accounts.values()) {
         ba.addInterest();
      }
   }
}
```

An important side effect of transparency is that it can reduce coupling between classes. In particular, note that the addInterest method no longer causes a dependency on SavingsAccount. The newAccount method is now the only place in Bank that mentions SavingsAccount and CheckingAccount. Eliminating these dependencies is a worthy goal, but involves the ability to remove the calls to the constructors. Techniques for doing so will be covered in Chapter 5.

The Open-Closed Rule

The advantage of a transparent interface is that adding a new implementing class requires very little modification to existing code. For example, suppose that the bank decides to introduce a new money-market account. Consider how you would have to change the version 6 banking demo:

- You would write a new class MoneyMarketAccount that implemented the BankAccount interface.

- You would modify the newAccount method of BankClient to display a different message to the user, indicating the account type for MoneyMarketAccount.

- You would modify the newAccount method in Bank to create new MoneyMarketAccount objects.

These changes fall into two categories: *modification*, in which existing classes change; and *extension*, in which new classes are written. In general, modification tends to be the source of bugs, whereas extension leads to a relatively bug-free "plug and play" situation. This insight leads to the following rule, called the Open/Closed rule:

The Open/Closed Rule

To the extent possible, a program should be open for extension
but closed for modification.

The Open/Closed rule is an ideal. Most changes to a program will involve some form of modification; the goal is to limit this modification as much as possible. For example, of the three tasks listed previously, the first one requires the most work but can be implemented using extension. The remaining two tasks require relatively small modifications. The techniques of Chapter 5 will make it possible to further reduce the modifications required for these two tasks.

The Comparable Interface

Suppose that the bank has asked you to modify the banking demo so that bank accounts can be compared according to their balances. That is, it wants ba1 > ba2 if ba1 has more money than ba2.

The Java library has an interface especially for this purpose, called Comparable<T>. Here is how the Java library declares the interface:

```java
public interface Comparable<T> {
    int compareTo(T t);
}
```

The call x.compareTo(y) returns a number greater than 0 if x>y, a value less than 0 if x<y, and 0 if x=y. Many classes from the Java library are comparable.

One such class is String, which implements Comparable<String>. Its compareTo method compares two strings by their lexicographic order. For a simple example, consider the following code. After executing it, the variable result will have a negative value because "abc" is lexicographically smaller than "x".

```
String s1 = "abc";
String s2 = "x";
int result = s1.compareTo(s2);
```

Version 6 of the banking demo modifies classes SavingsAccount and CheckingAccount to implement Comparable<BankAccount>. Each class now has a compareTo method and its header declares that it implements Comparable<BankAccount>. Listing 2-7 gives the relevant code for SavingsAccount. The code for CheckingAccount is similar.

Listing 2-7. The Version 6 SavingsAccount Class

```
public class SavingsAccount implements BankAccount,
                            Comparable<BankAccount> {
   ...
   public int compareTo(BankAccount ba) {
      int bal1 = getBalance();
      int bal2 = ba.getBalance();
      if (bal1 == bal2)
         return getAcctNum() - ba.getAcctNum();
      else
         return bal1 - bal2;
   }
}
```

The compareTo method needs to return a positive number if bal1>bal2 and a negative number if bal2>bal1. Subtracting the two balances has the desired effect. If the two balances are equal then the method uses their account numbers to arbitrarily break the tie. Thus the method will return 0 only if the comparison is between objects corresponding to the same account. This is the expected behavior of any compareTo method.

Listing 2-8 gives code for the demo program `CompareSavingsAccounts`, which illustrates the use of comparable objects. The program first calls the method `initAccts`, which creates some `SavingsAccount` objects, deposits money in them, and saves them in a list. The program then demonstrates two ways to calculate the account having the largest balance.

Listing 2-8. The CompareSavingsAccounts Class

```java
public class CompareSavingsAccounts {
   public static void main(String[] args) {
      ArrayList<SavingsAccount> accts = initAccts();
      SavingsAccount maxacct1 = findMax(accts);
      SavingsAccount maxacct2 = Collections.max(accts);
      System.out.println("Acct with largest balance is "
                        + maxacct1);
      System.out.println("Acct with largest balance is "
                        + maxacct2);
   }

   private static ArrayList<SavingsAccount> initAccts() {
      ArrayList<SavingsAccount> accts =
                                    new ArrayList<>();
      accts.add(new SavingsAccount(0));
      accts.get(0).deposit(100);
      accts.add(new SavingsAccount(1));
      accts.get(1).deposit(200);
      accts.add(new SavingsAccount(2));
      accts.get(2).deposit(50);
      return accts;
   }
```

```
private static SavingsAccount
              findMax(ArrayList<SavingsAccount> a) {
   SavingsAccount max = a.get(0);
   for (int i=1; i<a.size(); i++) {
      if (a.get(i).compareTo(max) > 0)
         max = a.get(i);
   }
   return max;
}
}
```

The first way to find the largest account is to call the local method findMax, which performs a linear search of the list. It initializes the current maximum to be the first element. The call to compareTo compares each remaining element with the current maximum; if that element is larger then it becomes the new current maximum.

The second way to find the largest account is to use the Java library method Collections.max. That method implicitly calls compareTo for each element of the list.

The main point of this example is that the program is able to find the account having the largest balance without ever explicitly mentioning account balances. All references to the balance occur in the compareTo method.

Subtypes

Although the version 6 code declares both SavingsAccount and CheckingAccount to be comparable, that is not the same as requiring that all bank accounts be comparable. This is a serious problem. For example, consider the following statements. The compiler will refuse to compile the third statement because BankAccount variables are not required to have a compareTo method.

```
BankAccount ba1 = new SavingsAccount(1);
BankAccount ba2 = new SavingsAccount(2);
int a = ba1.compareTo(ba2);  // unsafe!
```

This problem also occurs in the class CompareBankAccounts, which appears in Listing 2-9. The class is a rewritten version of CompareSavingsAccounts in which the account list is of type BankAccount instead of SavingsAccount. The differences from CompareSavingsAccounts are in bold. Although the changes are relatively minor, this code will no longer compile because the compiler cannot guarantee that every BankAccount object implements the compareTo method.

Listing 2-9. The CompareBankAccounts Class

```
public class CompareBankAccounts {
   public static void main(String[] args) {
      ArrayList<BankAccount> accts = initAccts();
      BankAccount maxacct1 = findMax(accts);
      BankAccount maxacct2 = Collections.max(accts);

      ...

   }

   private static BankAccount
                 findMax(ArrayList<BankAccount> a) {
      BankAccount max = a.get(0);
      for (int i=1; i<a.size(); i++) {
         if (a.get(i).compareTo(max) > 0)
            max = a.get(i);
      }
      return max;
   }
```

The solution to both examples is to assert that all classes that implement BankAccount also implement Comparable<BankAccount>. Formally speaking, we say that BankAccount needs to be a *subtype* of Comparable<BankAccount>. You specify subtypes in Java by using the keyword extends. Listing 2-10 shows the revised BankAccount interface.

Listing 2-10. The Version 6 BankAccount Interface

```
public interface BankAccount extends Comparable<BankAccount> {
   ...
}
```

The extends keyword indicates that if a class implements BankAccount then it must also implement Comparable<BankAccount>. Consequently, the classes SavingsAccount and CheckingAccount no longer need to explicitly implement Comparable<BankAccount> in their headers because they now implement the interface implicitly from BankAccount. With this change, CompareBankAccounts compiles and executes correctly.

A subtype relationship is represented in a class diagram by an open-headed arrow having a solid line. For example, the class diagram of the version 6 banking demo appears in Figure 2-2.

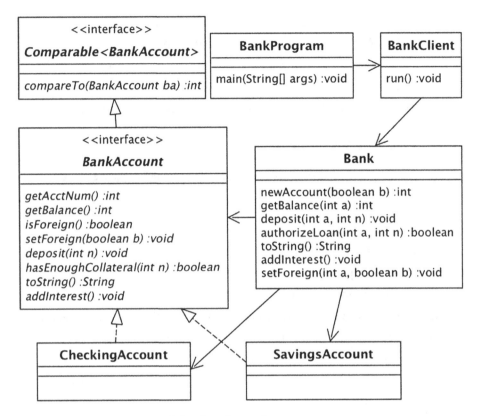

Figure 2-2. *Version 6 of the banking demo*

The Java Collection Library

The banking demo has one example of a subtype relationship. In general, a program might have several interfaces connected by subtype relationships. A good example of subtyping can be found in the collection interfaces from the Java library. These interfaces help manage objects that denote a group of elements. Figure 2-3 depicts their class diagram and some of their methods, together with four commonly used classes that implement them. Not only are these interfaces worth knowing well, they also illustrate some important design principles.

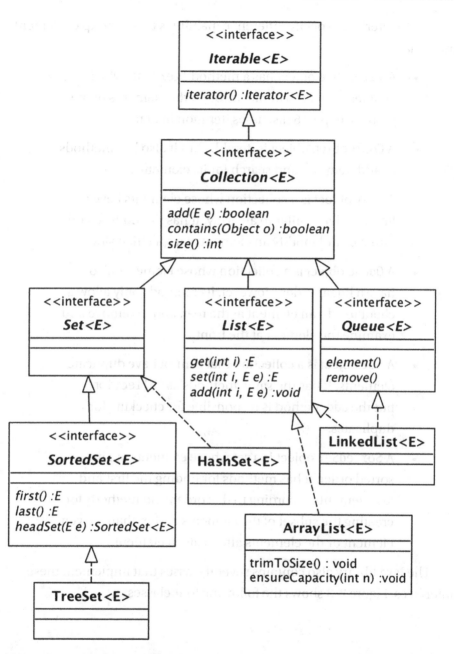

Figure 2-3. *The Java Collection interfaces*

These interfaces specify different capabilities that a group of elements might have.

- An Iterable object has a method iterator, which enables a client to iterate through the elements of the group. Chapter 6 discusses iteration in detail.

- A Collection object is iterable, but it also has methods to add, remove, and search for its elements.

- A List object is a collection whose elements have a linear order, similar to an array. It has methods to add, remove, and modify an element at a specified slot.

- A Queue object is a collection whose elements also have a linear order. However, its methods only allow a client to add an element at the rear, and to remove and examine the element at the front.

- A Set object is a collection that cannot have duplicate elements. It has the same methods as Collection but the add method is responsible for checking for duplicates.

- A SortedSet object is a set whose elements are in sorted order. It has methods for finding the first and last elements according to this order, and methods for creating the subset of the elements earlier than a given element or the elements after a given element.

The Java library also contains several classes that implement these interfaces. Figure 2-3 shows the following four classes.

ArrayList

The class ArrayList implements List, and thus also Collection and Iterable. Its code uses an underlying array to store the list elements, which gets resized as the list expands. The class has the methods trimToSize and ensureCapacity, which allow a client to manually adjust the size of the underlying array.

LinkedList

Like ArrayList, the class LinkedList implements List (and Collection and Iterable). It uses an underlying chain of nodes to store the list elements. Unlike ArrayList, it also implements Queue. The reason is that its chain implementation allows for fast removal from the front of the list, which is important for an efficient implementation of Queue.

HashSet

The class HashSet implements Set (and Collection and Iterable). It uses a hash table to avoid inserting duplicate elements.

TreeSet

The class TreeSet implements SortedSet (as well as Set, Collection, and Iterable). It uses a search tree to store elements in sorted order.

The Liskov Substitution Principle

The type hierarchy of Figure 2-3 seems quite natural and perhaps even obvious. However, significant effort went into the crafting of the hierarchy. An interesting discussion of some of the subtler design issues appears in

the Java Collections API Design FAQ, which is available at the URL
`https://docs.oracle.com/javase/8/docs/technotes/guides/`
`collections/designfaq.html`.

In general, how does one go about designing a type hierarchy?
The guiding principle is called the *Liskov Substitution Principle* (often
abbreviated as LSP). This rule is named for Barbara Liskov, who first
formulated it.

The Liskov Substitution Principle

If type X extends type Y then an object of type X can always be used
wherever an object of type Y is expected.

For example, consider the fact that `List` extends `Collection`. The
LSP implies that `List` objects can substitute for `Collection` objects. In
other words, if someone asks you for a collection then you can reasonably
give them a list because the list has all the methods it needs to behave
as a collection. Conversely, the LSP implies that `Collection` should not
extend `List`. If someone asks you for a list then you could not give them a
collection, because collections are not necessarily sequential and do not
support the corresponding list methods.

Another way to understand the LSP is to examine the intended
relationship between an interface and an interface it extends. For example,
consider my initial description of the collection interfaces. I said that "a set
is a collection that ...," "a sorted set is a set that ...," and so on.

In other words, each interface "is" the type that it extends, with added
functionality. Such a relationship is called an *IS-A relationship*, and we say
"Set IS-A Collection," "SortedSet IS-A Set," and so on. A good rule of thumb
is that if you can understand a type hierarchy in terms of IS-A relationships
then it satisfies the LSP.

A useful way to test your understanding of the LSP is to try to answer the following questions:

- Should SortedSet extend List?

- Why isn't there an interface SortedList?

- Should Queue extend List? Should List extend Queue?

- Why have the interface Set if it doesn't provide any added functionality?

Here are the answers.

Should SortedSet Extend List?

At first glance it seems like a sorted set is fairly similar to a list. After all, its sort order determines a sequentiality: given a value n, there is a well-defined n^{th} element. The list's get method could be useful for accessing any element by its current slot.

The problem is that a sorted set's modification methods would have undesirable side effects. For example, if you use the set method to change the value of the nth element then that element might change its position in the sort order (possibly along with several other elements). And it doesn't make sense to use the add method to insert a new element into a specific slot because the slot of each new element is determined by its sort order. Thus, a sorted set cannot do everything that a list can, which means that SortedSet cannot extend List without violating the LSP.

Why Isn't There an Interface SortedList?

Such an interface seems reasonable. The only question is where it would go in the hierarchy. If SortedList extends List then you run into the same problem that occurred with SortedSet—namely, there is no good way for SortedList to implement the set and add methods of List. The best option is to have SortedList extend Collection, and provide additional list-like methods for accessing elements according to their slot. This would satisfy the LSP.

So why doesn't the Java library have the interface SortedList? Most likely, the designers of the library decided that such an interface would not be that useful, and omitting it resulted in a more streamlined hierarchy.

Should Queue Extend List? Should List Extend Queue?

Queue cannot extend List because a list can access all its elements directly and insert anywhere, whereas a queue can only access the element at the front and insert at the rear.

A more interesting question is whether List should extend Queue. List methods can do everything that Queue methods can do, and more. Thus one can argue that lists are more general than queues; that is, List IS-A Queue. Declaring that List implements Queue would not violate the LSP.

The designers, on the other hand, felt that this functional relationship between lists and queues is somewhat coincidental and not very useful in practice. Conceptually, lists and queues are different beasts; nobody thinks of a list as being a more functional queue. Thus there is no such IS-A relationship and no such subtype declaration in Java.

Why Have the Interface Set if It Doesn't Provide any Added Functionality?

This question is related to the List IS-A Queue question. Conceptually, Set and Collection are two distinct types with a clear IS-A relationship: Set IS-A Collection. Although Set does not introduce any new methods, it does alter the meaning of the add method, and that is significant enough (and useful enough) to warrant a distinct type.

The Rule of Abstraction

Listing 2-11 gives code for a class named DataManager1. This class manages an ArrayList of data values. The list is passed into its constructor and its methods calculate some simple statistical properties of the list.

Listing 2-11. The DataManager1 Class

```
public class DataManager1 {
    private ArrayList<Double> data;

    public DataManager1(ArrayList<Double> d) {
        data = d;
    }

    public double max() {
        return Collections.max(data);
    }

    public double mean() {
        double sum = 0.0;
        for (int i=0; i<data.size(); i++)
            sum += data.get(i);
        return sum / data.size();
    }
}
```

Although this class executes correctly, it is poorly designed. Its problem is that it works only for data stored in ArrayList objects. This restriction is unnecessary because there is nothing in the code that applies only to array lists.

It is easy to rewrite the class so that it works for arbitrary lists of values. That code appears in Listing 2-12.

Listing 2-12. The Class DataManager2 Class

```
public class DataManager2 {
   private List<Double> data;

   public DataManager2(List<Double> d) {
      data = d;
   }
   ...
}
```

The code for DataManager1 and DataManager2 are identical, except for the two places where ArrayList has been replaced by List. These two classes and their dependencies can be expressed in the class diagram of Figure 2-4.

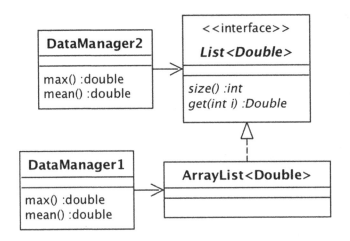

Figure 2-4. *DataManager1 vs. DataManager2*

The added flexibility of class DataManager2 results from the fact that it is dependent on the interface List, which is more abstract than the DataManager1 dependency on ArrayList. This insight is true in general, and can be expressed as the following rule of Abstraction.

> ### The Rule of Abstraction
>
> A class's dependencies should be as abstract as possible.

This rule suggests that a designer should examine each dependency in a design to see if it can be made more abstract. A special case of this rule is known as "Program to Interfaces," which asserts that it is always better to depend on an interface than a class.

Although DataManager2 is better than DataManager1, could it be made even better by changing its dependency on List to something more abstract, such as Collection? At first glance you would have to say "no" because the implementation of the mean method uses the List-based method get. If you want the class to work for any collection then you would need to write mean so that it uses only methods available to collections. Fortunately, such a rewrite is possible. Listing 2-13 gives the code for the even better class DataManager3.

Listing 2-13. The DataManager3 Class

```
public class DataManager3 {
    private Collection<Double> data;

    public DataManager3(Collection<Double> d) {
        data = d;
    }

    public double max() {
        return Collections.max(data);
    }
```

```
public double mean() {
    double sum = 0.0;
    for (double d : data)
        sum += d;
    return sum / data.size();
}
}
```

The rule of Abstraction can also be applied to the banking demo. Consider for example the dependency between Bank and HashMap. A Bank object has the variable accounts, which maps an account number to the corresponding BankAccount object. The type of the variable is HashMap<Integer,BankAccount>. The rule of Abstraction suggests that the variable should have the type Map<Integer,BankAccount> instead. That statement is changed in the version 6 code.

Adding Code to an Interface

At the beginning of this chapter I defined an interface to be a set of method headers, similar to an API. Under this definition, an interface cannot contain code. The Java 8 release loosened this restriction so that an interface can define methods, although it still cannot declare variables. This section examines the consequences of this new ability.

As an example, Listing 2-14 shows the version 6 modification to the BankAccount interface that adds the methods createSavingsWithDeposit and isEmpty.

Listing 2-14. The Version 6 BankAccount Interface

```
public interface BankAccount extends Comparable<BankAccount> {
   ...

   static BankAccount createSavingsWithDeposit(
                                   int acctnum, int n) {
      BankAccount ba = new SavingsAccount(acctnum);
      ba.deposit(n);
      return ba;
   }

   default boolean isEmpty() {
      return getBalance() == 0;
   }
}
```

Both methods are examples of *convenience methods*. A convenience method does not introduce any new functionality. Instead, it leverages existing functionality for the convenience of clients. The method createSavingsWithDeposit creates a savings account having a specified initial balance. The method isEmpty returns true if the account's balance is zero, and false otherwise.

Interface methods are either *static* or *default*. A static method has the keyword static, which means the same as it does in a class. A default method is nonstatic. The keyword default indicates that an implementing class may override the code if it wishes. The idea is that the interface provides a generic implementation of the method that is guaranteed to work for all implementing classes. But a specific class may be able to provide a better, more efficient implementation. For example, suppose that a money-market savings account requires a minimum balance of $100. Then it knows that the account will never be empty, and so it can overwrite the default isEmpty method to one that immediately returns false without having to examine the balance.

For a more interesting example of a default method, consider the question of how to sort a list. The Java library class Collections has the static method sort. You pass two arguments to the sort method—a list and a comparator— and it sorts the list for you. (A comparator is an object that specifies a sort order, and will be discussed in Chapter 4. It suffices here to know that passing null as the comparator causes the sort method to compare the list elements using their compareTo method.) For example, the code of Listing 2-15 reads ten words from standard input into a list and then sorts the list.

Listing 2-15. The Old Way to Sort a List

```
Scanner scanner = new Scanner(System.in);
List<String> words = new ArrayList<>();
for (int i=0; i<10; i++)
   words.add(scanner.next());
Collections.sort(words, null);
```

The problem with this sort method is that there is no good way to sort a list without knowing how it is implemented. The solution used by the Collections class is to copy the elements of the list into an array, sort the array, and then copy the sorted elements back to the list. Listing 2-16 gives the basic idea. Note that the method toArray returns an array of type Object because Java's restrictions on generic arrays make it impossible to return an array of type T. After sorting the array, the for-loop stores each array element back into L. The two typecasts are necessary to override the compiler's concern for type safety.

Listing 2-16. Code for the Sort Method

```
public class Collections {
   ...
   static <T> void sort(List<T> L, Comparator<T> comp) {
```

```
   Object[] a = L.toArray();
   Arrays.sort(a, (Comparator)comp);
   for (int i=0; i<L.size(); i++)
      L.set(i, (T)a[i]);
   }
}
```

Although this code will work for any list, it has the overhead of copying the list elements to an array and back. This overhead is wasted time for some list implementations. An array list, for example, saves its list elements in an array, so it would be more efficient to sort that array directly. This situation means that a truly efficient list sorting method cannot be transparent. It would need to determine how the list is implemented and then use a sorting algorithm specific to that implementation.

Java 8 addresses this problem by making sort be a default method of the List interface. The code for List.sort is a refactoring of the Collections.sort code; the basic idea appears in Listing 2-17.

Listing 2-17. A Default Sort Method for List

```
public interface List<T> extends Collection<T> {
   ...
   default void sort(Comparator<T> comp) {
      Object[] a = toArray();
      Arrays.sort(a, (Comparator)comp);
      for (int i=0; i<size(); i++)
         set(i, (T)a[i]);
   }
}
```

This default `sort` method has two benefits. The first is elegance: It is now possible to sort a list directly, instead of via a static method in `Collections`. That is, the following two statements are now equivalent:

```
Collections.sort(L, null);
L.sort(null);
```

The second, and more important benefit is that lists can be handled transparently. The default implementation of `sort` works for all implementations of `List`. However, any particular `List` implementation (such as `ArrayList`) can choose to override this method with a more efficient implementation of its own.

Summary

Polymorphism is the ability of a program to leverage the common functionality of classes. Java uses interfaces to support polymorphism—the methods of an interface specify some common functionality, and classes that support those methods can choose to implement that interface. For example, suppose classes `C1` and `C2` implement interface `I`:

```
public interface I {...}
public class C1 implements I {...}
public class C2 implements I {...}
```

A program can now declare variables of type `I`, which can then hold references to either `C1` or `C2` objects without caring which class they actually refer to.

This chapter examined the power of polymorphism and gave some basic examples of its use. It also introduced four design rules for using polymorphism appropriately:

- The rule of Transparency states that a client should be able to use an interface without needing to know the classes that implement that interface.

- The Open/Closed rule states that programs should be structured so that they can be revised by creating new classes instead of modifying existing ones.

- The Liskov Substitution Principle (LSP) specifies when it is meaningful for one interface to be a subtype of another. In particular, X should be a subtype of Y only if an object of type X can always be used wherever an object of type Y is expected.

- The rule of Abstraction states that a class's dependencies should be as abstract as possible.

CHAPTER 3

Class Hierarchies

Chapter 2 examined how interfaces can extend other interfaces, creating a hierarchy of types. One of the characteristics of an object-oriented language is that classes can extend other classes, creating a *class hierarchy*. This chapter investigates class hierarchies and the ways they can be used effectively.

Subclasses

Java allows one class to extend another. If class A extends class B, then A is said to be a *subclass* of B and B is a *superclass* of A. Subclass A inherits all public variables and methods of its superclass B, as well as all of B's code for these methods.

The most common example of subclassing in Java is the built-in class Object. By definition, every class in Java is a subclass of Object. That is, the following two class definitions are equivalent:

```
class Bank { ... }
class Bank extends Object { ... }
```

Consequently, the methods defined by Object are inherited by every object. Of these methods, two commonly-used ones are equals and toString. The equals method returns true if the two references being compared are to the same object. (That is, the method is equivalent to the "==" operation.) The toString method returns a string describing the object's class and its location in memory. Listing 3-1 demonstrates these methods.

© Edward Sciore 2019
E. Sciore, *Java Program Design*, https://doi.org/10.1007/978-1-4842-4143-1_3

Listing 3-1. Demonstrating the Default Equals Method

```
Object x = new Object();
Object y = new Object();
Object z = x;
boolean b1 = x.equals(y); // b1 is false
boolean b2 = x.equals(z); // b2 is true
System.out.println(x.toString());
// prints something like "java.lang.Object@42a57993"
```

A class can choose to *override* an inherited method. Often the code provided by a superclass is too generic and a subclass may be able to override the method with more appropriate code. The toString method is typically overridden. For example, the Bank, SavingsAccount, and CheckingAccount classes in the version 6 banking demo override toString.

It is also typical to override the equals method. A class that overrides the equals method typically compares the states of the two objects to determine whether they denote the same real-world thing. For example, consider the class SavingsAccount. Assuming that savings accounts have distinct account numbers, two SavingsAccount objects should be equal if their account numbers are the same. However, consider the following code.

```
SavingsAccount s1 = new SavingsAccount(123);
SavingsAccount s2 = new SavingsAccount(123);
boolean b = s1.equals(s2); // returns false
```

Since s1 and s2 refer to different objects, comparing them using the default equals method will return false. If you want the equals method to return true in this case then SavingsAccount needs to override it. See Listing 3-2.

Listing 3-2. The Version 6 Equals Method of SavingsAccount

```
boolean equals(Object obj) {
    if (! obj instanceof SavingsAccount)
        return false;
    SavingsAccount sa = (SavingsAccount) obj;
    return getAcctNum() == sa.getAcctNum();
}
```

This code is probably trickier than you expected. The reason is that the argument to the default equals method has the type Object, which means that any class that overrides equals must also declare its argument to be of type Object. That is, the equals method for SavingsAccount must handle the possibility of a client comparing a SavingsAccount object to an object from some other class. The code of Listing 3-2 surmounts this problem by using instanceof and typecasting, as in Chapter 2. If the argument is not a savings account then the method immediately returns false. Otherwise, it casts the argument to the type SavingsAccount and compares their account numbers.

A method defined in class Object never needs to be declared in an interface. For example, consider the following code.

```
BankAccount ba = new SavingsAccount(123);
String s = ba.toString();
```

This code is legal regardless of whether or not the BankAccount interface declares the toString method, because every implementing class will inherit toString from Object if it has not been otherwise overridden. However, there is still a value in having the interface declare toString—it requires each of its implementing classes to override the method explicitly.

To represent a class–superclass relationship in a class diagram, use a solid-head arrow with a solid line; this is the same arrow that is used for an interface–superinterface relationship. For example, Figure 3-1 shows the part of the class diagram related to the version 6 bank account classes, revised to include the Object class. In general, class diagrams usually omit Object because its presence is implied and adding it tends to make the diagram unnecessarily complex.

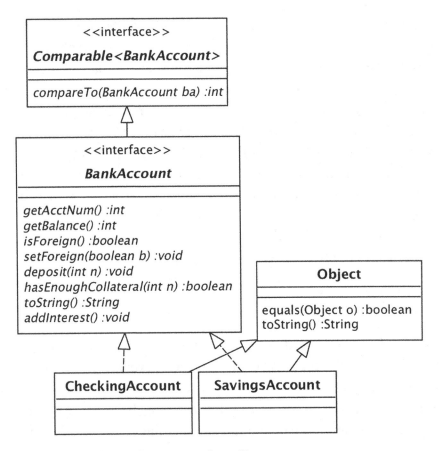

Figure 3-1. *Adding Object to a class diagram*

Chapter 2 introduced the Liskov Substitution Principle as it relates to interfaces. The principle also applies to classes. It states that if class A extends class B then an A-object can be used anywhere that a B-object is expected. In other words, if A extends B then A IS-A B.

As an example, suppose that you want to modify the banking demo to have the new bank account type "interest checking." An interest checking account is exactly like a regular checking account except that it gives periodic interest. Call this class InterestChecking.

Should InterestChecking extend CheckingAccount? When I described interest checking I said that it "is exactly like" regular checking. This suggests an IS-A relationship, but let's be sure. Suppose that the bank wants a report listing all checking accounts. Should the report include the interest checking accounts? If the answer is "yes" then there is an IS-A relationship and InterestChecking should extend CheckingAccount. If the answer is "no" then it shouldn't.

Suppose that InterestChecking should indeed be a subclass of CheckingAccount. An interest checking account differs from a regular checking account in two ways: its toString method prints "Interest checking," and its addInterest method gives interest. Consequently, the code for InterestChecking will override toString and addInterest, and inherit the code for the remaining methods from its superclass. A possible implementation of the class appears in Listing 3-3.

Listing 3-3. A Proposed InterestChecking Class

```
public class InterestChecking extends CheckingAccount {
   private double rate = 0.01;
   public InterestChecking(int acctnum) {
      super(acctnum);
   }
```

```java
public String toString() {
    return "Interest checking account " + getAcctNum()
            + ": balance=" + getBalance() + ", is "
            + (isForeign() ? "foreign" : "domestic");
}

public void addInterest() {
    int newbalance = (int) (getBalance() * rate);
    deposit(newbalance);
}
}
```

Note that the constructor calls the method super. The super method is a call to the superclass's constructor and is used primarily when the subclass needs the superclass to handle its constructor's arguments. If a subclass's constructor calls super then Java requires that the call must be the first statement of the constructor.

The private variables of a class are not visible to any other class, including its subclasses. This forces the subclass code to access its inherited state by calling the superclass's public methods. For example, consider again the proposed InterestChecking code of Listing 3-3. The toString method would like to access the variables acctnum, balance, and isforeign from its superclass. However, these variables are private, which forces toString to call the superclass methods getAcctNum, getBalance, and isForeign to get the same information. Similarly, the addInterest method has to call getBalance and deposit instead of simply updating the variable balance.

It is good practice to encapsulate a class from its subclasses as much as possible. But sometimes (as in the case of the addInterest code) the result is awkward. Consequently, Java provides the modifier protected as an alternative to public or private. A protected variable is accessible to its descendent classes in the hierarchy but not to any other classes. For example, if CheckingAccount declares the variable balance to be protected then the addInterest method of InterestChecking can be written as follows:

```
public void addInterest() {
    balance += (int) (balance * RATE);
}
```

Abstract Classes

Consider again version 6 of the banking demo. The CheckingAccount and SavingsAccount classes currently have several identical methods. If these methods need not remain identical in the future then the classes are designed properly. However, suppose that the bank's policy is that deposits always behave the same regardless of the account type. Then the two deposit methods will always remain identical; in other words, they contain duplicate code.

The existence of duplicate code in a program is problematic because this duplication will need to be maintained as the program changes. For example, if there is a bug fix to the deposit method of CheckingAccount then you will need to remember to make the same bug fix to SavingsAccount. This situation leads to the following design rule, called Don't Repeat Yourself (or "DRY"):

The "Don't Repeat Yourself" Rule

A piece of code should exist in exactly one place.

The DRY rule is related to the Most Qualified Class rule, which implies that a piece of code should only exist in the class that is most qualified to perform it. If two classes seem equally qualified to perform the code then there is probably a flaw in the design – most likely, the design is missing a class that can serve as the most qualified one. In Java, a common way to provide this missing class is to use an *abstract class.*

Version 6 of the banking demo illustrates a common cause of duplicate code: two related classes implementing the same interface. A solution is to create a superclass of CheckingAccount and SavingsAccount and move the duplicate methods to it, together with the state variables they use. Call this superclass AbstractBankAccount. The classes CheckingAccount and SavingsAccount will each hold their own class-specific code and will inherit their remaining code from AbstractBankAccount. This design is version 7 of the banking demo. The code for AbstractBankAccount appears in Listing 3-4. This class contains

- the state variables acctnum, balance, and isforeign. These variables have the protected modifier so that the subclasses can access them freely.

- a constructor that initializes acctnum. This constructor is protected so that it can only be called by its subclasses (via their super method).

- code for the common methods getAcctNum, getBalance, deposit, compareTo, and equals.

Listing 3-4. The Version 7 AbstractBankAccount Class

```
public abstract class AbstractBankAccount
                      implements BankAccount {
    protected int acctnum;
    protected int balance = 0;
    protected boolean isforeign = false;
```

```java
protected AbstractBankAccount(int acctnum) {
    this.acctnum = acctnum;
}

public int getAcctNum() {
    return acctnum;
}

public int getBalance() {
    return balance;
}

public boolean isForeign() {
    return isforeign;
}

public void setForeign(boolean b) {
    isforeign = b;
}

public void deposit(int amt) {
    balance += amt;
}

public int compareTo(BankAccount ba) {
    int bal1 = getBalance();
    int bal2 = ba.getBalance();
    if (bal1 == bal2)
        return getAcctNum() - ba.getAcctNum();
    else
        return bal1 - bal2;
}
```

95

```
public boolean equals(Object obj) {
   if (! (obj instanceof BankAccount))
      return false;
   BankAccount ba = (BankAccount) obj;
   return getAcctNum() == ba.getAcctNum();
}

public abstract boolean hasEnoughCollateral(int loanamt);
public abstract String toString();
public abstract void addInterest();
}
```

Note the declarations for the methods hasEnoughCollateral, toString, and addInterest. These methods are declared to be abstract and have no associated code. The issue is that AbstractBankAccount implements BankAccount, so those methods need to be in its API; however, the class has no useful implementation of the methods because the code is provided by its subclasses. By declaring those methods to be abstract, the class asserts that its subclasses will provide code for them.

A class that contains an abstract method is called an *abstract class* and must have the abstract keyword in its header. An abstract class cannot be instantiated directly. Instead, it is necessary to instantiate one of its subclasses so that its abstract methods will have some code. For example:

```
BankAccount xx = new AbstractBankAccount(123); // illegal
BankAccount ba = new SavingsAccount(123);      // legal
```

Listing 3-5 gives the version 7 code for SavingsAccount; the code for CheckingAccount is similar. This code is basically the same as the version 6 code except that it only contains implementations of the three abstract methods of AbstractBankAccount; the other methods of BankAccount can be omitted because they are inherited from AbstractBankAccount. The implementations of the abstract methods are able to reference the variables balance, acctnum, and isforeign because they are protected in AbstractBankAccount.

Listing 3-5. The Version 7 SavingsAccount Class

```
public class SavingsAccount extends AbstractBankAccount {
   private double rate = 0.01;

   public SavingsAccount(int acctnum) {
      super(acctnum);
   }

   public boolean hasEnoughCollateral(int loanamt) {
      return balance >= loanamt / 2;
   }

   public String toString() {
      return "Savings account " + acctnum + ": balance="
               + balance + ", is "
               + (isforeign ? "foreign" : "domestic");
   }

   public void addInterest() {
      balance += (int) (balance * rate);
   }
}
```

The version 7 code for InterestChecking is similar to the code in
Listing 3-3 except that its methods refer to the protected variables of
AbstractBankAccount; its code is therefore not shown.

The version 7 BankClient and Bank classes have minor revisions to
handle the creation of InterestChecking objects. Listing 3-6 gives the
relevant portion of the newAccount method in BankClient. Listing 3-7 gives
the revised method for newAccount in Bank. The changes are in bold.

Listing 3-6. The Version 7 newAccount Method of BankClient

```
private void newAccount() {
   System.out.print("Enter account type(1=savings,
                      2=checking, 3=interest checking): ");
   int type = scanner.nextInt();
   boolean isforeign = requestForeign();
   current = bank.newAccount(type, isforeign);
   System.out.println("Your new account number is "
                      + current);
}
```

Listing 3-7. The Version 7 newAccount Method of Bank

```
public int newAccount(int type, boolean isforeign) {
   int acctnum = nextacct++;
   BankAccount ba;
   if (type == 1)
      ba = new SavingsAccount(acctnum);
   else if (type == 2)
      ba = new CheckingAccount(acctnum);
   else
      ba = new InterestChecking(acctnum);
   ba.setForeign(isforeign);
   accounts.put(acctnum, ba);
   return acctnum;
}
```

The class diagram for the version 7 bank account classes appears in Figure 3-2. From it you can deduce that AbstractBankAccount implements all the methods in BankAccount except hasEnoughCollateral, toString, and addInterest; that CheckingAccount and SavingsAccount implement those three methods; and that `InterestChecking` overrides `toString` and `addInterest`. Note that the rectangle for `AbstractBankAccount` italicizes the class name and the abstract methods, to denote that they are abstract.

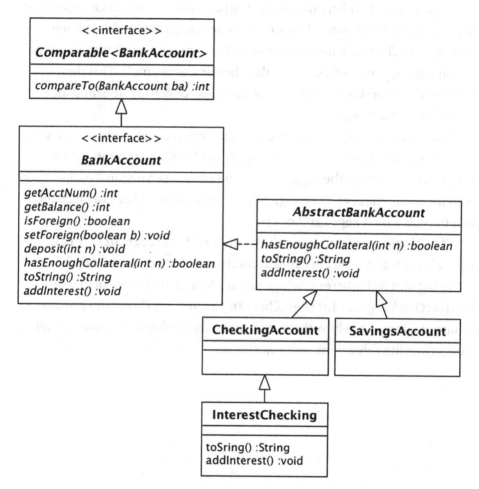

Figure 3-2. *The version 7 bank account classes*

An abstract class defines a category of related classes. For example, the class AbstractBankAccount defines the category "bank accounts," whose descendent classes—savings accounts, checking accounts, and interest checking accounts—are members of this category.

On the other hand, a non-abstract superclass such as CheckingAccount plays both roles: it defines the category "checking accounts" (of which InterestChecking is a member) and it also denotes a particular member of that category (namely, the "regular checking accounts"). This dual usage of CheckingAccount makes the class less easy to understand and complicates the design.

A way to resolve this issue is to split CheckingAccount into two pieces: an abstract class that defines the category of checking accounts and a subclass that denotes the regular checking accounts. Version 8 of the banking demo makes this change: the abstract class is CheckingAccount and the subclass is RegularChecking.

CheckingAccount implements the method hasEnoughCollateral, which is common to all checking accounts. Its abstract methods are toString and addInterest, which are implemented by the subclasses RegularChecking and InterestChecking. Figure 3-3 shows the version 8 class diagram. Note how the two abstract classes form a taxonomy that categorizes the three bank account classes.

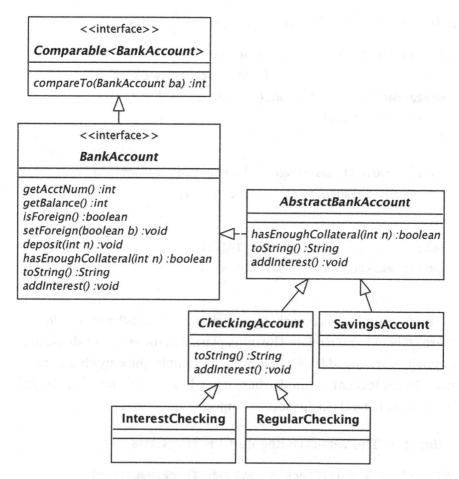

Figure 3-3. *The version 8 bank account classes*

The revised code for CheckingAccount appears in Listing 3-8. The methods toString and addInterest are abstract because its subclasses are responsible for calculating interest and knowing their account type. Its constructor is protected because it should be called only by subclasses.

Listing 3-8. The Version 8 CheckingAccount Class

```
public abstract class CheckingAccount
                      extends AbstractBankAccount {
   protected CheckingAccount(int acctnum) {
      super(acctnum);
   }

   public boolean hasEnoughCollateral(int loanamt) {
      return balance >= 2 * loanamt / 3;
   }

   public abstract String toString();
   public abstract void addInterest();
}
```

The code for RegularChecking appears in Listing 3-9; the code for InterestChecking is similar. The other classes in the version 8 demo are essentially unchanged from version 7. For example, the only change to Bank is its newAccount method, where it needs to create a RegularChecking object instead of a CheckingAccount object.

Listing 3-9. The Version 8 RegularChecking Class

```
public class RegularChecking extends CheckingAccount {
   public RegularChecking(int acctnum) {
      super(acctnum);
   }

   public String toString() {
      return "Regular checking account " + acctnum
              + ": balance=" + balance + ", is "
              + (isforeign ? "foreign" : "domestic");
   }
}
```

```
public void addInterest() {
   // do nothing
}
}
```

Abstract classes are by far the most common use of subclassing. The Java library contains numerous examples of subclass–superclass relationships, but in nearly all of them the superclass is abstract. The InterestChecking example illustrates why this is so: A design that involves a non-abstract superclass can often be improved by turning it into an abstract class.

Writing Java Collection Classes

Chapter 2 introduced the Java collection library, its interfaces, and the classes that implement these interfaces. These classes are general purpose and appropriate for most situations. However, a program may have a specific need for a custom collection class. The problem is that the collection interfaces have lots of methods, which complicates the task of writing custom classes. Moreover, many of the methods have straightforward implementations that would be the same for each implementing class. The result is duplicated code, violating the DRY rule.

The Java collection library contains abstract classes to remedy this problem. Most of the collection interfaces have a corresponding abstract class, whose name is "Abstract" followed by the interface name. That is, the class corresponding to List<E> is named AbstractList<E>, and so on. Each abstract class leaves a few of its interface methods abstract and implements the remaining methods in terms of the abstract ones.

For example, the abstract methods of AbstractList<E> are size and get. If you want to create your own class that implements List<E> then it suffices to extend AbstractList<E> and implement these two methods. (You also need to implement the method set if you want the list to be modifiable.)

As an example, suppose that you want to create a class RangeList that implements List<Integer>. A RangeList object will denote a collection that contains the n integers from 0 to n-1, for a value n specified in the constructor. Listing 3-10 gives the code for a program RangeListTest, which uses a RangeList object to print the numbers from 0 to 19:

Listing 3-10. The RangeListTest Class

```
public class RangeListTest {
   public static void main(String[] args) {
      List<Integer> L = new RangeList(20);
      for (int x : L)
         System.out.print(x + " ");
      System.out.println();
   }
}
```

The code for RangeList appears in Listing 3-11. Note how a RangeList object acts as if it actually contains a list of values, even though it doesn't. In particular, its get method acts as if each slot i of the list contains the value i. This technique is remarkable and significant. The point is that if an object declares itself to be a list and behaves like a list, then it is a list. There is no requirement that it actually contain the list's elements.

Listing 3-11. The RangeList Class

```
public class RangeList extends AbstractList<Integer> {
   private int limit;

   public RangeList(int limit) {
      this.limit = limit;
   }
```

```
public int size() {
   return limit;
}

public Integer get(int n) {
   return n;
}
}
```

Byte Streams

The Java library contains the abstract class InputStream, which denotes the category of data sources that can be read as a sequence of bytes. This class has several subclasses. Here are three examples:

- The class FileInputStream reads bytes from a specified file.

- The class PipedInputStream reads bytes from a pipe. Pipes are what enable different processes to communicate. For example, internet sockets are implemented using pipes.

- The class ByteArrayInputStream reads bytes from an array. This class enables a program to access the contents of a byte array as if it were a file.

Similarly, the abstract class OutputStream denotes objects to which you can write a sequence of bytes. The Java library has OutputStream classes that mirror the InputStream classes. In particular, FileOutputStream writes to a specified file, PipedOutputStream writes to a pipe, and ByteArrayOutputStream writes to an array. The class diagrams for these classes appear in Figure 3-4.

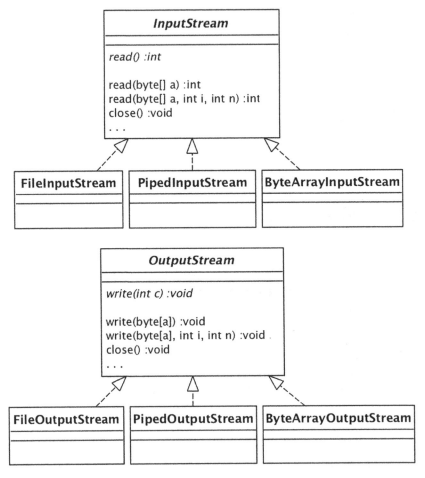

Figure 3-4. *Class diagrams for InputStream and OutputStream*

The public variable System.in belongs to an unspecified class that extends InputStream and by default reads bytes from the console. For example, the class BankProgram in the banking demo contains the following statement:

```
Scanner sc = new Scanner(System.in);
```

This statement can be written equivalently as follows:

```
InputStream is = System.in;
Scanner sc = new Scanner(is);
```

One of the great values of the abstract classes InputStream and OutputStream is their support of polymorphism. Client classes that use InputStream and OutputStream need not depend on the specific input or output source they use. The class Scanner is a good example. The argument to the Scanner's constructor can be any input stream whatsoever. For example, to create a scanner that reads from the file "testfile" you can write:

```
InputStream is = new FileInputStream("testfile");
Scanner sc = new Scanner(is);
```

The demo class EncryptDecrypt illustrates a typical use of byte streams. The code for this class appears in Listing 3-12. Its encrypt method takes three arguments: the name of the source and output files, and an encryption offset. It reads each byte from the source, adds the offset to it, and writes the modified byte value to the output. The main method calls encrypt twice. The first time, it encrypts the bytes of the file "data.txt" and writes them to the file "encrypted.txt"; the second time, it encrypts the bytes of "encrypted.txt" and writes them to "decrypted.txt." Since the second encryption offset is the negative of the first, the bytes in "decrypted. txt" will be a byte-by-byte copy of "data.txt."

Listing 3-12. The EncryptDecrypt Class

```java
public class EncryptDecrypt {
    public static void main(String[] args) throws IOException {
        int offset = 26;  // any value will do
        encrypt("data.txt", "encrypted.txt", offset);
        encrypt("encrypted.txt", "decrypted.txt", -offset);
    }
```

```
private static void encrypt(String source, String output,
                           int offset) throws IOException {
    try ( InputStream  is = new FileInputStream(source);
          OutputStream os = new FileOutputStream(output) ) {
        int x;
        while ((x = is.read()) >= 0) {
            byte b = (byte) x;
            b += offset;
            os.write(b);
        }
    }
}
```

Note that this "decryption by double encryption" algorithm works properly regardless of the encryption offset. The reason has to do with the properties of byte arithmetic. When an arithmetic operation causes a byte value to go outside of its range, the overflow is discarded; the result is that addition and subtraction become cyclic. For example, 255 is the largest byte value, so 255+1 = 0. Similarly, 0 is the smallest byte value, so 0-1 = 255.

The encrypt method illustrates the use of the read and write methods. The write method is straightforward; it writes a byte to the output stream. The read method is more intricate. It returns an integer whose value is either the next byte in the input stream (a value between 0 and 255) or a -1 if the stream has no more bytes. Client code typically calls read in a loop, stopping when the returned value is negative. When the returned value is not negative, the client should cast the integer value to a byte before using it.

Unbeknown to clients, input and output streams often request resources from the operating system on their behalf. Consequently, InputStream and OutputStream have the method close, whose purpose is to return those resources to the operating system. A client can call close explicitly, or can instruct Java to *autoclose* the stream. The encrypt method illustrates the autoclose feature. The streams are opened as "parameters" to the try clause and will be automatically closed when the try clause completes.

Most stream methods throw IO exceptions. The reason is that input and output streams are often managed by the operating system and therefore are subject to circumstances beyond the control of the program. The stream methods need to be able to communicate unexpected situations (such as a missing file or unavailable network) so that their client has a chance to handle them. For simplicity, the two EncryptDecrypt methods do not handle exceptions and instead throw them back up the call chain.

In addition to the zero-argument read method used in Listing 3-12, InputStream has two methods that read multiple bytes at a time:

- A one-argument read method, where the argument is a byte array. The method reads enough bytes to fill the array.

- A three-argument read method, where the arguments are a byte array, the offset in the array where the first byte should be stored, and the number of bytes to read.

The value returned by these methods is the number of bytes that were read, or -1 if no bytes could be read.

As a simple example, consider the following statements:

```
byte[] a = new byte[16];
InputStream is = new FileInputStream("fname");
int howmany = is.read(a);
if (howmany == a.length)
    howmany = is.read(a, 0, 4);
```

The third statement tries to read 16 bytes into array a; the variable howmany contains the actual number of bytes read (or -1 if no bytes were read). If that value is less than 16 then the stream must have run out of bytes, and the code takes no further action. If the value is 16 then the next statement tries to read four more bytes, storing them in slots 0-3 of the array. Again, the variable howmany will contain the number of bytes actually read.

The class OutputStream has analogous write methods. The primary difference between the write and read methods is that the write methods return void.

For a concrete example that uses the multibyte read and write methods, consider the banking demo. Suppose that you want the bank's account information to be written in a file so that its state can be restored upon each execution of BankProgram.

The revised BankProgram code appears in Listing 3-13. The code makes use of a class SavedBankInfo that behaves as follows. Its constructor reads account information from the specified file and constructs the account map. Its method getAccounts returns the account map, which will be empty if the file does not exist. Its method nextAcctNum returns the number for the next new account, which will be 0 if the file does not exist. Its method saveMap writes the current account information to the file, overwriting any previous information.

Listing 3-13. The Version 8 BankProgram Class

```
public class BankProgram {
    public static void main(String[] args) {
        SavedBankInfo info = new SavedBankInfo("bank.info");
        Map<Integer,BankAccount> accounts = info.getAccounts();
        int nextacct = info.nextAcctNum();
        Bank bank = new Bank(accounts, nextacct);
        Scanner scanner = new Scanner(System.in);
        BankClient client = new BankClient(scanner, bank);
```

```
    client.run();
    info.saveMap(accounts, bank.nextAcctNum());
  }
}
```

The code for SavedBankInfo appears in Listing 3-14. The variables accounts and nextaccount are initialized for a bank having no accounts. The constructor is responsible for reading the specified file; if the file exists, it calls the local method readMap to use the saved account information to initialize nextaccount and populate the map. The method saveMap opens an output stream for the file and calls writeMap to write the account information to that stream.

Listing 3-14. The Version 8 SavedBankInfo Class

```
public class SavedBankInfo {
    private String fname;
    private Map<Integer,BankAccount> accounts
                            = new HashMap<Integer,BankAccount>();
    private int nextaccount = 0;
    private ByteBuffer bb = ByteBuffer.allocate(16);

    public SavedBankInfo(String fname) {
        this.fname = fname;
        if (!new File(fname).exists())
            return;
        try (InputStream is = new FileInputStream(fname)) {
            readMap(is);
        }
        catch (IOException ex) {
            throw new RuntimeException("file read exception");
        }
    }
```

```
public Map<Integer,BankAccount> getAccounts() {
   return accounts;
}

public int nextAcctNum() {
   return nextaccount;
}

public void saveMap(Map<Integer,BankAccount> map,
                    int nextaccount) {
   try (OutputStream os = new FileOutputStream(fname)) {
      writeMap(os, map, nextaccount);
   }
   catch (IOException ex) {
      throw new RuntimeException("file write exception");
   }
}
... // definitions for readMap and writeMap
}
```

SavedBankInfo has a variable of type ByteBuffer. The ByteBuffer class defines methods for converting between values and bytes. A ByteBuffer object has an underlying byte array. Its method putInt stores the 4-byte representation of an integer into the array at the specified offset; its method getInt converts the 4 bytes at the specified offset into an integer. SavedBankInfo creates a single 16-byte ByteBuffer object, whose underlying array will be used for all reading and writing to the file.

The code for the writeMap and readMap methods appears in Listing 3-15. These methods determine the overall structure of the data file. First, writeMap writes an integer denoting the next account number; then it writes the values for each account. The readMap method reads these values back. It first reads an integer and saves it in the global variable nextaccount. Then it reads the account information, saving each account in the map.

Listing 3-15. The Methods writeMap and readMap

```
private void writeMap(OutputStream os,
                      Map<Integer,BankAccount> map,
                      int nextacct) throws IOException {
   writeInt(os, nextacct);
   for (BankAccount ba : map.values())
      writeAccount(os, ba);
}

private void readMap(InputStream is) throws IOException {
   nextaccount = readInt(is);
   BankAccount ba = readAccount(is);
   while (ba != null) {
      accounts.put(ba.getAcctNum(), ba);
      ba = readAccount(is);
   }
}
```

The code for writeInt and readInt appears in Listing 3-16. The writeInt method stores an integer in the first four bytes of the byte buffer's underlying array, and then uses the 3-argument write method to write those bytes to the output stream. The readInt method uses the 3-argument read method to read four bytes into the beginning of the ByteBuffer array, and then converts those bytes to an integer.

Listing 3-16. The writeInt and readInt Methods

```
private void writeInt(OutputStream os, int n)
                                      throws IOException {
   bb.putInt(0, n);
   os.write(bb.array(), 0, 4);
}
```

```
private int readInt(InputStream is) throws IOException {
    is.read(bb.array(), 0, 4);
    return bb.getInt(0);
}
```

The code for writeAccount and readAccount appears in Listing 3-17. The writeAccount method extracts the four crucial values from a bank account (its account number, type, balance, and isforeign flag), converts them to four integers, places them into the byte buffer, and then writes the entire underlying byte array to the output stream. The readAccount method reads 16 bytes into the underlying byte array and converts it into four integers. It then uses these integers to create a new account and configure it properly. The method indicates end of stream by returning a null value.

Listing 3-17. The writeAccount and readAccount Methods

```
private void writeAccount(OutputStream os, BankAccount ba)
                                        throws IOException {
    int type = (ba instanceof SavingsAccount)  ? 1
             : (ba instanceof RegularChecking) ? 2 : 3;
    bb.putInt(0, ba.getAcctNum());
    bb.putInt(4, type);
    bb.putInt(8, ba.getBalance());
    bb.putInt(12, ba.isForeign() ? 1 : 2);
    os.write(bb.array());
}

private BankAccount readAccount(InputStream is)
                                        throws IOException {
    int n = is.read(bb.array());
```

```
if (n < 0)
   return null;
int num      = bb.getInt(0);
int type     = bb.getInt(4);
int balance  = bb.getInt(8);
int isforeign = bb.getInt(12);

BankAccount ba;
if (type == 1)
   ba = new SavingsAccount(num);
else if (type == 2)
   ba = new RegularChecking(num);
else
   ba = new InterestChecking(num);
ba.deposit(balance);
ba.setForeign(isforeign == 1);
return ba;
}
```

As you can see, this way of preserving account information is very low level. Saving the information involves converting each account to a specific sequence of bytes, and restoring it requires reversing the process. As a result, the coding is difficult and somewhat painful. Chapter 7 will introduce the concept of an *object stream*, which enables clients to read and write objects directly and let the underlying code perform the tedious translation to bytes.

Now that you have seen how to use byte streams, it is time to examine how they are implemented. I will consider input streams only. Output streams are implemented analogously.

InputStream is an abstract class. It has one abstract method, namely the zero-argument read method, and provides default implementations of the other methods. A simplified version of the InputStream code appears in Listing 3-18.

Listing 3-18. A Simplified InputStream Class

```
public abstract class InputStream {
    public abstract int read() throws IOException;

    public void close() { }

    public int read(byte[] buf, int offset, int len)
                                        throws IOException {
        for (int i=0; i<len; i++) {
            int x = read();
            if (x < 0)
                return (i==0) ? -1 : i;
            buf[offset+i] = (byte) x;
        }
        return len;
    }

    public int read(byte[] buf) throws IOException {
        read(buf, 0, buf.length);
    }
    ...
}
```

The default implementations of the three non-abstract methods are straightforward. The close method does nothing. The three-argument read method fills the specified portion of the array by making repeated calls to the zero-argument read method. And the one-argument read method is just a special case of the three-argument method.

Each subclass of InputStream needs to implement the zero-argument read method and can optionally override the default implementation of other methods. For example, if a subclass acquires resources (such as the file descriptor acquired by FileInputStream) then it should override the close method to release those resources.

A subclass may choose to override the three-argument read method
for efficiency. For example, classes such as FileInputStream and
PipedInputStream obtain their bytes via operating system calls. Since
calls to the operating system are time consuming, the classes will be more
efficient when they minimize the number of these calls. Consequently,
they override the default three-argument read method by a method that
makes a single multibyte call to the operating system.

The code for ByteArrayInputStream provides an example of an
InputStream subclass. A simple implementation appears in Listing 3-19.

Listing 3-19. A Simplified ByteArrayInputStream Class

```java
public class ByteArrayInputStream extends InputStream {
   private byte[] a;
   private int pos = 0;

   public ByteArrayInputStream(byte[] a) {
      this.a = a;
   }

   public int read() throws IOException {
      if (pos >= a.length)
         return -1;
      else {
         pos++;
         return a[pos-1];
      }
   }
}
```

The way that the InputStream methods act as defaults for their
subclasses is akin to the way that the abstract collection classes help their
subclasses implement the collection interfaces. The difference is that
the collection library makes a difference between an abstract class (such

as AbstractList) and its corresponding interface (such as List). The abstract classes InputStream and OutputStream have no corresponding interface. In effect, they act as their own interface.

The Template Pattern

The abstract collection classes and the byte stream classes illustrate a particular way to use an abstract class: The abstract class implements some of the methods of its API, and declares the other methods to be abstract. Each of its subclasses will then implement these abstract public methods (and possibly override some of the other methods).

Here is a slightly more general way to design an abstract class. The abstract class will implement all the methods of its API, but not necessarily completely. The partially-implemented methods call "helper" methods, which are protected (that is, they are not visible from outside the class hierarchy) and abstract (that is, they are implemented by subclasses).

This technique is called the *template pattern*. The idea is that each partial implementation of an API method provides a "template" of how that method should work. The helper methods enable each subclass to appropriately customize the API methods.

In the literature, the abstract helper methods are sometimes called "hooks." The abstract class provides the hooks, and each subclass provides the methods that can be hung on the hooks.

The version 8 BankAccount class hierarchy can be improved by using the template pattern. The problem with the version 8 code is that it still violates the DRY rule. Consider the code for method hasEnoughCollateral in the classes SavingsAccount (Listing 3-5) and CheckingAccount (Listing 3-8). These two methods are almost identical. They both multiply the account balance by a factor and compare that value to the loan amount. Their only difference is that they multiply by different factors. How can we remove this duplication?

The solution is to move the multiplication and comparison up to the AbstractBankAccount class and create an abstract helper method that returns the factor to multiply by. This solution is implemented in the version 9 code. The code for the hasEnoughCollateral method in AbstractBankAccount changes to the following:

```
public boolean hasEnoughCollateral(int loanamt) {
    double ratio = collateralRatio();
    return balance >= loanamt * ratio;
}
protected abstract double collateralRatio();
```

That is, the hasEnoughCollateral method is no longer abstract. Instead, it is a template that calls the abstract helper method collateralRatio, whose code is implemented by the subclasses. For example, here is the version 9 code for the collateralRatio method in SavingsAccount.

```
protected double collateralRatio() {
    return 1.0 / 2.0;
}
```

The abstract methods addInterest and toString also contain duplicate code. Instead of having each subclass implement these methods in their entirety, it is better to create a template for them in AbstractBankAccount. Each template method can call abstract helper methods, which the subclasses can then implement. In particular, the addInterest method calls the abstract method interestRate and the toString method calls the abstract method accountType.

Figure 3-5 displays the class diagram for the version 9 banking demo. From it you can deduce that:

- AbstractBankAccount implements all of the methods in BankAccount, but itself has the abstract methods collateralRatio, accountType, and interestRate.

- SavingsAccount implements all three of these methods.

- CheckingAccount implements collateralRatio only, and leaves the other two methods for its subclasses.

- RegularChecking and InterestChecking implement accountType and interestRate.

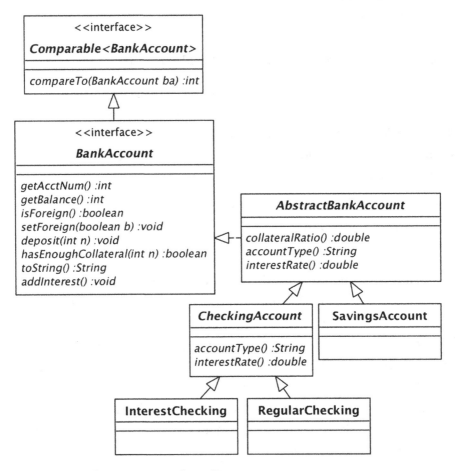

Figure 3-5. *The version 9 class diagram*

The following listings show the revised classes for version 9. The
code for AbstractBankAccount appears in Listing 3-20; the code for
SavingsAccount appears in Listing 3-21; the code for CheckingAccount
appears in Listing 3-22; and the code for RegularChecking appears
in Listing 3-23. The code for InterestChecking is similar to that for
RegularChecking, and is omitted. Note that because of the template
pattern, these classes are remarkably compact. There is no repeated code
whatsoever!

Listing 3-20. The Version 9 AbstractBankAccount Class

```java
public abstract class AbstractBankAccount
                    implements BankAccount {
   protected int acctnum;
   protected int balance;

   ...

   public boolean hasEnoughCollateral(int loanamt) {
      double ratio = collateralRatio();
      return balance >= loanamt * ratio;
   }

   public String toString() {
      String accttype = accountType();
      return accttype + " account " + acctnum
            + ": balance=" + balance + ", is "
            + (isforeign ? "foreign" : "domestic");
   }

   public void addInterest() {
      balance += (int) (balance * interestRate());
   }
```

```
    protected abstract double collateralRatio();
    protected abstract String accountType();
    protected abstract double interestRate();
}
```

Listing 3-21. The Version 9 SavingsAccount Class

```
public class SavingsAccount extends BankAccount {
    public SavingsAccount(int acctnum) {
        super(acctnum);
    }

    public double collateralRatio() {
        return 1.0 / 2.0;
    }

    public String accountType() {
        return "Savings";
    }

    public double interestRate() {
        return 0.01;
    }
}
```

Listing 3-22. The Version 9 CheckingAccount Class

```
public abstract class CheckingAccount extends BankAccount {
    public CheckingAccount(int acctnum) {
        super(acctnum);
    }

    public double collateralRatio() {
        return 2.0 / 3.0;
    }
```

```
    protected abstract String accountType();
    protected abstract double interestRate();
}
```

Listing 3-23. The Version 9 RegularChecking Class

```
public class RegularChecking extends CheckingAccount {
    public RegularChecking(int acctnum) {
        super(acctnum);
    }

    protected String accountType() {
        return "Regular Checking";
    }

    protected double interestRate() {
        return 0.0;
    }
}
```

For another illustration of the template pattern, consider the Java library class Thread. The purpose of this class is to allow a program to execute code in a new thread. It works as follows:

- Thread has two methods: start and run.

- The start method asks the operating system to create a new thread. It then executes the object's run method from that thread.

- The run method is abstract and is implemented by a subclass.

- A client program defines a class X that extends Thread and implements the run method. The client then creates a new X-object and calls its start method.

The class ReadLine in Listing 3-24 is an example of a Thread subclass. Its run method does very little. The call to sc.nextLine blocks until the user presses the Return key. When that occurs, the run method stores the input line in variable s, sets its variable done to true, and exits. Note that the method does nothing with the input line. The only purpose of the input is to set the variable done to true when the user presses Return.

Listing 3-24. The ReadLine Class

```
class ReadLine extends Thread {
    private boolean done = false;

    public void run() {
        Scanner sc = new Scanner(System.in);
        String s = sc.nextLine();
        sc.close();
        done = true;
    }

    public boolean isDone() {
        return done;
    }
}
```

Listing 3-25 gives the code for the class ThreadTest. That class creates a ReadLine object and calls its start method, causing its run method to execute from a new thread. The class then proceeds (from the original thread) to print integers in increasing order until the isDone method of ReadLine returns true. In other words, the program prints integers until the user presses the Return key. The new thread makes it possible for the user to interactively decide when to stop the printing.

Listing 3-25. The ThreadTest Class

```java
public class ThreadTest {
    public static void main(String[] args) {
        ReadLine r = new ReadLine();
        r.start();
        int i = 0;
        while(!r.isDone()) {
            System.out.println(i);
            i++;
        }
    }
}
```

Note how the Thread class uses the template pattern. Its start method is part of the public API and acts as the template for thread execution. Its responsibility is to create and execute a new thread, but it doesn't know what code to execute. The run method is the helper method. Each Thread subclass customizes the template by specifying the code for run.

One common mistake when using threads is to have the client call the thread's run method instead of its start method. After all, the Thread subclass contains the method run and the start method is hidden from sight. Moreover, calling run is legal; doing so has the effect of running the thread code, but not in a new thread. (Try executing Listing 3-25 after changing the statement r.start() to r.run(). What happens?) However, once you understand that threading uses the template pattern, the reason for calling the start method becomes clear and the design of the Thread class finally makes sense.

Summary

Classes in an object-oriented language can form subclass-superclass relationships. The creation of these relationships should be guided by the Liskov Substitution Principle: Class X should be a subclass of class Y if X-objects can be used wherever Y-objects are needed. A subclass inherits the code of its superclass.

One reason for creating superclass–subclass relationships is to satisfy the DRY rule, which states that a piece of code should exist in exactly one place. If two classes contain common code then that common code can be placed in a common superclass of the two classes. The classes can then inherit this code from their superclass.

If the two subclasses are different implementations of the same interface then their common superclass should also implement that interface. In this case the superclass becomes an abstract class and the interface methods that it does not implement are declared as abstract. An abstract class cannot be instantiated, and instead acts as a *category* for its implementing classes. The categorization produced by a hierarchy of abstract classes is called a *taxonomy*.

There are two ways for an abstract class to implement its interface. The first way is exemplified by the Java abstract collection classes. The abstract class declares a few of the interface methods to be abstract and then implements the remaining methods in terms of the abstract ones. Each subclass only needs to implement the abstract methods, but can override any of the other methods if desired.

The second way is exemplified by the Java Thread class. The abstract class implements all of the interface methods, calling abstract "helper" methods when needed. Each subclass implements these helper methods. This technique is called the *template pattern*. The abstract class provides a "template" of how each interface method should work, with each subclass providing the subclass-specific details.

CHAPTER 4

Strategies

Class hierarchies are a fundamental feature of object-oriented programming languages. Chapter 3 examined their capabilities. This chapter examines their (often significant) limitations and introduces the more flexible concept of a *strategy hierarchy*. Strategy hierarchies are a central component of several design techniques. This chapter examines two such techniques—the *strategy pattern* and the *command pattern*—and their uses.

The Strategy Pattern

Let's begin by reviewing the template pattern from Chapter 3. In it, an abstract class (known as the template) provides a skeletal implementation of each public method, and relies on nonpublic abstract methods to provide the implementation-specific details. These abstract methods get implemented by the template subclasses. Each subclass is called a *strategy class* because it provides a particular strategy for implementing the template's abstract methods.

Listing 4-1 gives a simple example. The class IntProcessor is the template class. It has an abstract method f that computes an output value from a given integer. The method operateOn passes an integer to f and prints its output value. There are two strategy subclasses, AddOne and AddTwo, that provide different implementations of f. The class TestClient demonstrates the use of these classes. It creates an instance of each subclass and calls the operateOn method of each instance.

© Edward Sciore 2019
E. Sciore, *Java Program Design*, https://doi.org/10.1007/978-1-4842-4143-1_4

Listing 4-1. Example Template Pattern Classes

```java
public abstract class IntProcessor {
   public void operateOn(int x) {
      int y = f(x);
      System.out.println(x + " becomes " + y);
   }
   protected abstract int f(int x);
}

public class AddOne extends IntProcessor {
   protected int f(int x) {
      return x+1;
   }
}

public class AddTwo extends IntProcessor {
   protected int f(int x) {
      return x+2;
   }
}

public class TestClient {
   public static void main(String[] args) {
      IntProcessor p1 = new AddOne();
      IntProcessor p2 = new AddTwo();
      p1.operateOn(6); // prints "6 becomes 7"
      p2.operateOn(6); // prints "6 becomes 8"
   }
}
```

Another way to design this program is to not use subclassing. Instead of implementing the strategy classes as subclasses of IntProcessor, you can give them their own hierarchy, called a *strategy hierarchy*. The hierarchy's interface is named Operation, and has the method f. The IntProcessor class, which no longer has any subclasses or abstract methods, holds a reference to an Operation object and uses that reference when it needs to call f. The revised code appears in Listing 4-2. The TestClient class creates the desired Operation objects and passes each to IntProcessor via dependency injection.

Listing 4-2. Refactoring Listing 4-1 to Use a Strategy Hierarchy

```java
public class IntProcessor {
    private Operation op;

    public IntProcessor(Operation op) {
        this.op = op;
    }
    public void operateOn(int x) {
        int y = f(x);
        System.out.println(x + " becomes " + y);
    }
    private int f(int x) {
        return op.f(x);
    }
}

interface Operation {
    public int f(int x);
}

class AddOne implements Operation {
    public int f(int x) {
        return x+1;
    }
}
```

```
class AddTwo implements Operation {
    public int f(int x) {
        return x+2;
    }
}

public class TestClient {
    public static void main(String[] args) {
        Operation op1 = new AddOne();
        Operation op2 = new AddTwo();
        IntProcessor p1 = new IntProcessor(op1);
        IntProcessor p2 = new IntProcessor(op2);
        p1.operateOn(6); p2.operateOn(6);
    }
}
```

If you compare the two listings you will see that they are refactorings of each other, with nearly identical code. The primary difference is how the strategy classes are attached to the IntProcessor class. Figure 4-1 shows the corresponding class diagrams for the two different designs.

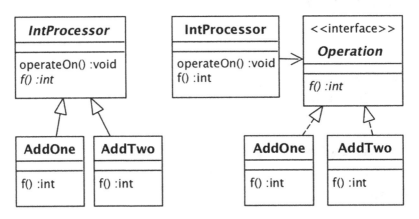

Figure 4-1. *Class diagrams for Listings 4-1 and 4-2*

The technique of organizing strategy classes into a hierarchy is called the *strategy pattern.* The strategy pattern is depicted by the class diagram of Figure 4-2. The strategy interface defines a set of methods. Each class that implements the interface provides a different strategy for performing those methods. The client has a variable that holds an object from one of the strategy classes. Because the variable is of type StrategyInterface, the client has no idea which class the object belongs to and consequently does not know which strategy is being used.

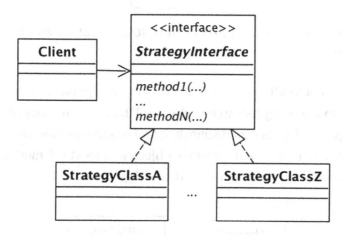

Figure 4-2. *The strategy pattern*

The class diagram on the right side of Figure 4-1 corresponds to the strategy pattern. IntProcessor is the client, Operation is the strategy interface, and AddOne and AddTwo are the strategy classes.

The Java Thread class provides a real-life example of the duality between the template and strategy patterns. Recall the ThreadTest program from Listing 3-25. The class Thread is the template class, whose public method start calls the abstract method run. Its subclass ReadLine is the strategy class that implements run. Figure 4-3 depicts the relationship between Thread and ReadLine.

131

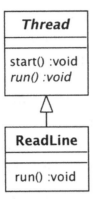

Figure 4-3. *Using the template pattern to connect Thread to its strategy class*

In the corresponding design that uses the strategy pattern, ReadLine will belong to a strategy hierarchy, which will be a dependency of Thread. The strategy interface is called Runnable and has the method run. A Thread object holds a reference to a Runnable object, and its start method will call the Runnable object's run method. See Figure 4-4.

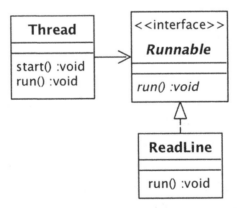

Figure 4-4. *Using the strategy pattern to connect Thread to its strategy class*

Compare Figure 4-3 with Figure 4-4. Figure 4-3 requires that ReadLine extend Thread, whereas Figure 4-4 requires that ReadLine implement Runnable. Syntactically, this difference is minor. In fact, revising the code for ReadLine does not involve any change to its code apart from its class header. The revised class appears in Listing 4-3, with differences from Listing 3-24 in bold.

Listing 4-3. The Revised ReadLine Class

```
public class ReadLine implements Runnable {
    private boolean done = false;

    public void run() {
        Scanner sc = new Scanner(System.in);
        String s = sc.nextLine();
        sc.close();
        done = true;
    }

    public boolean isDone() {
        return done;
    }
}
```

A Thread object obtains its Runnable object via dependency injection. That is, the client passes the desired Runnable object into the Thread constructor. Listing 4-4 gives code for the client program RunnableThreadTest, which revises the ThreadTest class of Listing 3-25 to use the strategy pattern. Differences are in bold.

Listing 4-4. The RunnableThreadTest Class

```
public class RunnableThreadTest {
   public static void main(String[] args) {
      ReadLine r = new ReadLine();
      Thread t = new Thread(r);
      t.start();
      int i = 0;
      while(!r.isDone()) {
         System.out.println(i);
         i++;
      }
   }
}
```

Although ThreadTest and RunnableThreadTest have practically the same code, their designs are conceptually very different. In ThreadTest, the class ReadLine is a subclass of Thread, which means that ReadLine IS-A Thread. In RunnableThreadTest, the ReadLine object is unrelated to Thread and is merely passed into the constructor of a new Thread object.

Current wisdom holds that creating threads using the strategy pattern produces better designs than creating threads using the template pattern. The primary reason is that the strategy pattern creates two objects—in this case, the runnable and the thread—which keeps their concerns separate. In contrast, the template pattern combines both concerns into a single object. A second reason is that the strategy pattern is more flexible, in that a runnable object is able to extend another class. For example, suppose for some reason that you want each SavingsAccount object to run in its own thread. The template pattern approach would not be possible here because Java does not allow SavingsAccount to extend both Thread and AbstractBankAccount.

You may have noticed that the Thread class is depicted differently in Figures 4-3 and 4-4. In Figure 4-3 it is an abstract class, with run as its abstract method. In Figure 4-4 it is a non-abstract class, whose run method calls the run method of its strategy class.

The Thread class was designed so that it can be used either way. Listing 4-5 shows the basic idea. The key issue is how to implement the run method. There are two potential run methods: the method defined in Thread, and the method defined in a subclass of Thread. If the strategy pattern is used (as in Listing 4-4) then the run method defined in Thread is executed, which calls the run method of the Runnable object passed to it. If the template pattern is used (as in Listing 3-25) then the run method defined in the subclass overrides the method defined in Thread, and is executed.

Listing 4-5. A Simplified Implementation of Thread

```java
public class Thread {
   private Runnable target;

   public Thread() {
      this(null); // if no Runnable is specified, use null
   }

   public Thread(Runnable r) {
      target = r;
   }

   public void start() {
      ...            // allocate a new thread
      run();         // and run it
   }

   // This method can be overridden by a subclass.
   public void run() {
```

```
    if (target != null)
        target.run();
}
}
```

You might be perplexed by why null is used as a possible value for the variable target, especially since it complicates the code. The reason stems from the need to handle the following statements:

```
Thread t1 = new Thread();
t1.start();

Runnable r = null;
Thread t2 = new Thread(r);
t2.start();
```

These statements execute two threads, neither of which has a run method. Although the code is pointless, it is legal, and the Thread class must handle it. The solution taken in Listing 4-5 is to store a null value as the target Runnable object in these cases. The run method can then check to see if the target is null; if so, it does nothing.

Comparators

Recall from Chapter 2 how the Comparable interface makes it possible to compare objects. This interface has one method, named compareTo, which specifies an ordering on the objects. If a class implements Comparable then its objects can be compared by calling compareTo. The order defined by CompareTo is called the object's *natural order*.

The problem is that Comparable hardcodes a specific ordering, which makes it essentially impossible to compare objects in any other way. For example, the AbstractBankAccount class implements Comparable<BankAccount>, and its compareTo method (given in Listing 3-4)

compares bank accounts by their balance from low to high. It does not
allow you to compare accounts by account number or by balance from
high to low.

How can you specify different comparison orders? Use the strategy
pattern! The strategy interface declares the comparison method, and the
strategy classes provide specific implementations of that method.

Because object comparison is so common, the Java library provides
this strategy interface for you. The interface is called Comparator and
the method it declares is called compare. The compare method is similar
to compareTo except that it takes two objects as parameters. The call
compare(x,y) returns a value greater than 0 if x>y, a value less than 0 if
x<y, and 0 if x=y.

The code for the example comparator class AcctByMinBal appears in
Listing 4-6. Its compare method compares two BankAccount arguments,
using essentially the same code as the compareTo method of Listing 3-4. The
primary difference is syntactic: the compare method has two arguments,
whereas compareTo has one argument. The other difference is that
Listing 4-6 subtracts the account balances in the opposite order from
Listing 3-4, meaning that it compares balances from high to low. That is,
the account having the smallest balance will be the "maximum."

Listing 4-6. The AcctByMinBal Class

```
class AcctByMinBal implements Comparator<BankAccount> {
   public int compare(BankAccount ba1, BankAccount ba2) {
      int bal1 = ba1.getBalance();
      int bal2 = ba2.getBalance();
      if (bal1 == bal2)
         return ba1.getAcctNum() - ba2.getAcctNum();
      else
         return bal2 - bal1;
   }
}
```

Listing 4-7 gives code for the program ComparatorBankAccounts, which revises the CompareBankAccounts class of Listing 2-9. Unlike CompareBankAccounts, which found the maximum bank account using the natural ordering, ComparatorBankAccounts finds the maximum element according to four specified orderings. Each ordering is represented by a different comparator object. Two of the comparators are passed to the local method findMax. The other two are passed to the Java library method Collections.max.

Listing 4-7. The ComparatorBankAccounts Class

```
public class ComparatorBankAccounts {
   public static void main(String[] args) {
      List<BankAccount> accts = initAccts();
      Comparator<BankAccount> minbal = new AcctByMinBal();
      Comparator<BankAccount> maxbal = innerClassComp();
      Comparator<BankAccount> minnum = lambdaExpComp1();
      Comparator<BankAccount> maxnum = lambdaExpComp2();

      BankAccount a1 = findMax(accts, minbal);
      BankAccount a2 = findMax(accts, maxbal);
      BankAccount a3 = Collections.max(accts, minnum);
      BankAccount a4 = Collections.max(accts, maxnum);

      System.out.println("Acct with smallest bal is " + a1);
      System.out.println("Acct with largest bal is "  + a2);
      System.out.println("Acct with smallest num is " + a3);
      System.out.println("Acct with largest num is "  + a4);
   }

   private static BankAccount findMax(List<BankAccount> a,
                             Comparator<BankAccount> cmp) {
      BankAccount max = a.get(0);
      for (int i=1; i<a.size(); i++) {
```

```
      if (cmp.compare(a.get(i),max) > 0)
         max = a.get(i);
   }
   return max;
}
... // code for the three comparator methods goes here
}
```

The findMax method of Listing 4-7 revises the corresponding method of Listing 2-9. It now takes two parameters: a list of bank accounts and a comparator. It returns the largest account, where "largest" is determined by the comparator.

The Collections.max method, like other library methods that involve comparison, is able to handle both the Comparable and Comparator interfaces. If you call Collections.max with one argument (as in Listing 2-9) then it will compare elements according to their natural order. On the other hand, if you call Collections.max with a comparator as its second argument (as in Listing 4-7) then the elements will be compared according to the order specified by the comparator.

The main method of Listing 4-7 creates four objects of type Comparable<BankAccount>. The first object is an instance of the AcctByMinBal class of Listing 4-6. The other three objects are created by the methods innerClassComp, lambdaExpComp1, and lambdaExpComp2; the code for these methods will appear in listings 4-8 to 4-10. Each of these methods creates an object from an *anonymous inner class*; anonymous inner classes are discussed in the next section.

The class diagram for the ComparatorBankAccounts program appears in Figure 4-5. Note how it follows the strategy pattern.

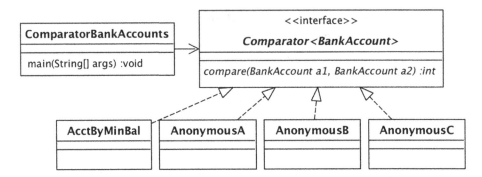

Figure 4-5. *The Class Diagram for ComparatorBankAccounts*

Anonymous Inner Classes

The rule of Abstraction (from Chapter 2) asserts that the type of a variable should be an interface when possible. In such a case the name of the class that implements the interface is relatively unimportant, as it will only be used when the class constructor is called. This section examines how to create unnamed classes, called *anonymous inner classes,* and the convenience that they provide.

Explicit Anonymous Classes

An anonymous inner class defines a class without giving it a name. Suppose that T is an interface. The general syntax is:

```
T v = new T() { ... };
```

This statement causes the compiler to do three things:

- It creates a new class that implements T and has the code appearing within the braces.

- It creates a new object of that class by calling the class's default constructor.

- It saves a reference to that object in variable v.

Note that the client will never need to know the class of the new object, because it interacts with the object only via the variable of type T.

The code for the method `innerClassComp` in `ComparatorBankAccounts` appears in Listing 4-8. The bold code highlights the anonymous inner class syntax. The code within the braces implements the `compare` method, which in this case happens to be the same as the `compareTo` method of Listing 3-4. This class is named AnonymousA in the class diagram of Figure 4-5, but of course we don't know (or care) what its name really is.

Listing 4-8. The innerClassComp Method

```
private static Comparator<BankAccount> innerClassComp() {
    Comparator<BankAccount> result =
        new Comparator<BankAccount>() {
            public int compare(BankAccount ba1,
                                BankAccount ba2) {
                int bal1 = ba1.getBalance();
                int bal2 = ba2.getBalance();
                if (bal1 == bal2)
                  return ba1.getAcctNum() - ba2.getAcctNum();
                else
                  return bal1 - bal2;
            }
        };
    return result;
}
```

Lambda Expressions

An anonymous inner class provides a convenient way to define a class and create a single instance of it, as both the class and its instance can be created inline. This section shows how it is often possible to shorten the definitions of anonymous inner classes, making them even more convenient.

An interface is said to be *functional* if it has only one method, not counting any default or static methods. The interface `Comparator<T>` is an example of a functional interface. An anonymous inner class for a functional interface can be written very compactly. Since there is only one method to define, its name and return type are determined by the interface, so you don't need to write them; you only need to write the code for the method. This notation is called a *lambda expression*. Its syntax is:

```
(T1 t1, ..., Tn tn) -> {...}
```

The method's parameter list is to the left of the "arrow" and its code is to its right, within braces. The method `lambdaExpComp1` in `Comparator BankAccounts` uses this syntax; see the bold portion of Listing 4-9. Its `compare` method compares accounts by their account numbers, from high to low.

Listing 4-9. The lambdaExpComp1 Method

```
private static Comparator<BankAccount> lambdaExpComp1() {
    Comparator<BankAccount> result =
        (BankAccount ba1, BankAccount ba2) -> {
            return ba2.getAcctNum() - ba1.getAcctNum();
        };
    return result;
}
```

Although lambda expressions can be written reasonably compactly, Java lets you abbreviate them even further.

- You don't have to specify the types of the parameters.

- If there is only one parameter then you can omit the parentheses around it.

- If the body of the method consists of a single statement then you can omit the braces; if a single-statement method also returns something then you also omit the "return" keyword.

The method `lambdaExpComp2` in `ComparatorBankAccounts` uses this syntax; see the bold portion of Listing 4-10. The `compare` method compares accounts by their account numbers, from low to high.

Listing 4-10. The lambdaExpComp2 Method

```
private static Comparator<BankAccount> lambdaExpComp2() {
   Comparator<BankAccount> result =
      (ba1, ba2) -> ba1.getAcctNum() - ba2.getAcctNum();
   return result;
}
```

For another example of a lambda expression, consider again the implementation of the `Thread` class in Listing 4-5. Its variable `target` held the specified runnable object, with a null value denoting a nonexistent runnable. The `run` method had to use an if-statement to ensure that it only executed nonnull runnables.

The use of the null value to mean "do nothing" is poor design, as it forces the `run` method to make the decision to "do something" or "do nothing" each time it is executed. A better idea is to have the class make the decision once, in its constructor. The solution is to use a lambda expression. The code of Listing 4-11 revises Listing 4-5.

Listing 4-11. A revised Implementation of Thread

```
public class Thread {
   private static Runnable DO_NOTHING = () -> {};
   private Runnable target;

   public Thread() {
      this(DO_NOTHING); // use the default runnable
   }
```

```
public Thread(Runnable r) {
    target = (r == null) ? DO_NOTHING : r;
}

public void start() {
    ...            // allocate a new thread
    run();
}

// This method can be overridden by a subclass.
public void run() {
    target.run(); // no need to check for null!
}
}
```

The class creates a Runnable object via the lambda expression ()->{}. This lambda expression defines a run method that takes no arguments and does nothing. This Runnable object is saved in the constant DO_NOTHING. If no Runnable object is passed into the Thread constructor then the variable target will receive a reference to DO_NOTHING instead of a null value. Since this object is runnable, the run method can execute it without the need for an if-statement.

The Strategy Pattern as a Design Tool

Let's return to the design of the banking demo. Chapter 3 introduced version 9 of the demo, which supported three kinds of bank account organized into the class hierarchy of Figure 4-6.

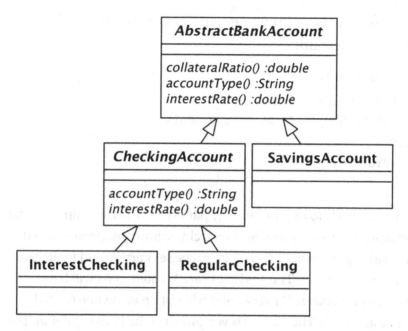

Figure 4-6. *The version 9 BankAccount hierarchy*

Suppose that the bank wants to add another feature to the design. It already distinguishes between domestic accounts and foreign accounts; it now wants to charge a yearly maintenance fee of $5 for foreign-owned accounts. The BankAccount interface will get a new method named fee, which returns the fee for that account.

A simple way to implement the fee method is from within the class AbstractBankAccount, as shown in Listing 4-12. Although this code is straightforward, its use of the if-statement is bad design. The method will need to be modified each time the bank changes the fee categories—which is a blatant violation of the Open/Closed rule.

Listing 4-12. A Naïve Implementation of the Fee method in
AbstractBankAccount

```
public int fee() {
   if (isforeign)
      return 500;    // $5 is 500 cents
   else
      return 0;
}
```

A better idea is to use the strategy pattern. The ownership information
will be moved to its own strategy hierarchy, whose interface is called
OwnerStrategy and whose two strategy classes correspond to the two
different fee categories. The AbstractBankAccount class will have
a dependency on OwnerStrategy and will obtain all owner-related
information from it. This design is version 10 of the banking demo. The
relevant portion of its class diagram is in Figure 4-7, with changes from
Figure 3-5 in bold.

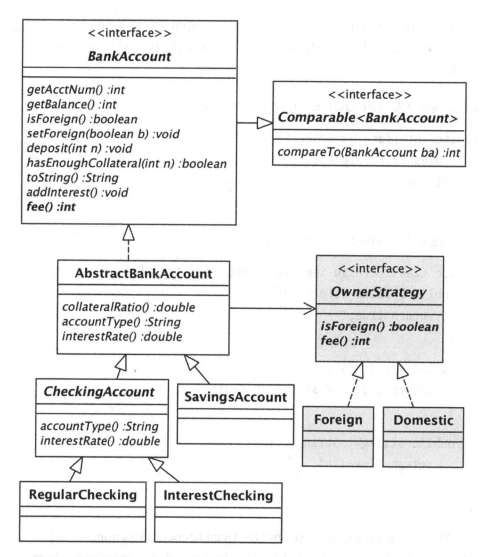

Figure 4-7. The version 10 bank account classes

This diagram shows the fee method added to the BankAccount interface. The class AbstractBankAccount implements the method by calling the fee method of its OwnerStrategy object. The OwnerStrategy classes also implement the additional method isForeign.

The code for the OwnerStrategy interface appears in Listing 4-13. Listing 4-14 gives the code for the Foreign class; the Domestic class is similar.

Listing 4-13. The OwnerStrategy Interface

```
public interface OwnerStrategy {
   boolean isForeign();
   int fee();
}
```

Listing 4-14. The Foreign Class

```
public class Foreign implements OwnerStrategy {
   public boolean isForeign() {
      return true;
   }

   public int fee() {
      return 500;  // $5 is 500 cents
   }

   public String toString() {
      return "foreign";
   }
}
```

The code for the version 10 AbstractBankAccount class appears in Listing 4-15, with changes in bold. Its boolean variable isforeign has been replaced by the strategy variable owner. Its isForeign and fee methods call the isForeign and fee strategy methods of owner. Its toString method calls the toString method of the strategy object to obtain the string indicating that the account is "domestic" or "foreign." Initially, the owner variable is bound to a Domestic strategy object. The setForeign method rebinds that variable to the OwnerStrategy object determined by its argument value.

Listing 4-15. The Version 10 AbstractBankAccount Class

```
public abstract class AbstractBankAccount
                      implements BankAccount {
   protected int acctnum;
   protected int balance = 0;
   private OwnerStrategy owner = new Domestic();

   protected AbstractBankAccount(int acctnum) {
      this.acctnum = acctnum;
   }

   public boolean isForeign() {
      return owner.isForeign();
   }

   public int fee() {
      return owner.fee();
   }

   public void setForeign(boolean b) {
      owner = b ? new Foreign() : new Domestic();
   }

   public String toString() {
      String accttype = accountType();
         return accttype + " account " + acctnum
            + ": balance=" + balance + ", is "
            + owner.toString() + ", fee=" + fee();
   }
   ...
}
```

The Command Pattern

The OwnerStrategy strategy hierarchy arose from the problem of how to implement multiple ways to calculate the fee of a bank account. The initial solution, given in Listing 4-12, used an if-statement to determine which calculation to perform. This use of an if-statement was problematic: not only was it inefficient but it would need to be modified each time a new type of fee was added. Replacing the if-statement with a strategy hierarchy elegantly resolved both issues.

A similar situation exists in the BankClient class. It assigns a number to eight different input commands and its processCommand method uses an if-statement to determine which code to execute for a given command number. The code for the method appears in Listing 4-16.

Listing 4-16. The Version 9 processCommand Method

```java
private void processCommand(int cnum) {
    if      (cnum == 0) quit();
    else if (cnum == 1) newAccount();
    else if (cnum == 2) select();
    else if (cnum == 3) deposit();
    else if (cnum == 4) authorizeLoan();
    else if (cnum == 5) showAll();
    else if (cnum == 6) addInterest();
    else if (cnum == 7) setForeign();
    else
        System.out.println("illegal command");
}
```

A better design for this method is to create a strategy interface InputCommand and an implementing strategy class for each command type. BankClient can then hold a polymorphic array of type InputCommand, containing one object from each strategy class. The command number passed to processCommand becomes an index into that array. The revised processCommand method appears in Listing 4-17. Note how the indexed array access replaces the if-statement.

Listing 4-17. The Version 10 processCommand Method

```
private void processCommand(int cnum) {
   InputCommand cmd = commands[cnum];
   current = cmd.execute(scanner, bank, current);
   if (current < 0)
     done = true;
}
```

The strategy interface InputCommand has eight implementing classes— one class for each type of command. These classes are named QuitCmd, NewCmd, DepositCmd, and so on. Figure 4-8 shows their class diagram.

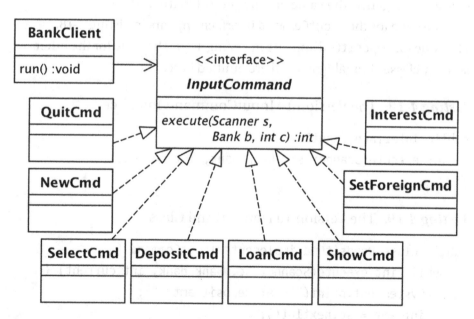

Figure 4-8. *The InputCommand Strategy Hierarchy*

The strategy method declared by InputCommand is named execute. The execute method for each strategy class contains the code required to perform its designated command. The code for these strategy classes is taken from the methods referenced in Listing 4-16. For example, the execute method of DepositCmd contains the same code as the version 9 deposit method.

One complicating issue is that the version 9 methods are able to modify the global variables of BankClient; in particular, the version 9 newAccount and select commands change the value of the variable current, and the quit command changes the value of done. However, the strategy classes have no such access to the BankClient variables. The solution taken in version 10 is for the execute method to return the new value of current (or the old value, if it did not change). A value of -1 indicates that done should be set to true. The code of Listing 4-17 reflects this decision: the return value of execute is assigned to current, and if current is negative, the value of done gets set to true.

The code for the InputCommand interface appears in Listing 4-18. The code for DepositCmd appears in Listing 4-19. The code for the other strategy classes is analogous and are omitted here.

Listing 4-18. The Version 10 InputCommand Interface

```
public interface InputCommand {
    int execute(Scanner sc, Bank bank, int current);
}
```

Listing 4-19. The Version 10 DepositCmd Class

```
public class DepositCmd implements InputCommand {
    public int execute(Scanner sc, Bank bank, int current) {
        System.out.print("Enter deposit amt: ");
        int amt = sc.nextInt();
        bank.deposit(current, amt);
```

```
      return current;
   }

   public String toString() {
      return "deposit";
   }
}
```

The use of command objects also solves another problem of the version 9 BankClient class, which is related to its run method. The code in question is the string beginning "Enter command..." in Listing 4-20. This string explicitly assigns numbers to commands and must be kept in synch with the processCommand method. If new commands are added to processCommand or if the numbers assigned to existing commands change, then this string will need to be rewritten.

Listing 4-20. The Version 9 BankClient Run Method

```
public void run() {
   while (!done) {
      System.out.print("Enter command (0=quit, 1=new,
                        2=select, 3=deposit, 4=loan,
                        5=show, 6=interest, 7=setforeign): ");
      int cnum = scanner.nextInt();
      processCommand(cnum);
   }
}
```

The version 10 BankClient class has a better design, which appears in Listing 4-21. It takes advantage of the fact that the commands array contains an object for each command. When the run method is called, it calls the method constructMessage to traverse that array and construct the "Enter command..." string. Consequently, that string will always be accurate no matter how the commands change.

Listing 4-21. The Version 10 BankClient Class

```
public class BankClient {
   private Scanner scanner;
   private boolean done = false;
   private Bank bank;
   private int current = 0;
   private InputCommand[] commands = {
         new QuitCmd(),
         new NewCmd(),
         new SelectCmd(),
         new DepositCmd(),
         new LoanCmd(),
         new ShowCmd(),
         new InterestCmd(),
         new SetForeignCmd() };

   public BankClient(Scanner scanner, Bank bank) {
      this.scanner = scanner;
      this.bank = bank;
   }

   public void run() {
      String usermessage = constructMessage();
      while (!done) {
         System.out.print(usermessage);
         int cnum = scanner.nextInt();
         processCommand(cnum);
      }
   }
```

```
private String constructMessage() {
    int last = commands.length-1;
    String result = "Enter Account Type (";
    for (int i=0; i<last; i++)
        result += i + "=" + commands[i] + ", ";
    result += last + "=" + commands[last] + "): ";
    return result;
}

private void processCommand(int cnum) {
    InputCommand cmd = commands[cnum];
    current = cmd.execute(scanner, bank, current);
    if (current < 0)
        done = true;
}
}
```

The method constructMessage creates the user message. In doing so, it appends each InputCommand object to the string. Java interprets this as implicitly appending the result of the object's toString method. That is, the following statements are equivalent:

```
result += i + "=" + commands[i] + ", ";
result += i + "=" + commands[i].toString() + ", ";
```

The use of a strategy hierarchy shown in Figure 4-8 is called the *command pattern*. The structure of the command pattern is the same as for the strategy pattern. For example, in Figure 4-8, BankClient is the client and depends on the strategy hierarchy headed by InputCommand. The only difference between the two patterns is the purpose of their strategies. In the strategy pattern the strategies are *computational*—they provide alternative ways to compute a value. In the command pattern the strategies are *procedural*—they provide alternative tasks that can be performed.

Eliminating the Class Hierarchy

The duality between the template pattern and the strategy pattern implies that any design using the template pattern can be redesigned to use the strategy pattern. This section shows how to redesign the banking demo so that its BankAccount class hierarchy is replaced by a strategy hierarchy. This redesign is version 11 of the banking demo.

The idea of the redesign is to implement SavingsAccount, RegularChecking, and InterestChecking as strategy classes, headed by a strategy interface named TypeStrategy. The interface declares the three methods collateralRatio, accountType, and interestRate. Consequently, AbstractBankAccount will no longer need subclasses. Instead, it will implement these three methods via its reference to a TypeStrategy object.

Figure 4-9 shows the version 11 class diagram. In this design, AbstractBankAccount has two strategy hierarchies. The OwnerStrategy hierarchy is the same as in version 10. The TypeStrategy hierarchy contains the code for the methods of AbstractBankAccount that were previously abstract.

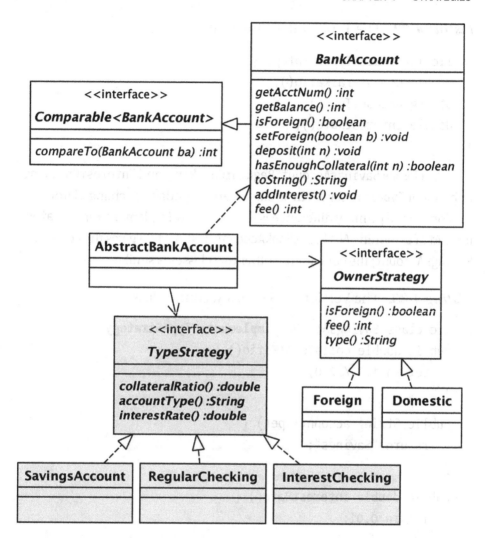

Figure 4-9. *Version 11 of the Banking Demo*

The TypeStrategy interface appears in Listing 4-22.

Listing 4-22. The TypeStrategy Interface

```
public interface TypeStrategy {
    double collateralRatio();
    String accountType();
    double interestRate();
}
```

The classes SavingsAccount, RegularChecking, and InterestChecking implement TypeStrategy. These classes are essentially unchanged from version 10; the primary difference is that they now implement TypeStrategy instead of extending AbstractBankAccount. Listing 4-23 gives the code for SavingsAccount; the code for the other two classes is similar.

Listing 4-23. The Version 11 SavingsAccount Class

```
public class SavingsAccount implements TypeStrategy {
    public double collateralRatio() {
        return 1.0 / 2.0;
    }

    public String accountType() {
        return "Savings";
    }

    public double interestRate() {
        return 0.01;
    }
}
```

In version 10, the newAccount method of class Bank used the type number entered by the user to determine the subclass of the new account. The newAccount method in version 11 uses the type number to determine the TypeStrategy of the new account. It then passes the TypeStrategy object to the AbstractBankAccount constructor, as shown in Listing 4-24. Analogous changes are needed to the class SavedBankInfo, but are not shown here.

Listing 4-24. The Version 11 newAccount Method of Bank

```
public int newAccount(int type, boolean isforeign) {
    int acctnum = nextacct++;
    TypeStrategy ts;
    if (type==1)
        ts = new SavingsAccount();
    else if (type==2)
        ts = new RegularChecking();
    else
        ts = new InterestChecking();
    BankAccount ba = new AbstractBankAccount(acctnum, ts);
    ba.setForeign(isforeign);
    accounts.put(acctnum, ba);
    return acctnum;
}
```

The code for AbstractBankAccount appears in Listing 4-25, with changes in bold. The primary difference from version 10 is that the class is no longer abstract and implements the previously abstract methods collateralRatio, accountType, and interestRate. The code of these methods simply calls the corresponding methods of the TypeStrategy variable ts.

Listing 4-25. The AbstractBankAccount Class

```
public class AbstractBankAccount implements BankAccount {
    private int acctnum;
    private int balance = 0;
    private OwnerStrategy owner = new Domestic();
    private TypeStrategy ts;

    public AbstractBankAccount(int acctnum, TypeStrategy ts) {
        this.acctnum = acctnum;
        this.ts = ts;
```

```
    }
    ...
    private double collateralRatio() {
        return ts.collateralRatio();
    }

    private String accountType() {
        return ts.accountType();
    }

    private double interestRate() {
        return ts.interestRate();
    }
}
```

Templates vs. Strategies

The template pattern and the strategy pattern use different mechanisms to accomplish similar goals—the template pattern uses the class hierarchy, whereas the strategy pattern uses a separate strategy hierarchy. Can we derive any insight into when one technique is preferable over the other?

In the template pattern the class hierarchy forms a structure that organizes the different strategy classes. A class hierarchy takes a general concept (such as "bank account") and divides it into increasingly narrower concepts (such as "savings account," "regular checking," and "interest checking"). Such an organization is known as a *taxonomy*.

A taxonomy is a useful organizational concept. For example, this book's table of contents is a taxonomy of its information. One characteristic of a taxonomy is that membership in a category is permanent. For example in the version 10 banking demo, a savings account cannot become a checking account. The only way to "convert" a savings account into a checking account is to create a new checking account, transfer the savings account's balance to it, and then delete the savings account. But this conversion is not exact—in particular, the checking account will have a different account number from the savings account.

Another characteristic of a taxonomy is that it can only represent a hierarchical relationship between its members. For example, the banking demo organizes accounts according to "savings" vs. "checking." That organization cannot handle the added distinction of "foreign" vs. "domestic."

On the other hand, the strategy pattern is much more fluid. Each strategy hierarchy corresponds to a completely independent way of organizing the objects. Moreover, the strategy pattern allows an object to change its choice of strategies. For example, the setForeign method in BankAccount changes that object's membership in the OwnerStrategy hierarchy.

Version 11 of the banking demo demonstrated how strategies can even subsume the functionality of subclasses. In that version, every bank account belongs to the same class, namely AbstractBankAccount. The concept of "checking account" or "savings account" is no longer embedded in a class hierarchy. Instead, a savings account is merely a bank account that has a specific implementation of the TypeStrategy methods (namely, savings accounts pay interest, have a low collateral ratio, and have the name "Savings"). Similarly, the two kinds of checking accounts are just bank accounts with their own TypeStrategy implementations. Such a design is tremendously flexible. It is possible to create various combinations of checking-savings accounts simply by mixing and matching their strategy implementations.

Is this a good idea? Not necessarily. A class hierarchy provides a structure that helps tame the unbridled complexity that strategies enable. The decision of how to mix strategy hierarchies and template subclasses requires careful consideration, and will depend on the situation being modeled. For example, my sense is that version 10 of the banking demo is a better design. The division into checking and savings accounts seems reasonable and corresponds to how banks operate. Version 11, by giving up the hierarchy, seems to be less realistic and less easily understood.

In this book I take the position that the version 11 demo is interesting and educational, but ultimately a dead end. The revisions of Chapter 5 will be based on version 10.

Summary

In the template pattern, each subclass of the template defines a different strategy for implementing the template's abstract methods, and is called a *strategy class*. This chapter investigated the technique of organizing these strategy classes into their own strategy hierarchy. When the strategy classes perform computation this technique is called the *strategy pattern*; when they denote tasks it is called the *command pattern*.

These two design patterns model situations where a class can have multiple ways to perform a computation or a task. A common example is object comparison. The Java library has the interface `Comparator` for precisely this purpose. A client can implement customized comparison code by writing an appropriate class that implements `Comparator`.

Strategy classes are often written as anonymous inner classes. If the strategy interface is functional then a strategy class for it can be written compactly and elegantly as a *lambda expression*.

The strategy pattern is more flexible than the template pattern, and this flexibility can lead to better designs. An example is the problem of how to calculate fees based on account ownership. Since the class hierarchy is organized by account type, the fee calculations do not neatly fit into the existing class structure. Instead, the creation of a separate `OwnerStrategy` hierarchy was easy and elegant, and did not impact the existing class hierarchy.

The strategy pattern can in fact be used to eliminate class hierarchies altogether, but this is not necessarily a good idea. As a class designer, you need to understand your options. It is then up to you to weigh their tradeoffs for a given situation.

CHAPTER 5

Encapsulating Object Creation

Polymorphism enables code to be more abstract. When your code references an interface instead of a class, it loses its coupling to that class and becomes more flexible in the face of future modifications. This use of abstraction was central to many of the techniques of the previous chapters.

Class constructors are the one place where such abstraction is not possible. If you want to create an object, you need to call a constructor; and calling a constructor is not possible without knowing the name of the class. This chapter addresses that problem by examining the techniques of *object caching* and *factories*. These techniques help the designer limit constructor usage to a relatively small, well-known set of classes, in order to minimize their potential liability.

Object Caching

Suppose you want to write a program that analyzes the status of a large number of motion-detecting sensors, whose values are either "on" or "off." As part of that program, you write a class Sensors that stores the sensor information in a list and provides methods to get and set individual sensor values. The code for that class appears in Listing 5-1.

© Edward Sciore 2019
E. Sciore, *Java Program Design*, https://doi.org/10.1007/978-1-4842-4143-1_5

Listing 5-1. Version 1 of the Sensors Class

```java
public class Sensors {
   private List<Boolean> L = new ArrayList<>();

   public Sensors(int size) {
      for (int i=0; i<size; i++)
         L.add(new Boolean(false));
   }

   public boolean getSensor(int n) {
      Boolean val = L.get(n);
      return val.booleanValue();
   }

   public void setSensor(int n, boolean b) {
      L.set(n, new Boolean(b));
   }
}
```

This code creates a lot of Boolean objects: the constructor creates one object per sensor and the setSensor method creates another object each time it is called. However, it is possible to create far fewer objects. Boolean objects are immutable (that is, their state cannot be changed), which means that Boolean objects having the same value are indistinguishable from each other. Consequently, the class only needs to use two Boolean objects: one for true and one for false. These two objects can be shared throughout the list.

Listing 5-2 shows a revision of Sensors that takes advantage of immutability. This code uses the variables off and on as a cache. When it needs a Boolean object for true it uses on; and when it needs a Boolean object for false it uses off.

Listing 5-2. Version 2 of the Sensors Class

```
public class Sensors {
    private List<Boolean> L = new ArrayList<>();
    private static final Boolean off = new Boolean(false);
    private static final Boolean on  = new Boolean(true);

    public Sensors(int size) {
        for (int i=0; i<size; i++)
            L.add(off);
    }

    public boolean getSensor(int n) {
        Boolean val = L.get(n);
        return val.booleanValue();
    }

    public void setSensor(int n, boolean b) {
        Boolean val = b ? on : off;
        L.set(n, val);
    }
}
```

This use of caching is a good idea, but in this case it is limited to the Sensors class. If you want to use Boolean objects in another class, it could be awkward to share the cached objects between the two classes. Fortunately, there is a better way—the Boolean class has caching built into it. Listing 5-3 gives a simplified version of the Boolean source code.

Listing 5-3. A Simplified Boolean Class

```
public class Boolean {
    public static final Boolean TRUE  = new Boolean(true);
    public static final Boolean FALSE = new Boolean(false);
    private boolean value;
```

```java
    public Boolean(boolean b) {value = b;}

    public boolean booleanValue() {
        return value;
    }

    public static Boolean valueOf(boolean b) {
        return (b ? TRUE : FALSE);
    }
    ...
}
```

The constants TRUE and FALSE are static and public. They are created once, when the class is loaded, and are available everywhere. The static method valueOf returns TRUE or FALSE based on the supplied boolean value.

Listing 5-4 shows a revision of the Sensors class that uses the valueOf method and public constants of Boolean instead of its constructor. This is the preferred use of the Boolean class. The Java documentation states that valueOf should be used in preference to the constructor, as its caching saves time and space. In fact, I cannot think of a reason why anyone's Java code would ever need to call the Boolean constructor.

Listing 5-4. Version 3 of the Sensors Class

```java
public class Sensors {
    private List<Boolean> L = new ArrayList<>();

    public void init(int size) {
        for (int i=0; i<size; i++)
            L.add(Boolean.FALSE);
    }
```

```
public void setSensor(int n, boolean b) {
   Boolean value = Boolean.valueOf(b);
   L.set(n, value);
}
}
```

Although there is a sharp distinction between the primitive type boolean and the class Boolean, the Java concept of *autoboxing* blurs that distinction. With autoboxing you can use a boolean value anywhere that a Boolean object is expected; the compiler automatically uses the valueOf method to convert the boolean to a Boolean for you. Similarly, the concept of *unboxing* lets you use a Boolean object anywhere that a boolean value is expected; the compiler automatically uses the booleanValue method to convert the Boolean to a boolean.

Listing 5-5 gives yet another revision of Sensors, this time without any explicit mention of Boolean objects. It is functionally equivalent to Listing 5-4. This code is interesting because it has a lot going on behind the scenes. Although it doesn't explicitly mention Boolean objects, they exist because of autoboxing. Moreover, because autoboxing calls valueOf, the code will not create new objects but will use the cached versions.

Listing 5-5. Version 4 of the Sensors Class

```
public class Sensors {
   private List<Boolean> L = new ArrayList<>();

   public void init(int size) {
      for (int i=0; i<size; i++)
         L.add(false);
   }
   public void setSensor(int n, boolean b) {
      L.set(n, b);
   }
}
```

The Java library class Integer also performs caching. It creates a cache of 256 objects, for the integers between -128 and 127. Its valueOf method returns a reference to one of these constants if its argument is within that range; otherwise it creates a new object and returns it.

For example, consider the code of Listing 5-6. The first two calls to valueOf will return a reference to the cached Integer object for the value 127. The third and fourth calls will each create a new Integer object for the value 128. In other words, the code creates two new Integer objects, both having the value 128.

Listing 5-6. An Example of Integer Caching

```
List<Integer> L = new ArrayList<>();
L.add(Integer.valueOf(127)); // uses cached object
L.add(Integer.valueOf(127)); // uses cached object
L.add(Integer.valueOf(128)); // creates new object
L.add(Integer.valueOf(128)); // creates new object
```

The Java compiler uses autoboxing and unboxing to convert between int values and Integer objects. As with Boolean, it uses the valueOf method to perform the boxing and the intValue method to perform the unboxing. The code of Listing 5-7 is functionally equivalent to Listing 5-6.

Listing 5-7. An Equivalent Example of Integer Caching

```
List<Integer> L = new ArrayList<>();
L.add(127); // uses cached object
L.add(127); // uses cached object
L.add(128); // creates new object
L.add(128); // creates new object
```

Singleton Classes

One important use of caching is to implement *singleton classes.* A singleton class is a class that has a fixed number of objects, created when the class is loaded. It does not have a public constructor, so no additional objects can be created. It is called "singleton" because the most common situation is a class having a single instance.

For example, if the Java designers had made the Boolean constructor private (which would have been a good idea) then Boolean would be a singleton class. On the other hand, Integer cannot be a singleton class, even if its constructor were private, because its valueOf method creates new objects when needed.

The Java *enum* syntax simplifies the creation of singleton classes and is the preferred way of writing singletons. For example, Listing 5-8 shows how the code for Boolean can be rewritten as an enum. Differences from Listing 5-3 are in bold.

Listing 5-8. Writing Boolean as an Enum

```
public enum Boolean {
   TRUE(true), FALSE(false);

   private boolean value;

   private Boolean(boolean b) {value = b;}

   public boolean booleanValue() {
      return value;
   }

   public static Boolean valueOf(boolean b) {
      return (b ? TRUE : FALSE);
   }
   ...
}
```

Note that the syntactic differences are incredibly minor. The main difference concerns the definitions of the constants TRUE and FALSE, which omit both the declaration of their type and their call to the Boolean constructor. The values inside the parentheses denote the arguments to the constructor. That is, the statement

```
TRUE(true), FALSE(false);
```

is equivalent to the two statements

```
public static final Boolean TRUE  = new Boolean(true);
public static final Boolean FALSE = new Boolean(false);
```

Conceptually, an enum is a class that has no public constructors, and therefore no objects other than its public constants. In all other respects an enum behaves like a class. For example, the code of Listing 5-4 would be the same if Boolean were implemented as an enum or a class.

Beginners are often unaware of the correspondence between enums and classes because an enum is typically introduced as a named set of constants. For example, the following enum defines the three constants Speed.SLOW, Speed.MEDIUM, and Speed.FAST:

```
public enum Speed {SLOW, MEDIUM, FAST};
```

This enum is equivalent to the class definition of Listing 5-9. Note that each Speed constant is a reference to a Speed object having no functionality of interest.

Listing 5-9. The Meaning of the Speed Enum

```java
public class Speed {
    public static final Speed SLOW   = new Speed();
    public static final Speed MEDIUM = new Speed();
    public static final Speed FAST   = new Speed();

    private Speed() { }
}
```

As with classes, an enum constructor with no arguments and no body (such as the constructor for Speed) is called a *default constructor.* Default constructors can be omitted from enum declarations just as they can be omitted from class declarations.

Because the constants in an enum are objects, they inherit the equals, toString, and other methods of Object. In the simple case of the Speed enum, its objects can do nothing else. The elegant thing about the Java enum syntax is that enum constants can be given as much additional functionality as desired.

The default implementation of an enum's toString method is to return the name of the constant. For example, the following statement assigns the string "SLOW" to variable s.

```java
String s = Speed.SLOW.toString();
```

Suppose instead that you want the Speed constants to display as musical tempos. Then you could override the toString method as shown in Listing 5-10. In this case the preceding statement would assign the string "largo" to variable s.

Listing 5-10. Overriding the toString Method of Speed

```java
public enum Speed {
    SLOW("largo"), MEDIUM("moderato"), FAST("presto");

    private String name;
```

171

```
    private Speed(String name) {
        this.name = name;
    }

    public String toString() {
        return name;
    }
}
```

Singleton Strategy Classes

Let's return to version 10 of the banking demo. The OwnerStrategy interface has two implementing classes, Domestic and Foreign. Both of these classes have empty constructors and their objects are immutable. Consequently, all Domestic objects can be used interchangeably, as can all Foreign objects.

Instead of creating new Domestic and Foreign objects on demand (which is what the AbstractBankAccount class currently does), it would be better for the classes to be singletons. Listing 5-11 shows how to rewrite Foreign as an enum; the code for Domestic is similar. The two differences from the version 10 code are in bold.

Listing 5-11. Rewriting Foreign as an Enum

```
public enum Foreign implements OwnerStrategy {
    INSTANCE;

    public boolean isForeign() {
        return true;
    }

    public int fee() {
        return 500;
    }
```

```
public String toString() {
   return "foreign";
}
}
```

The constant INSTANCE holds the reference to the singleton Foreign object that was created by calling the enum's default constructor. The class Domestic also has a constant INSTANCE. Listing 5-12 shows how the class AbstractBankAccount can use these constants instead of creating new strategy objects.

Listing 5-12. Revising AbstractBankAccount to Use the Enums

```
public class AbstractBankAccount implements BankAccount {
   protected int acctnum;
   protected int balance = 0;
   protected OwnerStrategy owner = Domestic.INSTANCE;
   ...
   public void setForeign(boolean b) {
      owner = b ? Foreign.INSTANCE : Domestic.INSTANCE;
   }
}
```

Although this use of enums is reasonable, the version 12 banking demo uses a different implementation technique in which both constants belong to a single enum named Owners. Its code appears in Listing 5-13. This enum defines the constants Owners.DOMESTIC and Owners.FOREIGN, which correspond to the earlier constants Domestic.INSTANCE and Foreign.INSTANCE.

Listing 5-13. The Version 12 Owners Enum

```
public enum Owners implements OwnerStrategy {
   DOMESTIC(false,0,"domestic"), FOREIGN(true,500,"foreign");

   private boolean isforeign;
   private int fee;
   private String name;

   private Owners(boolean isforeign, int fee, String name) {
      this.isforeign = isforeign;
      this.fee = fee;
      this.name = name;
   }

   public boolean isForeign() {
      return isforeign;
   }

   public int fee() {
      return fee;
   }

   public String toString() {
      return name;
   }
}
```

The revised code for the version 12 class AbstractBankAccount appears in Listing 5-14.

Listing 5-14. The Version 12 AbstractBankAccount Class

```
public class AbstractBankAccount implements BankAccount {
   protected int acctnum;
   protected int balance = 0;
```

```java
protected OwnerStrategy owner = Owners.DOMESTIC;
...
public void setForeign(boolean b) {
    owner = (b ? Owners.FOREIGN : Owners.DOMESTIC);
}
}
```

From a design point of view, using a single enum that has two constants is roughly equivalent to using two enums that have one constant each. I chose the single enum approach because I happen to prefer its aesthetics—having constants named FOREIGN and DOMESTIC appeals to me more than having two constants named INSTANCE.

Another strategy interface in the version 10 banking demo is InputCommand. Its implementing classes are also immutable and can be rewritten using enums. Listing 5-15 shows how to rewrite the code for SelectCmd; the other seven strategy classes are similar.

Listing 5-15. Rewriting SelectCmd as an Enum

```java
public enum SelectCmd implements InputCommand {
    INSTANCE;

    public int execute(Scanner sc, Bank bank, int current) {
        System.out.print("Enter acct#: ");
        current = sc.nextInt();
        int balance = bank.getBalance(current);
        System.out.println("The balance of account " + current
                        + " is " + balance);
        return current;
    }

    public String toString() {
        return "select";
    }
}
```

The only required modification to the version 10 BankClient code is the way it creates its array of input commands. The array now consists of enum constants instead of new InputCommand objects. See Listing 5-16.

Listing 5-16. Rewriting BankClient to Reference Enums

```
public class BankClient {
    private Scanner scanner;
    private boolean done = false;
    private Bank bank;
    private int current = 0;
    private InputCommand[] commands = {
        QuitCmd.INSTANCE,
        NewCmd.INSTANCE,
        SelectCmd.INSTANCE,
        DepositCmd.INSTANCE,
        LoanCmd.INSTANCE,
        ShowCmd.INSTANCE,
        InterestCmd.INSTANCE,
        SetForeignCmd.INSTANCE };

    ...
}
```

An alternative to having a separate enum for each command is to create a single enum containing all the commands. The version 12 code takes this approach. The enum is named InputCommands and its code appears in Listing 5-17. The InputCommands constructor has two arguments: a string used by the toString method, and a lambda expression that defines its execute method. The code for the constant SELECT is in bold so that you can compare it with Listing 5-15.

Listing 5-17. The Version 12 InputCommands Enum

```
public enum InputCommands implements InputCommand {
    QUIT("quit", (sc, bank, current)->{
        sc.close();
        System.out.println("Goodbye!");
        return -1;
    }),
    NEW("new", (sc, bank, current)->{
        System.out.print("Enter account type(1=savings,
                        2=checking, 3=interest checking): ");
        int type = sc.nextInt();
        boolean isforeign = requestForeign(sc);
        current = bank.newAccount(type, isforeign);
        System.out.println("Your new account number is "
                        + current);
        return current;
    }),
    SELECT("select", (sc, bank, current)->{
        System.out.print("Enter account#: ");
        current = sc.nextInt();
        int balance = bank.getBalance(current);
        System.out.println("The balance of account " + current
                        + " is " + balance);
        return current;
    }),
    DEPOSIT("deposit", (sc, bank, current)->{
        System.out.print("Enter deposit amount: ");
        int amt = sc.nextInt();
        bank.deposit(current, amt);
        return current;
    }),
```

```
LOAN("loan", (sc, bank, current)->{
    System.out.print("Enter loan amount: ");
    int amt = sc.nextInt();
    boolean ok = bank.authorizeLoan(current, amt);
    if (ok)
        System.out.println("Your loan is approved");
    else
        System.out.println("Your loan is denied");
    return current;
}),
SHOW("show", (sc, bank, current)->{
    System.out.println(bank.toString());
    return current;
}),
INTEREST("interest", (sc, bank, current)-> {
    bank.addInterest();
    return current;
}),
SET_FOREIGN("setforeign", (sc, bank, current)-> {
    bank.setForeign(current, requestForeign(sc));
    return current;
});

private String name;
private InputCommand cmd;

private InputCommands(String name, InputCommand cmd) {
    this.name = name;
    this.cmd = cmd;
}

public int execute(Scanner sc, Bank bank, int current) {
    return cmd.execute(sc, bank, current);
}
```

```
    public String toString() {
        return name;
    }

    private static boolean requestForeign(Scanner sc) {
        System.out.print("Enter 1 for foreign,
                            2 for domestic: ");
        int val = sc.nextInt();
        return (val == 1);
    }
}
```

An enum has the static method values, which returns an array of its constants. The BankClient class can take advantage of this method. Instead of constructing the array of commands shown in Listing 5-16, BankClient can now call InputCommands.values(). See Listing 5-18.

Listing 5-18. The Version 12 BankClient Class

```
public class BankClient {
    private Scanner scanner;
    private boolean done = false;
    private Bank bank;
    private int current = 0;
    private InputCommand[] commands = InputCommands.values();
    ...
}
```

Although the use of InputCommands.values is certainly convenient, you may be wondering whether the single enum design is a good idea. One issue is that it violates the Single Responsibility rule—the InputCommands enum has the responsibility for eight different commands, which leads to a larger and more complex enum than having eight separate enums.

Having a single enum also violates the Open/Closed rule—adding a new command requires a modification to `InputCommands` instead of the creation of another enum.

These violations are mitigated by the fact that enums are much safer to modify than arbitrary code, as modification only involves adding or deleting a constant. Perhaps the most compelling reason to use a single enum is to take advantage of its `values` method. Without it, the addition of a new command requires creating the new enum and modifying the code that creates the list of commands; and since that code exists separately from the enum, there is a significant chance that the modification will be overlooked. That possibility seems too dangerous to ignore, and tips the scales in favor of the single enum design.

Static Factory Methods

Recall from the beginning of this chapter that the `Boolean` and `Integer` classes have a method `valueOf`, which takes a primitive value, boxes it, and returns the boxed object. This method hides certain details about its return object—in particular, the caller does not know whether the returned object is a new object or a previously created one. The `valueOf` method assumes responsibility for determining the best course of action, which is why using it is preferable to using a constructor.

The `valueOf` method is called a *static factory method*. A factory method is a method whose job is to create objects. It encapsulates the details of object creation, and can hide the class of a newly constructed object. It can even hide the fact that it is returning a previously-created object instead of a new one.

The Java library contains many other static factory methods. One example is the static method `asList` in the class `Arrays`. The argument to this method is an array of object references and its return value is a list containing those references. The following code illustrates its use.

```
String[] names = {"joe", "sue", "max"};
List<String> L = Arrays.asList(names);
```

The asList method returns a list containing the elements of the supplied array, but it gives no other details. The method not only hides the algorithm for creating the list, it also hides the class of the list. This encapsulation gives the factory method considerable flexibility in how it chooses to create the list. For example, one option is for the method to create a new ArrayList object and then add each element of the array into it. But other options are possible. Chapter 7 will discuss a very efficient solution that uses an adapter class.

The library class ByteBuffer provides other examples of static factory methods. A ByteBuffer object denotes an area of memory and has methods to store and retrieve primitive values at arbitrary locations within the area. Formally, ByteBuffer is an abstract class that has two subclasses. The subclass DirectByteBuffer allocates its space from the operating system's I/O buffers. The subclass HeapByteBuffer allocates its space from the Java VM.

Neither of these subclasses has a public constructor. The only way to construct a ByteBuffer object is to use one of three static factory methods. The method allocateDirect creates a new direct buffer; the method allocate creates a new, uninitialized heap buffer; and the method wrap creates a new heap buffer based on the contents of its argument array.

The following statements illustrate the use of these three factory methods. The first statement creates a 200-byte direct buffer. The second statement creates a 200-byte heap buffer. The last two statements create a heap buffer based on the array variable *bytes*.

```
ByteBuffer bb  = ByteBuffer.allocateDirect(200);
ByteBuffer bb2 = ByteBuffer.allocate(200);
byte[]    bytes = new byte[200];
ByteBuffer bb3 = ByteBuffer.wrap(bytes);
```

The benefit of these static factory methods is that they hide the existence of the ByteBuffer subclasses. Note how the class ByteBuffer acts as a mediator between its clients and its subclasses, ensuring that its clients are unable to discern anything about how ByteBuffer objects are created and what classes they belong to.

For a final example of a static factory method, consider the banking demo. The version 10 BankAccount interface has the static factory method createSavingsWithDeposit. In this case the purpose of the factory method is for convenience. It enables a client to create a SavingsAccount object and perform an initial deposit, using a single method.

Let's examine how to improve the banking demo by adding additional static factory methods. Consider for example how the version 10 Bank class creates bank accounts. Listing 5-19 shows its newAccount method, which performs the account creation.

Listing 5-19. The Version 10 newAccount Method

```
public int newAccount(int type, boolean isforeign) {
    int acctnum = nextacct++;
    BankAccount ba;
    if (type == 1)
        ba = new SavingsAccount(acctnum);
    else if (type == 2)
        ba = new RegularChecking(acctnum);
    else
        ba = new InterestChecking(acctnum);
    ba.setForeign(isforeign);
    accounts.put(acctnum, ba);
    return acctnum;
}
```

The if-statement in bold is the only part of the entire Bank class that is aware of the BankAccount subclasses. Everywhere else, the code manipulates bank accounts transparently, using variables of type BankAccount. This situation is similar to what occurs with ByteBuffer, and the solution is also similar: there needs to be a mediator that can handle the calls to the constructors, thereby shielding Bank from the BankAccount subclasses.

Version 12 of the demo introduces the interface AccountFactory for this purpose; its code appears in Listing 5-20. The interface contains the static factory methods createSavings, createRegularChecking, createInterestChecking, and createAccount.

Listing 5-20. The Version 12 AccountFactory Interface

```
public interface AccountFactory {
   static BankAccount createSavings(int acctnum) {
      return new SavingsAccount(acctnum);
   }

   static BankAccount createRegularChecking(int acctnum) {
      return new RegularChecking(acctnum);
   }

   static BankAccount createInterestChecking(int acctnum) {
      return new InterestChecking(acctnum);
   }

   static BankAccount createAccount(int type, int acctnum) {
      BankAccount ba;
      if (type == 1)
         ba = createSavings(acctnum);
      else if (type == 2)
         ba = createRegularChecking(acctnum);
```

```
        else
            ba = createInterestChecking(acctnum);
        return ba;
    }
}
```

The first three methods hide the subclass constructors. The createAccount method encapsulates the decision about which account type has which type number. This decision had previously been made by Bank (as was shown in Listing 5-19) as well as SavedBankInfo (see Listing 3-17). By moving the decision to AccountFactory, those classes can now call createAccount without needing to know anything about how account types are implemented.

For example, Listing 5-21 shows the version 12 newAccount method of Bank, modified to call the createAccount method. The SavedBankInfo class is modified similarly but is not shown here.

Listing 5-21. The Version 12 newAccount Method of Bank

```
public int newAccount(int type, boolean isforeign) {
    int acctnum = nextacct++;
    BankAccount ba =
                AccountFactory.createAccount(type, acctnum);
    ba.setForeign(isforeign);
    accounts.put(acctnum, ba);
    return acctnum;
}
```

Recall the static method createSavingsWithDeposit from the BankAccount interface, which creates savings accounts having a specified initial balance. This method can now be revised to call a factory method instead of a constructor. Its code appears in Listing 5-22.

Listing 5-22. The Version 12 BankAccount Interface

```
public interface BankAccount extends Comparable<BankAccount> {
   ...
   static BankAccount createSavingsWithDeposit(
                                   int acctnum, int n) {
      BankAccount ba = AccountFactory.createSavings(acctnum);
      ba.deposit(n);
      return ba;
   }
}
```

Factory Objects

The AccountFactory class greatly improves the banking demo, because the demo now has a single place to hold its knowledge about the BankAccount subclasses. Of course, AccountFactory is coupled to every BankAccount subclass, which implies that any changes to the subclasses will require a modification to AccountFactory—thereby violating the Open/Closed rule. But at least this violation has been limited to a single, well-known place.

It is possible to improve on this design. The idea is that a static factory method is essentially a *command* to create an object. If you have several related static factory methods (as AccountFactory does) then you can create a more object-oriented design by using the command pattern from Chapter 4.

Recall that in the command pattern, each command is an object. To execute a command you first obtain the desired command object and then call its execute method. Analogously, to execute a factory command you first obtain the desired factory object and then call its create method. The following code illustrates how these two steps combine to create a new BankAccount object from a factory object.

```
AccountFactory af = new SavingsFactory();
BankAccount ba = af.create(123);
```

Variable af holds a factory object of type SavingsFactory. Assuming that the create method of SavingsFactory calls the SavingsAccount constructor, the variable ba will hold a new SavingsAccount object.

Version 13 of the banking demo takes this approach. It has three factory classes: SavingsFactory, RegularCheckingFactory, and InterestCheckingFactory. Each factory class has the method create, which calls the appropriate class constructor. Listing 5-23 shows the version 13 code for SavingsFactory, whose create method calls the SavingsAccount constructor. The code for the other two factory classes is similar.

Listing 5-23. The SavingsFactory Class

```
public class SavingsFactory implements AccountFactory {
    public BankAccount create(int acctnum) {
        return new SavingsAccount(acctnum);
    }
}
```

The factory classes form a strategy hierarchy with AccountFactory as its interface. Listing 5-24 shows the version 13 code for AccountFactory. In addition to the new nonstatic method create, the interface also revises its static createAccount method to use the strategy classes.

Listing 5-24. The Version 13 AccountFactory Interface

```
public interface AccountFactory {
    BankAccount create(int acctnum);

    static BankAccount createAccount(int type, int acctnum) {
        AccountFactory af;
        if (type == 1)
            af = new SavingsFactory();
```

```
    else if (type == 2)
        af = new RegularCheckingFactory();
    else
        af = new InterestCheckingFactory();
    return af.create(acctnum);
    }
}
```

The loss of the static factory method createSavings means that the method createSavingsWithDeposit in BankAccount needs to be modified to use a factory object instead. Listing 5-25 gives the revised code.

Listing 5-25. The Version 13 BankAccount Interface

```
public interface BankAccount extends Comparable<BankAccount> {
    ...
    static BankAccount createSavingsWithDeposit(
                                    int acctnum, int n) {
        AccountFactory af = new SavingsFactory();
        BankAccount ba = af.create(acctnum);
        ba.deposit(n);
        return ba;
    }
}
```

Figure 5-1 shows the class diagram for the factory hierarchy and its connection to the BankAccount hierarchy. Note that there is a dependency arrow from each factory class to its corresponding BankAccount class.

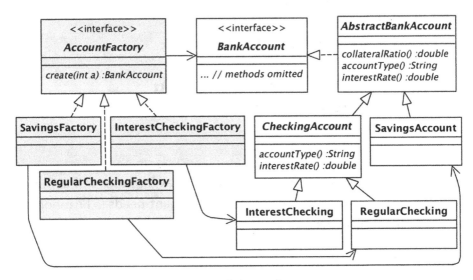

Figure 5-1. *The AccountFactory hierarchy*

Cached Factory Objects

The code of Listings 5-24 and 5-25 should help solidify your understanding of how factories work—namely that the creation of an object requires two steps: creating a factory object, and calling its create method. The code may also leave you with the question of why anyone would want to do things this way. What is the advantage of using factory objects?

The answer has to do with the fact that factory objects do not need to be created at the same time as the objects they create. In fact, it usually makes sense to create the factory objects early and cache them. Listing 5-26 revises Listing 5-24 to perform this caching.

Listing 5-26. Revising AccountFactory to Use Caching

```
public interface AccountFactory {
    BankAccount create(int acctnum);

    static AccountFactory[] factories = {
                        new SavingsFactory(),
```

```
new RegularCheckingFactory(),
new InterestCheckingFactory() };
```

```
static BankAccount createAccount(int type, int acctnum) {
    AccountFactory af = factories[type-1];
    return af.create(acctnum);
}
}
```

Note the implementation of the createAccount method. It no longer needs to use an if-statement to choose which type of account to create. Instead, it can simply index into the precomputed array of factory objects. This is a big breakthrough in the design of AccountFactory. Not only does it eliminate the annoying if-statement but it also brings the interface very close to satisfying the Open/Closed rule. To add a new account factory, you now only need to create a new factory class and add an entry for that class into the factories array.

Of course, instead of caching the factory objects manually, it would be better to implement them as enum constants. This is the approach taken in version 14 of the banking demo. Listing 5-27 gives the code for the enum AccountFactories, which creates a constant for each of the three factory class objects. The constructor has two arguments: a string indicating the display value of the constant, and a lambda expression giving the code for the create method.

Listing 5-27. The Version 14 AccountFactories Enum

```
public enum AccountFactories implements AccountFactory {
    SAVINGS("Savings",
            acctnum -> new SavingsAccount(acctnum)),
    REGULAR_CHECKING("Regular checking",
            acctnum -> new RegularChecking(acctnum)),
    INTEREST_CHECKING("Interest checking",
            acctnum -> new InterestChecking(acctnum));
```

```
    private String name;
    private AccountFactory af;

    private AccountFactories(String name, AccountFactory af) {
        this.name = name;
        this.af = af;
    }

    public BankAccount create(int acctnum) {
        return af.create(acctnum);
    }

    public String toString() {
        return name;
    }
}
```

Listing 5-28 gives the version 14 code for AccountFactory. As with the InputCommands enum, the call to AccountFactories.values() enables AccountFactory to completely satisfy the Open/Closed rule. Now the only action required to add a new account factory is to create a new constant for it in AccountFactories.

Listing 5-28. The Version 14 AccountFactory Class

```
public interface AccountFactory {
    BankAccount create(int acctnum);
    static AccountFactory[] factories =
                            AccountFactories.values();
    static BankAccount createAccount(int type, int acctnum) {
        AccountFactory af = factories[type-1];
        return af.create(acctnum);
    }
}
```

The version 14 code for the createSavingsWithDeposit method appears in Listing 5-29.

Listing 5-29. The Version 14 BankAccount Interface

```java
public interface BankAccount extends Comparable<BankAccount> {
    ...
    static BankAccount createSavingsWithDeposit(
                                    int acctnum, int n) {
        AccountFactory af = AccountFactory.SAVINGS;
        BankAccount ba = af.create(acctnum);
        ba.deposit(n);
        return ba;
    }
}
```

One final point: You might recall that the constant NEW in the version 13 InputCommands enum asks the user to choose from a list of account types. How can you ensure that the type numbers presented to the user stay in synch with the type numbers associated with the AccountFactory array?

The solution is to modify NEW so that it constructs the user message based on the contents of the AccountFactories.values array. Listing 5-30 shows the relevant code.

Listing 5-30. The Version 14 InputCommands Enum

```java
public enum InputCommands implements InputCommand {
    ...
NEW("new", (sc, bank, current)->{
        printMessage();
        int type = sc.nextInt();
        current = bank.newAccount(type);
        System.out.println("Your new account number is "
                        + current);
```

```
        return current;
    }),
...
    private static String message;

    static {
        AccountFactory[] factories = AccountFactories.values();
        message = "Enter Account Type (";
        for (int i=0; i<factories.length-1; i++)
            message += (i+1) + "=" + factories[i] + ", ";
        message += factories.length + "="
                + factories[factories.length-1] +")";
    }

    private static void printMessage() {
        System.out.print(message);
    }
}
```

The construction of the message string is in a static block to ensure that it only occurs once. The code iterates through the constants in the AccountFactories enum. For each constant, it adds the index of that constant (plus one) to the message, followed by the toString value of the constant.

The Factory Pattern

The class diagram of Figure 5-1 illustrates a typical use of factory classes, namely that the classes in the factory hierarchy create objects belonging to a second, parallel hierarchy called the *result hierarchy*. Each class in the factory hierarchy has a corresponding class in the result hierarchy. In Figure 5-1 the parallel hierarchies are AccountFactory and BankAccount.

This design is sufficiently common that is has a name: the *factory pattern*. Figure 5-2 shows the general form of the factory pattern with its parallel hierarchies.

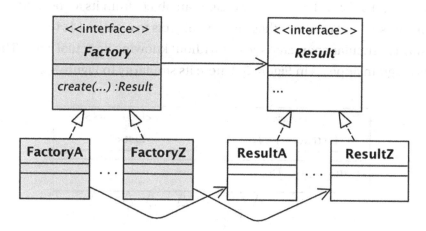

Figure 5-2. *The factory pattern*

Typically, the need for the factory pattern arises when you have a result hierarchy and you want clients to be able to create result objects without knowing the names of each result subclass. The factory pattern says that you should create a parallel factory hierarchy so that your clients can create a result object by calling the create method of the appropriate factory object.

For an example, consider the List interface. The Java library has several classes that implement List, with each class having a different purpose. For example, Vector is thread-safe; CopyOnWriteArrayList enables safe concurrent access; ArrayList is random-access; and LinkedList supports fast inserts and deletes. Suppose that you want your clients to be able to create List objects based on these characteristics, but you don't want them to choose the classes themselves. You might have several reasons for this decision: perhaps you don't want your clients to have to know the name of each class and its characteristics, or you want clients to choose from only these four classes, or you want the flexibility to change the class associated with a given characteristic as time goes on.

193

Your solution is to use the factory pattern. You create an interface
ListFactory, whose factory classes are ThreadSafeFactory,
ConcurrentAccessFactory, RandomAccessFactory, and
FastUpdateFactory. Each factory creates an object from its associated
result class. Clients can use these factory objects to create a List object
having a particular characteristic but without knowing its actual class. The
class diagram appears in Figure 5-3; note its similarity to Figure 5-2.

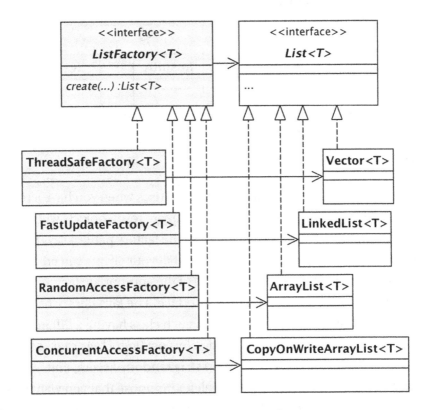

Figure 5-3. *The ListFactory strategy hierarchy*

Factories for Customized Objects

The factory pattern assumes that the classes in a factory hierarchy create objects from different result classes. Another way to use a factory hierarchy is to have the factory classes create objects from the same result class. In this case, the purpose of each factory is to *customize* its result object in a particular way. This section examines three examples of this design technique.

For the first example, consider version 11 of the banking demo (i.e., the aborted version from the end of Chapter 4). In that version, AbstractBankAccount has no subclasses; all bank accounts are instances of AbstractBankAccount. The different types of account are distinguished by a TypeStrategy object passed to the AbstractBankAccount constructor. How would you use factory classes here?

Even though there is no AbstractBankAccount hierarchy, it would still make sense to have an AccountFactory hierarchy. Each factory object would choose the appropriate TypeStrategy object and pass it to the AbstractBankAccount constructor. Listing 5-31 shows what the SavingsFactory class might look like, with differences from the version 11 code in bold. Each factory class creates an AbstractBankAccount object, customized with a different type strategy.

Listing 5-31. An Alternative SavingsFactory Class

```java
public class SavingsFactory implements AccountFactory {
    public BankAccount create(int acctnum) {
        TypeStrategy ts = new SavingsAccount();
        return new AbstractBankAccount(acctnum, ts);
    }
}
```

For a second example of customization, return to version 14 of the banking demo. Suppose that the bank decides that savings accounts opened by new customers will have an initial balance of $10. A reasonable way to implement this feature is to create a "new customer" factory by adding NEW_CUSTOMER to the AccountFactories enum as its fourth constant. See Listing 5-32. Note that the "new customer" factory does not create "new customer" accounts. Instead, it creates savings accounts that have been customized to have a non-zero initial balance.

Listing 5-32. Adding Promotional Accounts to AccountFactories

```java
public enum AccountFactories implements AccountFactory {
    SAVINGS("Savings",
            acctnum -> new SavingsAccount(acctnum)),
    REGULAR_CHECKING("Regular checking",
            acctnum -> new RegularChecking(acctnum)),
    INTEREST_CHECKING("Interest checking",
            acctnum -> new InterestChecking(acctnum)),
    NEW_CUSTOMER("New Customer Savings",
            acctnum -> {
                BankAccount result = new SavingsAccount(acctnum);
                result.deposit(1000); // $10 for free!
                return result; });
    ...
}
```

The Java library interface ThreadFactory provides a third example of how factories can be used for object customization. This interface is defined as follows:

```java
interface ThreadFactory {
    Thread newThread(Runnable r);
}
```

The newThread method returns a customized Thread object. Each class that implements ThreadFactory will have its own way to customize the threads returned by newThread. As an example, Listing 5-33 defines the class PriorityThreadFactory, which generates new threads having a specified priority.

Listing 5-33. The Class PriorityThreadFactory

```
class PriorityThreadFactory implements ThreadFactory {
    private int priority;
    public PriorityThreadFactory(int p) {
        priority = p;
    }

    public Thread newThread(Runnable r) {
        Thread t = new Thread(r);
        t.setPriority(priority);
        return t;
    }
}
```

Listing 5-34 illustrates the use of PriorityThreadFactory. The code creates two ThreadFactory objects: one that creates high-priority Thread objects and one that creates low-priority Thread objects. It then creates two threads from each factory and runs them.

Listing 5-34. Using the PriorityThreadFactory Class

```
ThreadFactory important = new PriorityThreadFactory(9);
ThreadFactory menial = new PriorityThreadFactory(2);
Runnable r1 = ...; Runnable r2 = ...;
Runnable r3 = ...; Runnable r4 = ...;
```

```
Thread t1 = important.newThread(r1);
Thread t2 = important.newThread(r2);
Thread t3 = menial.newThread(r3);
Thread t4 = menial.newThread(r4);
t1.start(); t2.start(); t3.start(); t4.start();
```

Listing 5-34 demonstrates another benefit of using a factory class to customize objects. Given a factory object, a client can call its `create` method multiple times and the resulting objects will all be customized the same. (In Listing 5-34 the objects will all have the same priority. In Listing 5-31 they will all have the same account type.) You can think of each factory object as a cookie cutter, with each factory class producing a different shape of cookie. Moreover, factory objects can be passed from one method to another, so that the user of a factory object may have no idea which shape of cookie it creates.

Summary

Class constructors are problematic. When a class calls the constructor of another class the two classes become coupled. This coupling reduces the ability to write abstract and transparent code. This chapter examined two strategies for addressing this issue: *caching* and *factories*.

Caching reuses objects, thereby reducing the need for constructors. Immutable objects are good candidates for caching. If a class only needs a fixed number of immutable objects, then it can create and cache those objects when it is loaded. Such classes are called *singletons*. The Java enum syntax is the preferred way to define singleton classes.

A *factory* is a class that encapsulates constructor usage. When a class needs to create an object, it calls a method from the appropriate factory class. Factory classes can be static or nonstatic.

A static factory class typically consists of multiple static methods, each of which calls a different constructor. A static factory method hides the constructor it calls, as well as the class of the return value. An example is the static method ByteBuffer.allocate, which hides its call to the HeapByteBuffer constructor. A caller of the allocate method is not aware of the ByteBuffer subclass that the return value belongs to, or even that ByteBuffer has subclasses.

Nonstatic factory classes are organized into strategy hierarchies. Each class in the hierarchy implements a create method, which embodies a particular strategy for creating result objects. When all the classes in a factory hierarchy create objects belonging to the same result hierarchy then the design is called the *factory pattern*. When multiple factory classes create objects belonging to the same class then the factory classes are said to provide *customizations* of their result objects.

CHAPTER 6

Iterables and Iteration

This chapter addresses the following question: suppose that a variable holds a collection of objects; what code should you write to examine its elements? Technically speaking, this question is asking about *iterables* and *iteration*. A collection is an iterable, and the mechanism for examining its elements is iteration. The question can be rephrased as "How should I iterate through an iterable?"

Java supports multiple ways to iterate through an iterable, which can be divided into two categories: *external iteration*, in which you write a loop that examines each element of the iterable; and *internal iteration*, in which you call a method to perform the loop for you. This chapter covers the programming issues related to both uses of iteration, as well as the design issues of how to write classes that support iteration.

Iterators

Suppose that you have a variable L that holds a collection of objects. What code should you write to print its elements? One possibility is to write the following loop:

```java
for (int i=0; i<L.size(); i++)
    System.out.println(L.get(i));
```

© Edward Sciore 2019
E. Sciore, *Java Program Design*, https://doi.org/10.1007/978-1-4842-4143-1_6

There are two reasons why this code is not very good. First, it violates the rule of Abstraction because it uses the method get, which is only supported by collections that implement List. Second, it will execute much less efficiently in some List implementations than in others. In particular, the get method for ArrayList performs a constant-time array access whereas the get method for LinkedList searches the chain of nodes. Consequently, the loop will execute in linear time if L implements ArrayList but in quadratic time if L implements LinkedList.

The way to address both issues is to provide each collection class with methods that are specifically dedicated to iteration. In Java these methods are called hasNext and next. The method hasNext returns a boolean indicating whether an unexamined element remains. The method next returns one of the unexamined elements. These methods solve the first issue because they can be implemented for any kind of collection, not just lists; they solve the second issue because each class can have its own implementation of these methods, tuned to be as efficient as possible.

Where should these methods live? Recall from Figure 2-3 that the root of the collection hierarchy is the interface Iterable. All collections are iterables. These methods should be associated with Iterable, but how? The obvious design is to add the methods to the Iterable interface, meaning that each collection object would have its own hasNext and next methods. Under this design, the code to print the contents of a list L would look like this:

```
// Warning: This code is not legal Java.
while (L.hasNext())
    System.out.println(L.next());
```

This design is unsatisfactory because it can allow incorrect behavior to occur. Listing 6-1 provides an example. The noDuplicates method is intended to return true if its argument list has no duplicates. The code calls the helper method isUnique, which should return true if a specified string appears exactly once in the list. The idea is noDuplicates iterates through each string in L, calling isUnique for each one and returning false if isUnique ever returns false. The method isUnique also iterates through L, returning true if it finds exactly one occurrence of string s.

Listing 6-1. A Terrible Way to Test a List for Duplicates

```java
// Warning: This code is not legal Java.
// And even if it were, it wouldn't work.

public boolean noDuplicates(List<String> L) {
    while (L.hasNext()) {
        String s = L.next();
        if (!isUnique(L, s))
            return false;
    }
    return true;
}

private boolean isUnique(List<String> L, String s) {
    int count = 0;
    while (L.hasNext())
        if (L.next().equals(s))
            count++;
    return count == 1;
}
```

Incorrect behavior occurs because both methods iterate through L concurrently. The first time through the noDuplicates loop, the code examines the first element of L and calls isUnique. That method will iterate through L (starting with the second element) and return back to noDuplicates after having read all of L. Therefore, the second time through the noDuplicates loop the call to L.hasNext will immediately return false, and noDuplicates will exit prematurely.

203

The only way for this algorithm to work correctly is if both methods can iterate through L independently. That is, the functionality to iterate though a list must be separate from the list itself. Java takes this approach, moving the methods hasNext and next to a separate interface called Iterator.

The Iterable interface (and thus every collection) has a method iterator; each call to iterator returns a new Iterator object. For example, the following code prints the elements of L:

```
Iterator<String> iter = L.iterator();
while (iter.hasNext())
    System.out.println(iter.next());
```

It may seem awkward to create an Iterator object each time you need to iterate through a collection, but that is how Java separates the iteration from the collection. When a method creates an Iterator object for a collection, the method is guaranteed that its iteration will be independent of any other iteration of the collection. (And if some other method happens to modify the iterable while your iteration is still in progress, Java will throw a ConcurrentModificationException to inform you that your iteration has become invalid.)

Listing 6-2 gives the correct code for NoDuplicates. Note that each method has its own iterator. In fact, isUnique creates a new iterator for L each time it is called.

Listing 6-2. A Correct Way to Check a List for Duplicates

```
public class NoDuplicates {
    public boolean noDuplicates(List<String> L) {
        Iterator<String> iter = L.iterator();
        while (iter.hasNext()) {
            String s = iter.next();
            if (!isUnique(L, s))
                return false;
        }
```

```
        return true;
    }

    private boolean isUnique(List<String> L, String s) {
        int count = 0;
        Iterator<String> iter = L.iterator();
        while (iter.hasNext())
            if (iter.next().equals(s))
                count++;
        return count == 1;
    }
}
```

Writing an Iterator Class

This section explores some classes that implement Iterator. An iterator class needs to implement the hasNext and next methods. It need not be associated with an iterable. Listing 6-3 gives a very simple example of a "stand alone" iterator class named RandomIterator. The intent of this class is to generate arbitrarily many random numbers. Its next method returns another random integer and its hasNext method always returns true.

Listing 6-3. The RandomIterator Class

```
public class RandomIterator implements Iterator<Integer> {
    private Random rand = new Random();

    public boolean hasNext() {
        return true;
    }

    public Integer next() {
```

205

```
        return rand.nextInt();
    }
}
```

The code in Listing 6-4 tests RandomIterator. It generates random integers, savings them in a hash set and stopping when a duplicate occurs. It then prints the number of nonduplicate integers that were generated.

Listing 6-4. Using the RandomIterator Class

```
Iterator<Integer> iter = new RandomIterator();
Set<Integer> nums = new HashSet<>();
boolean dupNotFound = true;
while (dupNotFound)
    dupNotFound = nums.add(iter.next());
System.out.println(nums.size());
```

Listing 6-5 gives another example of an iterator class, named PrimeIterator. This class generates the first N prime numbers, where N is specified in the constructor. The code for next calculates the value of the next prime and keeps track of how many primes have been generated. The code for hasNext returns false as soon as the indicated number of primes has been generated. The code of Listing 6-6 tests this class by printing the first 20 primes.

Listing 6-5. The PrimeIterator Class

```
public class PrimeIterator implements Iterator<Integer> {
    private int current = 1;
    private int howmany;
    private int count = 0;

    public PrimeIterator(int howmany) {
        this.howmany = howmany;
    }
```

```java
public boolean hasNext() {
    return count < howmany;
}

public Integer next() {
    current++;
    while (!isPrime(current)) // Loop until
        current++;            // you find a prime.
    count++;
    return current;
}

private boolean isPrime(int n) {
    for (int i=2; i*i<=n; i++)
        if (n%i == 0)
            return false;
    return true;
}
}
```

Listing 6-6. Printing the First 20 Primes

```java
Iterator<Integer> iter = new PrimeIterator(20);
while (iter.hasNext()) {
    int p = iter.next();
    System.out.println(p);
}
```

Now suppose that you want to create a class PrimeCollection whose objects denote a collection of the first N primes for some N. The easiest way to create a class that implements Collection is to extend the abstract class AbstractCollection. To do so you need to implement its abstract methods size and iterator. The code for PrimeCollection appears in Listing 6-7. It uses the PrimeIterator class to implement the iterator method.

Listing 6-7. The PrimeCollection Class

```
public class PrimeCollection
              extends AbstractCollection<Integer> {
   private int size;

   public PrimeCollection(int size) {
      this.size = size;
   }

   public int size() {
      return size;
   }

   public Iterator<Integer> iterator() {
      return new PrimeIterator(size);
   }
}
```

A PrimeCollection object has a very interesting feature—its collection of primes is not stored within the object, nor are they stored within its iterator. Instead, the primes are generated by the iterator, on demand. Some people find it difficult to grasp the idea that a Collection object doesn't need to actually hold a collection. Instead, *it only needs to act as if it does,* by implementing the methods of the interface. This is the beauty of encapsulation.

The easy way to create a class that implements List is to extend AbstractList and implement its two abstract methods size and get. The code for AbstractList implements the remaining methods of the List interface. The class RangeList from Listing 3-11 was such an example.

The iterator method is one of the methods implemented by AbstractList. Listing 6-8 gives a simplified implementation of the method. Its code creates and returns a new AbstractListIterator object. The object holds a reference to the list and its current position in the list. Its next method calls the list's get method to retrieve the element from the list at the current position, and increments the current position. Its hasNext method calls the list's size method to determine when there are no more elements.

Listing 6-8. Simplified Code for the AbstractList and AbstractListIterator Classes

```
public abstract class AbstractList<T> {
   public abstract T get(int n);
   public abstract int size();

   public Iterator<T> iterator() {
      return new AbstractListIterator<T>(this);
   }
   ... // code for the other List methods
}

class AbstractListIterator<T> implements Iterator<T> {
   private int current = 0;
   private AbstractList<T> list;

   public AbstractListIterator(AbstractList<T> list) {
      this.list = list;
   }

   public boolean hasNext() {
      return current < list.size();
   }
```

```
public T next() {
    T val = list.get(current);
    current++;
    return val;
  }
}
```

Note that this implementation of iterator uses the get method, and therefore will exhibit the same inefficient behavior as the code at the very beginning of this chapter. As a result, whenever you create a class by extending AbstractList, you must decide if it makes sense to overwrite the default implementation of iterator with a more efficient one.

The Iterator Pattern

Figure 6-1 depicts the relationship between the classes and interfaces mentioned in the previous section. The interface Iterable, its two sub-interfaces, and three implementing classes constitute the shaded hierarchy on the left side of the diagram; Iterator and its three implementing classes form the hierarchy on the right side.

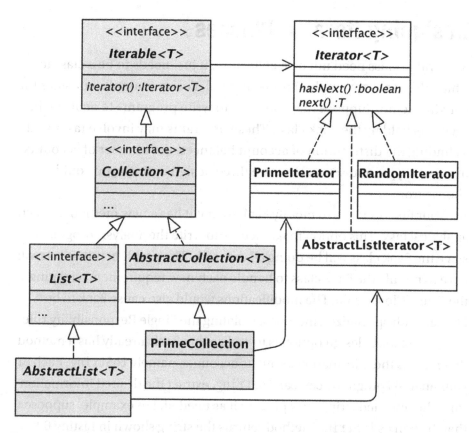

Figure 6-1. *Examples of the iterator pattern*

This separation between the Iterable and Iterator hierarchies is known as the *iterator pattern*. The iterator pattern asserts that every class that implements Iterable should be coupled to a corresponding class that implements Iterator. The Java collection class library was specifically designed to satisfy the iterator pattern.

The parallel hierarchies of the iterator pattern bear a strong resemblance to the parallel hierarchies of the factory pattern, as shown in Figure 5-2. This resemblance is not coincidental. An iterable can be thought of as an "iterator factory." Given an Iterable object L, each call to L.iterator() creates a new Iterator object customized with the elements of L.

Designing Iterable Classes

An iterable class need not be a collection; it just needs to be a class for which the `iterator` method is meaningful. For an example, consider the banking demo. Suppose that you want to write programs to analyze the accounts held by the Bank class. These programs may involve tasks such as finding the distribution of account balances, the number of accounts of a given type, and so on. Here are three design options you could choose from.

Your first option is to modify Bank so that it has a new method for each analytical task. This option makes it easy to write the analysis programs, since the Bank class will be doing all the work. The problem is that you will have to modify the Bank class to handle each new requirement, violating the Open/Closed rule. The modifications would also cause Bank to be bloated with specialized methods, violating the Single Responsibility rule.

Your second design option is to realize that Bank already has a method that returns the information about its accounts, namely `toString`. Each of your analysis programs can call `toString`, extract the desired information from the returned string, and process it as needed. For example, suppose that the bank's `toString` method returns the string shown in Listing 6-9. Each line except the first describes an account. To find the balance of each account, the analysis program can look for the number following "balance=" on each line. To find the foreign accounts, it can look for the string "is foreign". And so on.

Listing 6-9. Output of the Bank's toString Method

```
The bank has 3 accounts.
 Savings account 0: balance=3333, is foreign, fee=500
 Regular checking account 1: balance=6666, is domestic, fee=0
 Interest checking account 2: balance=9999, is domestic, fee=0
```

This technique is known as *screen scraping*. The term refers to the case when a program extracts information from the HTML contents of a web page. Screen scraping is an option of last resort. It is difficult to perform and will break when the format of the toString output changes.

The third and only good option is to modify the Bank class to have one (or more) general-purpose methods that clients can use to extract information. The iterator method is a good choice here. It allows clients to iterate through the desired accounts without breaking the encapsulated implementation of the account information. (For example, the clients won't be able to discover that the accounts are stored in a map.)

Version 15 of the banking demo makes this modification. The Bank class now implements Iterable<BankAccount>, which means that it must supply an iterator method that returns BankAccount objects. Listing 6-10 gives the relevant changes to *Bank*.

Listing 6-10. The Version 15 Bank Class

```
public class Bank implements Iterable<BankAccount> {
   ...
   public Iterator<BankAccount> iterator() {
      return accounts.values().iterator();
   }
}
```

Version 15 of the banking demo also has two new classes, IteratorAccountStats and StreamAccountStats, which are clients of Bank. The methods in these classes support two prototypical tasks: printing and finding the maximum balance of some selected accounts. These classes contain multiple methods for the two tasks, in order to illustrate different programming techniques. The remainder of this chapter examines the methods in these classes and the techniques behind them.

External Iteration

Iterators are the fundamental way to examine the elements of an iterable. Listing 6-11 shows the basic idiom for traversing an iterable. The examples in the previous sections of this chapter all used this idiom.

Listing 6-11. The Basic Idiom for Using Iterators

```
Iterable<E> c = ...
Iterator<E> iter = c.iterator();
while (iter.hasNext()) {
   E e = iter.next();
   ... // process e
}
```

Listing 6-12 gives the code for the methods printAccounts1 and maxBalance1 from the IteratorAccountStats class. Both methods use the basic idiom to iterate through the iterable class Bank. The method printAccounts1 prints all bank accounts and maxBalance1 returns the maximum balance of the accounts.

Listing 6-12. The printAccounts1 and maxBalance1 Methods

```
public void printAccounts1() {
   Iterator<BankAccount> iter = bank.iterator();
   while (iter.hasNext()) {
      BankAccount ba = iter.next();
      System.out.println(ba);
   }
}
```

```
public int maxBalance1() {
    Iterator<BankAccount> iter = bank.iterator();
    int max = 0;
    while (iter.hasNext()) {
        BankAccount ba = iter.next();
        int balance = ba.getBalance();
            if (balance > max)
                max = balance;
    }
    return max;
}
```

This idiom is so common that Java has a syntax specifically designed to simplify it. This syntax is the *for-each loop*. For example, the following loop is equivalent to the code of Listing 6-11.

```
for (E e : c) {
    ... // process e
}
```

The variable c in the above for-each loop can be any Iterable; it need not be a collection. Listing 6-13 gives the code for methods printAccounts2 and maxBalance2 of IteratorAccountStats. These methods revise their earlier versions, replacing the explicit iterator methods with a for-each loop. Note that the code is significantly easier to read and understand, primarily because it no longer mentions iterators explicitly.

Listing 6-13. The Methods printAccounts2 and maxBalance2

```
public void printAccounts2() {
    for (BankAccount ba : bank)
        System.out.println(ba);
}

public int maxBalance2() {
    int max = 0;
```

```
    for (BankAccount ba : bank) {
        int balance = ba.getBalance();
        if (balance > max)
            max = balance;
    }
    return max;
}
```

Although the for-each loop simplifies the use of iterators, it is not always applicable. The issue is that a for-each loop hides its calls to the iterator's next method, so there is no way to control when that method will be called. Here are two situations where such control is needed.

The first situation is finding the maximum element in an iterable. Listing 6-14 gives code for the method findMax, which rewrites the method from Listing 2-9 to use iterators.

Listing 6-14. Using an Iterator to Find the Maximum Element

```
public BankAccount findMax(Iterable<BankAccount> bank) {
    Iterator<BankAccount> iter = bank.iterator();
    BankAccount max = iter.next();
    while (iter.hasNext()) {
        BankAccount ba = iter.next();
        if (ba.compareTo(max) > 0)
            max = ba;
    }
    return max;
}
```

This code uses the first element of the iterator to initialize the variable max, and then loops through the remaining elements. Such a strategy is not possible with a for-each loop. The solution shown in Listing 6-15 initializes max to null. Unfortunately, it must check max for null each time through the loop, which is unsatisfactory.

Listing 6-15. Using a for-each Loop to Find the Maximum Element

```
public BankAccount findMax(Iterable<BankAccount> bank) {
    BankAccount max = null;
    for (BankAccount ba : bank)
        if (max == null || ba.compareTo(max) > 0)
            max = ba;
    return max;
}
```

The second situation is when you want to interleave the elements of two collections. Listing 6-16 shows how to perform this task using explicit iterators. I know of no good way to rewrite this code using for-each loops.

Listing 6-16. Interleaving Access to Two Collections

```
Iterator<String> iter1 = c1.iterator();
Iterator<String> iter2 = c2.iterator();
Iterator<String> current = iter1;
while (current.hasNext()) {
    String s = current.next();
    // process s
    current = (current == iter1) ? iter2 : iter1;
}
```

Internal Iteration

Each of the examples in the previous section used a loop to traverse its iterator. This looping was performed in two different ways: by calling the iterator methods explicitly, or by using a for-each loop. Both ways are examples of *external iteration*, because in each case the client writes the loop.

It is also possible to traverse the elements of an iterable object without writing a loop. This technique is called *internal iteration*.

For example, the method addInterest in Bank performs internal iteration for the client, invisibly looping through the bank's accounts.

The addInterest method is an internal iterator that is specialized to perform a single task. The Java Iterable interface has the default method forEach, which can be used for general-purpose internal iteration. The argument to forEach is an object that implements the Consumer interface. This interface, which also is part of the Java library, has a single void method accept and is defined as follows:

```
interface Consumer<T> {
    void accept(T t);
}
```

The purpose of the accept method is to perform an action to its argument object. Listing 6-17 gives an example of the creation and use of a Consumer object. Its first statement creates the Consumer object and saves a reference to it in the variable action. The Consumer object's accept method prints its BankAccount argument. The second statement obtains a reference to bank account 123, and saves in the variable x. The third statement performs the action on the specified account. In other words, the statement prints account 123.

Listing 6-17. Creating and Using a Consumer Object

```
Consumer<BankAccount> action = ba -> System.out.println(ba);
BankAccount x = bank.getAccount(123);
action.accept(x);
```

An iterable's forEach method performs an action on every object of the iterable's iterator; this action is defined by the Consumer object that is the argument to forEach. Listing 6-18 gives the code for the method printAccounts3, which uses forEach to print every element generated by the bank's iterator.

Listing 6-18. The Method printAccounts3

```java
public void printAccounts3() {
    Consumer<BankAccount> action = ba->System.out.println(ba);
    bank.forEach(action);
}
```

The interesting feature of listing 6-18 is that there is no explicit loop. Instead, the looping is performed internally within the forEach method. Listing 6-19 gives a simplified version of the Iterable interface, showing how the forEach method might perform its loop.

Listing 6-19. A Simplified Iterable Interface

```java
public interface Iterable<T> {
    Iterator<T> iterator();

    default void forEach(Consumer<T> action) {
        Iterator<T> iter = iterator();
        while (iter.hasNext())
            action.apply(iter.next());
    }
}
```

The Visitor Pattern

The Consumer object that is passed to the forEach method is called a *visitor*. As the forEach method encounters each element of the iterable, the Consumer object "visits" that element. This visitation could involve printing the element (as in printAccounts3), modifying it, or any other action that can be expressed as a Consumer.

The beauty of the forEach method is that it separates the code for visiting an element (the Consumer object) from the code to iterate through the elements. This separation is called the *visitor pattern*.

219

The demo class `IteratorAccountStats` has a method `visit1` that generalizes `printAccounts3` so that its argument can be any visitor. Its code appears in Listing 6-20. The statements in Listing 6-21 illustrate its use.

Listing 6-20. The Method visit1

```
public void visit1(Consumer<BankAccount> action) {
   bank.forEach(action);
}
```

Listing 6-21. Uses of the visit1 Method

```
// Print all accounts
visit1(ba -> System.out.println(ba));

// Add interest to all accounts
visit1(ba -> ba.addInterest());

// Print the balance of all domestic accounts
visit1(ba -> { if (!ba.isForeign())
                  System.out.println(ba.getBalance()); });
```

The problem with the `visit1` method is that it only applies to void actions—that is, actions that do not return a value. For example, it is not possible to use `visit1` to calculate the maximum account balance. To achieve this functionality, the definition of a visitor must also have a method that calculates a return value. Java does not have such a visitor interface in its library, but it is easy enough to create one. See Listing 6-22.

Listing 6-22. The Visitor Interface

```
public interface Visitor<T,R> extends Consumer<T> {
   R result();
}
```

This interface defines a visitor to be a consumer with the additional method result. A visitor has two generic types: Type T is the type of the elements it visits, and type R is the type of the result value.

Listing 6-23 gives code for the visitor class MaxBalanceVisitor, whose objects calculate the maximum balance of the accounts they visit. The variable max holds the maximum balance encountered so far. The accept method examines the balance of the currently-visited account and updates max if appropriate. The result method returns the final value of max.

Listing 6-23. The Class MaxBalanceVisitor

```java
public class MaxBalanceVisitor
            implements Visitor<BankAccount,Integer> {
   private int max = 0;

   public void accept(BankAccount ba) {
      int bal = ba.getBalance();
      if (bal > max)
         max = bal;
   }

   public Integer result() {
      return max;
   }
}
```

IteratorAccountStats contains two methods that use a visitor to find the maximum bank account balance. Their code appears in Listing 6-24. The method maxBalance3a creates a MaxBalanceVisitor object. The method maxBalance3b defines the equivalent visitor object inline. Since the Visitor interface has two nondefault methods, maxBalance3b cannot define its visitor using a lambda expression; instead, it must use an anonymous inner class. Note that a Visitor object can be legitimately passed to the forEach method because Visitor is a subtype of Consumer.

Listing 6-24. The maxBalance3a and maxBalance3b Methods

```java
public int maxBalance3a() {
   Visitor<BankAccount,Integer> v = new MaxBalanceVisitor();
   bank.forEach(v);
   return v.result();
}

public int maxBalance3b() {
   Visitor<BankAccount,Integer> v =
         new Visitor<BankAccount,Integer>() {
            private int max = 0;
            public void accept(BankAccount ba) {
               int bal = ba.getBalance();
               if (bal > max)
                  max = bal;
            }
            public Integer result() {
               return max;
            }
         };
   bank.forEach(v);
   return v.result();
}
```

Listing 6-25 gives the code for the method visit2, which generalizes visit1 so that its argument is a Visitor object instead of a Consumer object. Listing 6-26 gives the code for the method maxBalance3c, which uses visit2 to find the maximum account balance.

Listing 6-25. The visit2 Method

```
public <R> R visit2(Visitor<BankAccount, R> action) {
    bank.forEach(action);
    return action.result();
}
```

Listing 6-26. The maxBalance3c Method

```
public int maxBalance3c() {
    return visit2(new MaxBalanceVisitor());
}
```

Predicates

The previous section presented several methods that traversed the bank's iterator. Each method visited all the accounts, printing them or finding their maximum balance.

Suppose now that you want to write code to visit only some of the accounts; for example, suppose you want to print the domestic accounts. It might be an unwelcome surprise to discover that *none* of these methods will be of any use. Instead, you will need to write a new method, such as the method shown in Listing 6-27.

Listing 6-27. Printing the Domestic Accounts

```
public void printDomesticAccounts() {
    for (BankAccount ba : bank)
        if (!ba.isForeign())
            System.out.println(ba);
}
```

Note that this method contains most of the same code as printAccounts2, in violation of the Don't Repeat Yourself rule. Moreover, you will need to write a new method whenever you are interested in another subset of the accounts. This situation is unacceptable.

The solution is to rewrite the printAccounts and maxBalance methods to have an argument that specifies the desired subset of accounts. The Java library has the interface Predicate for this purpose. It has a method test, whose return value indicates whether the specified object satisfies the predicate. The Predicate interface is defined as follows:

```
interface Predicate<T> {
    boolean test(T t);
}
```

Since the interface is functional (that is, it has a single method), classes that implement Predicate can be defined by lambda expressions. For example, consider Listing 6-28. Its first statement creates a predicate that specifies accounts having a balance greater than $100. Its second statement obtains a reference to account 123. Its third statement uses the predicate to determine if the balance of that account is greater than $100, and prints it if it does.

Listing 6-28. Creating and Using a Predicate

```
Predicate<BankAccount> pred = ba -> ba.getBalance() > 10000;
BankAccount x = bank.getAccount(123);
if (pred.test(x))
    System.out.println(x);
```

Listing 6-29 gives code for the methods printAccounts4 and maxBalance4 of InteratorAccountStats. These methods take an arbitrary predicate as their argument and use that predicate to restrict the bank accounts they visit.

Listing 6-29. The printAccounts4 and maxBalance4 Methods

```java
public void printAccounts4(Predicate<BankAccount> pred) {
    for (BankAccount ba : bank)
        if (pred.test(ba))
            System.out.println(ba);
}

public int maxBalance4(Predicate<BankAccount> pred) {
    int max = 0;
    for (BankAccount ba : bank) {
        if (pred.test(ba)) {
            int balance = ba.getBalance();
            if (balance > max)
                max = balance;
        }
    }
    return max;
}
```

Predicates can also be embedded into the visitor pattern. Method printAccounts5 creates a Consumer object that visits each account. If the account satisfies the predicate then it prints the account. See Listing 6-30.

Listing 6-30. The printAccounts5 Method

```java
public void printAccounts5(Predicate<BankAccount> pred) {
    Consumer<BankAccount> action =
        ba -> { if (pred.test(ba))
                    System.out.println(ba);
              };
    bank.forEach(action);
}
```

The statements in Listing 6-31 illustrate three uses of printAccounts5. They print the accounts having a balance greater than $100, the domestic accounts, and all accounts.

Listing 6-31. Using the printAccounts5 Method

```
Predicate<BankAccount> p = ba -> ba.getBalance() > 10000;
printAccounts5(p);
printAccounts5(ba->!ba.isForeign());
printAccounts5(ba->true);
```

Listing 6-32 gives code for the method maxBalance5, which creates a Consumer object that incorporates both its argument predicate and its visitor.

Listing 6-32. The maxBalance5 Method

```
public int maxBalance5(Predicate<BankAccount> pred) {
    Visitor<BankAccount,Integer> r = new MaxBalanceVisitor();
    Consumer<BankAccount> action =
              ba -> {if (pred.test(ba))
                        r.accept(ba);};
    bank.forEach(action);
    return r.result();
}
```

The following statement shows how to use maxBalance5 to return the maximum balance of the domestic accounts.

```
int max = maxBalance5(ba->!ba.isForeign());
```

This ability to combine a predicate with a consumer can be generalized. The method visit3 takes two arguments: a predicate and a consumer. The arguments to method visit4 are a predicate and a visitor. Each method visits those elements that satisfy the predicate. The code for both methods appears in Listing 6-33.

Listing 6-33. The visit3 and visit4 Methods

```
public void visit3(Predicate<BankAccount> pred,
                   Consumer<BankAccount> action) {
   bank.forEach(ba -> {if (pred.test(ba))
                          action.accept(ba);});
}

public <R> R visit4(Predicate<BankAccount> pred,
                    Visitor<BankAccount, R> action) {
   bank.forEach(ba -> {if (pred.test(ba))
                          action.accept(ba);});
   return action.result();
}
```

The code in Listing 6-34 illustrates the use of visit3 and visit4. The first statement prints the balance of all domestic accounts whose balance is over $50. The second statement assigns the maximum balance of the domestic accounts to variable max.

Listing 6-34. Using the visit3 and visit4 Methods

```
visit3(ba->(!ba.isForeign() && ba.getBalance()>5000),
       ba->System.out.println(ba));
int max = visit4(ba->!ba.isForeign(),
                 new MaxBalanceVisitor());
```

Collection Streams

This section examines the Stream interface from the Java library. A Stream object is similar to an iterator, in that its methods allow you to iterate through a group of elements. The difference is that the Stream provides additional methods that simplify the use of internal iteration.

The code for Stream and six of its methods appears in Listing 6-35. The iterator method converts the stream into an iterator, so that clients can use the hasNext and next methods for external iteration. This method is not commonly used and exists only for the rare cases where internal iteration is not possible.

Listing 6-35. The Stream Interface

```
interface Stream<T> {
    Iterator<T> iterator();
    void forEach(Consumer<T> cons);
    Stream<T> filter(Predicate<T> p);
    <R> Stream<R> map(Function<T,R> f);
    T reduce(T id, BinaryOperator<T> op);
    boolean anyMatch(Predicate<T> p);

    ...
}
```

The other stream methods support internal iteration. The forEach method is the same as the forEach method of Iterator. The methods filter, map, reduce, and anyMatch will be discussed soon.

Objects that implement Stream are called *collection streams*. The elements of a collection stream come from a collection or something that can be viewed as a collection (such as an array). A collection stream has no relationship whatsoever to the byte streams discussed in Chapter 3.

The Collection interface contains the method stream, which creates a Stream object whose elements are the elements of the collection. This is the most common way to get a collection stream. A noncollection class (such as Bank) can also implement the stream method. Typically, the stream method for such a class calls the stream method of one of its collections. For example, the Bank class in the version 15 banking demo implements the method stream. Listing 6-36 gives the relevant code.

Listing 6-36. The version 15 Bank Class

```
public class Bank implements Iterable<BankAccount> {
   private Map<Integer,BankAccount> accounts;
   ...
   public Stream<BankAccount> stream() {
      return accounts.values().stream();
   }
}
```

The class StreamAcctStats in the version 15 banking demo illustrates the use of several Stream methods. The code for printAccounts6 appears in Listing 6-37. It uses the Stream methods filter and forEach to print the bank accounts satisfying the given predicate.

Listing 6-37. The printAccounts6 Method

```
public void printAccounts6(Predicate<BankAccount> pred) {
   Stream<BankAccount> s1 = bank.stream();
   Stream<BankAccount> s2 = s1.filter(pred);
   s2.forEach(ba->System.out.println(ba));
}
```

The forEach method behaves the same as the corresponding method in Iterable. The filter method transforms one stream to another. It takes a predicate as an argument and returns a new stream containing the elements that satisfy the predicate. In Listing 6-37, stream s2 contains those accounts from s1 that satisfy the predicate. Note how the filter method uses internal iteration to do what you otherwise would need a loop and an if-statement to do.

Because Java syntax allows method calls to be composed, it is possible to rewrite printAccounts6 so that the filter method is called by the output of the stream method. See Listing 6-38.

Listing 6-38. A Revised Version of the Method printAccounts6

```
public void printAccounts6(Predicate<BankAccount> pred) {
    Stream<BankAccount> s = bank.stream().filter(pred);
    s.forEach(ba->System.out.println(ba));
}
```

In fact, you could even rewrite printAccounts6 so that all method calls occur in a single statement. In this case you don't need the Stream variable s. See Listing 6-39.

Listing 6-39. Another Revsion of printAccounts6

```
public void printAccounts6(Predicate<BankAccount> pred) {
    bank.stream().filter(pred).forEach(
                            ba->System.out.println(ba));
}
```

This code is not particularly readable. However, it becomes nicely readable if it is rewritten so that each method call is on a different line. This is what the method printAccounts7 does. Its code appears in Listing 6-40.

Listing 6-40. The Method printAccounts7

```
public void printAccounts7(Predicate<BankAccount> pred) {
    bank.stream()
        .filter(pred)
        .forEach(ba->System.out.println(ba));
}
```

This programming style is called *fluent*. A fluent expression consists of several composed method calls. You can think of each method call as a transformation of one object to another. For example, Listing 6-41 gives a fluent statement that prints the bank accounts having a balance between $10 and $20.

Listing 6-41. A Fluent Statement

```
bank.stream()
    .filter(ba -> ba.getBalance() >= 1000)
    .filter(ba -> ba.getBalance() <= 2000)
    .forEach(ba->System.out.println(ba));
```

The `filter` method transforms a stream into another stream that contains a subset of the original elements. Another form of transformation is produced by the method `map`. The argument to `map` is an object that implements the `Function` interface. This interface, which is part of the Java library, has a single method `apply` and is defined as follows:

```
interface Function<T,R> {
    R apply(T t);
    ...
}
```

The `apply` method transforms an object of type T to an object of type R. The `map` method calls `apply` for each element in the input stream and returns the stream consisting of the transformed elements. You can use lambda expressions to create `Function` objects. For example, consider the following statement. The lambda expression transforms a `BankAccount` object to an integer that denotes its balance. The `map` method therefore returns a stream containing the balances of each account.

```
Stream<Integer> balances = bank.stream()
                        .map(ba -> ba.getBalance());
```

It is also useful to be able to construct a "return value" from a stream. This operation is called *reducing* the stream. The `Stream` interface has the method `reduce` for this purpose. For example, Listing 6-42 gives the code for the `maxBalance4` method of `StreamAcctStats`.

Listing 6-42. The Method maxBalance4

```
public int maxBalance4(Predicate<BankAccount> pred) {
   return bank.stream()
              .filter(pred)
              .map(ba->ba.getBalance())
              .reduce(0, (x,y)->Math.max(x,y));
}
```

The reduce method has two arguments. The first argument is the initial value of the reduction. The second argument is the reduction method, which reduces two values into a single value. The reduce method repeatedly calls its reduction method for each element of the stream. Its algorithm is given in Listing 6-43, where x is the initial value of the reduction and r is the reduction method.

Listing 6-43. The Reduction Algorithm

```
1. Set currentval = x.
2. For each element e in the stream:
       currentval = r(currentval, e).
3. Return currentval.
```

The Stream interface also has reduction methods that search for elements that match a given predicate. Three of these methods are allMatch, anyMatch, and findFirst. The code of Listing 6-44 uses anyMatch to determine if there is an account having a balance greater than $1,000.

Listing 6-44. Using the anyMatch Method

```
boolean result =
   bank.stream()
       .anyMatch(ba->ba.getBalance() > 100000);
```

Collection streams are the building blocks of *map-reduce* programs. Map-reduce programming is an effective, commonly used way to process Big data applications. Map-reduce programs have the structure given in Listing 6-45.

Listing 6-45. The Structure of a Map-Reduce Program

```
1. Obtain an initial collection stream.
2. Transform the stream, filtering and mapping its contents
until you get a stream containing the values you care about.
3. Reduce that stream to get the answer you want.
```

Map-reduce programming has two advantages. First, it allows you to divide your problem into a sequence of small transformations. People find this coding style easy to write, and easy to debug. Note that map-reduce code has no assignment statements and no control structures.

The second advantage is that you can easily change the code to run in parallel. Each collection has a method parallelStream as well as stream. Given a collection, if you use the parallelStream method to create the stream then the resulting stream will execute in parallel. That's it! The Java parallelSteam method does all the hard work behind the scenes.

Summary

An *iterator* generates a sequence of elements. It has the two methods next and hasNext. The method next returns the next element in the iterator and hasNext indicates whether the iterator has more elements left. An *iterable* is an object that has an associated iterator. Collections are the most common examples of iterables.

The *iterator pattern* organizes the iterable and iterator classes into separate, parallel hierarchies, with each iterable class having a corresponding iterator class. The Java library contains the interfaces Iterable and Iterator for exactly this purpose. Iterable declares the method iterator, which returns the Iterator object associated with that iterable.

The most fundamental way to iterate through an iterable L is to use the following *basic idiom*:

```
Iterator<T> iter = L.iterator();
while (iter.hasNext()) {
    T t = iter.next();
    process(t); // some code that uses t
}
```

Java has a special syntax for this idiom, called the *for-each loop*. The above code can be written more succinctly using the following for-each loop:

```
for (T t : L) {
    process(t);
}
```

Explicitly looping through the elements of an iterator is called *external iteration*. A method that encapsulates the looping (such as the bank's addInterest method) is said to perform *internal iteration*. The Java Iterable interface has a general-purpose internal iteration method called forEach. The argument to forEach is a Consumer object that specifies the body of the iteration loop. Using forEach, the preceding code can be written as follows:

```
L.forEach(t->process(t));
```

The Consumer object is said to *visit* each element of the iterable. The forEach method separates the specification of the visitor from the specification of the looping. This separation is called the *visitor pattern*.

Collection streams are a way to simplify the use of the visitor pattern. Instead of expressing iteration via a single visitor having a complex body, you can use the collection stream methods to express the iteration as a sequence of small *transformations*. Each transformation is itself a visitor that performs a limited action, such as a filter or a map. This technique is the foundation of *map-reduce* programming. The idea is that writing several small transformations is much simpler, more compact, and less error-prone than writing a single large one.

The use of collection streams, however, raises the question of efficiency. If the stream transformations were to execute sequentially, each via its own iteration loop, then a map-reduce program would take far more time than a traditional program that made a single iteration through the elements. Collection streams will be useful only if their transformations can be coalesced somehow. The technique for doing so is interesting, and will be discussed in Chapter 8.

CHAPTER 7

Adapters

The next two chapters examine a design technique known as *wrapping*.
Wrapping denotes a close relationship between two classes, called the
wrapper class and the *wrapped* class. The sole purpose of the wrapper
class is to modify or enhance the functionality of its wrapped class.
Wrapping corresponds perfectly to the Open/Closed design rule: If you
need a class to behave slightly differently then don't modify it. Instead,
create a new class that wraps it.

This chapter covers the concept of an *adapter*, which is a wrapper
that changes the functionality of the class it wraps. This chapter presents
several examples that illustrate the widespread applicability of adapter
classes. Of particular interest are the Java library classes that adapt the
byte streams of Chapter 3. These classes make it possible to read and write
streams of characters, primitive values, or objects simply by adapting the
existing classes that implement streams of bytes.

Inheritance for Reuse

Suppose you need to write a class. There is an existing class that has
methods similar to the methods you need. You therefore decide to define
your class as a subclass of this existing class, so that you can inherit those
methods and thereby simplify your code-writing task.

© Edward Sciore 2019

E. Sciore, *Java Program Design*, https://doi.org/10.1007/978-1-4842-4143-1_7

This sounds like a great idea, right? Unfortunately, it isn't. In fact, it's a very bad idea. As discussed in Chapter 3, the only good reason to create a subclass is because the subclass–superclass relationship satisfies the Liskov Substitution Principle—that is, if subclass objects can be used in place of a superclass objects. The possibility of inheriting code plays no part in the decision.

Nevertheless, it is hard to resist the temptation to create a subclass just to inherit code. The history of object-oriented software is littered with such classes. This design technique even has a name: *inheritance for reuse.*

In the early days of object-oriented programming, inheritance for reuse was touted as one of the big advantages of object orientation. Now we understand that this idea is completely wrong. The Java library class Stack provides a good example of the problems that arise.

Stack extends the Java library class Vector, which implements List. The advantage to extending Vector is that the stack methods empty, push, and pop become very easy to implement. Listing 7-1 gives a simplified version of the source code for Stack.

Listing 7-1. Simplified Code for the Stack Class

```java
public class Stack<E> extends Vector<E> {
    public boolean empty() {
        return size() == 0;
    }

    public void push(E item) {
        add(item);
    }

    public E pop() {
        return remove(size()-1);
    }
}
```

This code takes advantage of the inherited methods `size`, `add`, and `remove` from `Vector`. The designers of `Stack` were no doubt delighted that they could use the `Vector` methods for "free," without having to write any code for them. This is a perfect example of inheritance for reuse.

However, this design has significant problems. The decision to extend `Vector` violates the Liskov Substitution Principle because a stack in no way behaves like a list. For example, a stack only lets you look at its top element whereas a list lets you look at (and modify) every element.

Practically speaking, the problem is that clients can use a stack in non-stack-like ways. For a simple example, the last statement of the following code modifies the bottom of the stack:

```
Stack<String> s = new Stack<>();
s.push("abc");
s.push("xyz");
s.set(0,"glorp");
```

In other words, the `Stack` class is not sufficiently encapsulated. A client can take advantage of the fact that it is implemented in terms of `Vector`.

The `Stack` class was part of the first Java release. Since then the Java development community has admitted that this design was a mistake. In fact, the current documentation for the class recommends that it not be used.

Wrappers

The good news is that it is possible to write `Stack` so that it makes use of `Vector` without being a subclass of it. Listing 7-2 illustrates the technique: `Stack` holds a variable of type `Vector`, and uses this variable to implement its `empty`, `push`, and `pop` methods. Since the variable is private to `Stack`, it is inaccessible from the other classes, which ensures that `Stack` variables are not able to call `Vector` methods.

Listing 7-2. Using a Wrapper to Implement Stack

```
public class Stack<E> {
   private Vector<E> v = new Vector<>();

   public boolean empty() {
      return v.size() == 0;
   }

   public void push(E item) {
      v.add(item);
   }

   public E pop() {
      return v.remove(v.size()-1);
   }
}
```

This implementation technique is called *wrapping*. Wrapping is a specific use of a dependency relationship in which a class C implements its methods via a dependency to a class D, calling D's methods to do most (or all) of the work. The class D is called the *backing store* of the wrapper C. For example in Listing 7-2, Stack wraps Vector because it has a dependency to Vector, and implements its methods by calling the Vector methods.

Wrapping is a remarkably useful technique. If a design involves inheritance for reuse then it can always be redesigned to use wrapping instead. And experience has shown that the wrapper-based design is always better.

The Adapter Pattern

Wrapper classes are often used as *adapters*. The term "adapter" has an analogy with real life adapters. For example, suppose you want to plug a three-pronged vacuum cleaner into a two-prong electric outlet. One way to resolve this impasse is to purchase a new vacuum cleaner that works with a two-prong outlet. Another way is to rewire the outlet so that it accepts three prongs. Both of these options are expensive and impractical.

A third and far better option is to buy an adapter that has two prongs on one end and accepts three prongs on the other end. The device plugs into one end of the adapter and the adapter's other end plugs into the outlet. The adapter manages the transfer of electricity between its two ends.

An analogous situation exists with software. Suppose that your code needs a class having a particular interface but the best available class implements a slightly different interface. What should you do? You have the same three options.

Your first two options are to modify your code so that it uses the existing interface, or to modify the code for the existing class so that it implements the desired interface. As with the electrical adapter scenario, these options can be expensive and impractical. Moreover, they may not even be possible. For example, you are not allowed to modify classes in the Java library.

A simpler and better solution is to write an adapter class. The adapter class wraps the existing class and uses it to implement the desired interface. This solution is known as the *adapter pattern.* Its class diagram appears in Figure 7-1.

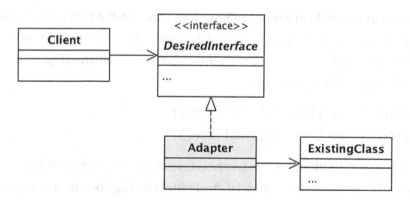

Figure 7-1. The adapter pattern

The Stack class in Listing 7-2 is an example of the adapter pattern. The existing class is Vector. The desired interface consists of the methods {push, pop, empty}. The adapter class is Stack. Figure 7-2 shows their relationship. In this case there is no formal Java interface, so the diagram uses "StackAPI" to denote the desired methods.

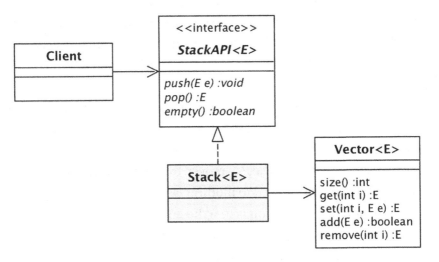

Figure 7-2. *Stack as an adapter class*

Another example of the adapter pattern arises in the Java library class Arrays. Recall from Chapter 5 that Arrays has a static factory method asList that returns a list containing the contents of a given array. The following code illustrates its use:

```
String[] a = {"a", "b", "c", "d"};
List<String> L = Arrays.asList(a);
```

One way to implement this method is to create a new ArrayList object, add the array elements to it, and return it. This idea is not very good because copying the elements of a large array is inefficient.

A much better idea is to use the adapter pattern. The object returned by the asList method will belong to an adapter class that wraps the array and implements the List methods. The code in Listing 7-3 implements the Arrays class using this idea. The adapter class is called ArrayAsList.

Listing 7-3. A Simplified Implementation of the Arrays Class

```
public class Arrays {
    ...
    public static <T> List<T> asList(T[] vals) {
        return new ArrayAsList<T>(vals);
    }
}

class ArrayAsList<T> extends AbstractList<T> {
    private T[] data;

    public ArrayAsList(T[] data) {
        this.data = data;
    }

    public int size() {
        return data.length;
    }

    public T get(int i) {
        return data[i];
    }

    public T set(int i, T val) {
        T oldval = data[i];
        data[i] = val;
        return oldval;
    }
}
```

The asList method simply creates and returns an object from its ArrayAsList adapter class. ArrayAsList extends the Java library class

AbstractList, implementing the methods size, get, and set. Note that the code does not copy the array, but instead accesses the array elements on demand. The design is elegant and efficient. Figure 7-3 gives the class diagram showing how ArrayAsList fits into the adapter pattern.

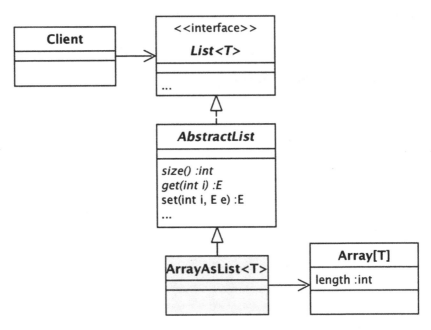

Figure 7-3. *The adapter class ArrayAsList*

Another example of an adapter is the class RandomIterator from Chapter 6, whose code appeared in Listing 6-3. The class wrapped an object of type Random and used it to implement the Iterator interface.

Text Streams

Chapter 3 introduced the abstract class InputStream, whose subclasses are able to read bytes from files, pipes, and other input sources; it also introduced OutputStream, which has analogous subclasses for writing bytes. The sequences of bytes managed by these classes are called *byte streams* (and are totally unrelated to the collection streams of Chapter 6). This section is concerned with streams of characters, which are called *text streams*.

The character stream hierarchies are headed by the abstract classes Reader and Writer. These classes closely parallel InputStream and OutputStream. Their methods are similar, the major difference being that the read and write methods for Reader and Writer manipulate characters instead of bytes. Their subclasses are also analogous. For example, the classes FileReader and PipedReader parallel FileInputStream and PipedInputStream.

As an example, Listing 7-4 gives the code for a program that reads the text file "mobydick.txt" and writes its first 500 characters to the file "shortmoby.txt."

Listing 7-4. Reading and Writing a Text File

```
public class FilePrefix {
    public static void main(String[] args) throws IOException {
        try (Reader r = new FileReader("mobydick.txt");
             Writer w = new FileWriter("shortmoby.txt")) {
            for (int i=0; i<500; i++) {
                int x = r.read();
                if (x < 0)
                    break;
                char c = (char) x;
                w.write(c);
            }
        }
    }
}
```

From a design perspective, the most interesting question about text streams is how the various `Reader` and `Writer` classes are implemented. It turns out that adapters play a big part, as discussed in the following subsections.

The Adapter OutputStreamWriter

Suppose you are asked to implement the `FileWriter` class; what would you do? Your code will need to address two issues. First, it will need to manage the file—opening it, writing values to it, and closing it. Second, your code will need to translate each output character to one or more bytes, because files understand bytes and not characters. You can handle the first issue by looking at the code for `FileOutputStream`. It has already dealt with that issue, so you can copy the relevant code. You can handle the second issue by using the class `CharEncoder` from the Java library, in a way that will be discussed soon. So everything seems under control. But before you proceed further you should stop and reread this paragraph. Is the proposed design a good one?

The answer is "no." Copying code from `FileOutputStream` violates the Don't Repeat Yourself design rule, and is a terrible idea. A much better design is to use an adapter class to leverage the existing implementation. In other words, `FileWriter` should be a class that adapts `FileOutputStream` and implements `Writer`.

In fact, you can do even better. Note that `FileWriter`'s only real responsibility is to encode each character into bytes and write those bytes to its wrapped output stream. This code is applicable to any output stream, not just `FileOutputStream`. In other words, instead of writing an adapter class for `FileOutputStream`, a more general solution is to write an adapter class for `OutputStream`.

The Java library provides exactly such an adapter class, called OutputStreamWriter. This class wraps an object that has existing functionality (namely OutputStream, which has the ability to write bytes) and uses it to implement the desired interface (namely Writer, which gives you the ability to write chars).

The usefulness of the OutputStreamWriter adapter is that it can convert *any* output stream into a writer. In particular, you can use it to write FileWriter. The following two statements are equivalent:

```
Writer fw = new FileWriter(f);
Writer fw = new OutputStreamWriter(new FileOutputStream(f));
```

In other words, FileWriter is a convenience class. It can be implemented as a subclass of OutputStreamWriter whose constructor creates the wrapped FileOutputStream object. Its code looks something like Listing 7-5.

Listing 7-5. The Code for the FileWriter Class

```
public class FileWriter extends OutputStreamWriter {
   public FileWriter(String f) throws IOException {
      super(new FileOutputStream(f));
   }
}
```

The class diagram in Figure 7-4 shows the relationship between the Writer, OutputStream, and FileWriter classes, and the key role played by the adapter class OutputStreamWriter.

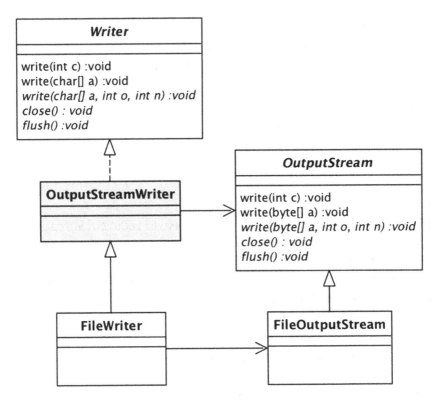

Figure 7-4. *OutputStreamWriter as an adapter*

Now that the purpose of OutputStreamWriter is clear, it is time to consider its implementation. A simplified version of the code appears in Listing 7-6. The class extends the abstract class Writer and therefore needs to implement three abstract methods: close, flush, and the 3-arg write method. OutputStreamWriter implements these three methods using its wrapped OutputStream object. The implementation of close and flush simply call the corresponding OutputStream methods. The write method encodes the specified characters, places the encoded bytes into a byte buffer, and writes each byte to the wrapped output stream.

Listing 7-6. A Simplified OutputStreamWriter Class

```
public class OutputStreamWriter extends Writer {
    private CharsetEncoder encoder;
    private OutputStream os;

    public OutputStreamWriter(OutputStream os,
                    String charsetname) throws IOException {
        this.os = os;
        encoder = Charset.forName(charsetname).newEncoder();
    }

    public OutputStreamWriter(OutputStream os)
                                throws IOException {
        this(os, Charset.defaultCharset().name());
    }

    public void write(char cbuf[], int offset, int len)
                                throws IOException {
        CharBuffer cb = CharBuffer.wrap(cbuf, offset, len);
        ByteBuffer bb = encoder.encode(cb);
        for (int i=0; i<bb.limit(); i++)
            os.write(bb.get(i));
    }

    public void close() throws IOException {
        os.close();
    }

    public void flush() throws IOException {
        os.flush();
    }
}
```

The complexity of this class arises from the fact that there are many ways to encode characters. For example, Java uses *16-bit Unicode* for its in-memory character encoding, which requires two bytes to store most characters. (Some characters require four bytes, which complicates matters considerably for Java but fortunately is irrelevant to this discussion.) However, 16-bit Unicode is not necessarily the best way to encode files. Many text editors use an encoding such as ASCII, which assumes a smaller character set that requires only one byte per character. A Java program that reads and writes files needs to be able to interact with multiple character encodings.

The Java library has the class Charset, whose objects denote character encodings. The class supports several standard encodings, each of which has a name. For example, the encodings for ASCII, 8-bit Unicode, and 16-bit Unicode are named "US-ASCII," "UTF-8," and "UTF-16." Its forName method is a static factory method that returns the Charset object corresponding to the specified name.

The OutputStreamWriter class has two constructors. The first constructor has an argument that specifies the name of the desired charset. The second constructor uses a predetermined default charset.

The Charset method newEncoder returns a CharsetEncoder object. CharsetEncoder has the method encode, which performs the encoding. The argument to encode is a CharBuffer object. A CharBuffer is similar to a ByteBuffer except that it uses an underlying array of chars instead of bytes. The encode method encodes those characters and places their encoded bytes into a ByteBuffer object, whose bytes can then be written to the output stream.

The Adapter InputStreamReader

The correspondence between the Reader and InputStream classes is analogous to that between Writer and OutputStream. In particular, the Java library contains the adapter class InputStreamReader that wraps

InputStream and extends Reader. FileReader is a convenience class
that extends InputStreamReader. The FileReader code is analogous to
FileWriter and appears in Listing 7-7.

Listing 7-7. The FileReader Class

```
public class FileReader extends InputStreamReader {
    public FileReader(String f) throws IOException {
        super(new FileInputStream(f));
    }
}
```

The code for the InputStreamReader adapter class appears in
Listing 7-8. It is more complex than OutputStreamWriter because
decoding bytes is trickier than encoding chars. The problem is that the
characters in some encodings need not encode to the same number
of bytes, which means that you cannot know how many bytes to read
to decode the next character. The InputStreamReader class solves this
problem by buffering the input stream. It reads ahead some number of
bytes and stores those bytes in a ByteBuffer object. The read method
gets its input from that buffer.

The read method performs the conversion from bytes to chars by
calling the method decode of class CharDecoder. Two of the arguments
it provides to decode are the input byte buffer and the output char
buffer. The decode method reads bytes from the byte buffer and places
the decoded characters into the char buffer. It stops either when the
char buffer is full or the byte buffer is empty. The situation when the
char buffer is full is called *overflow*. In this case the read method can
stop, retaining the remaining input bytes for the next call to read. The
situation when the byte buffer is empty is called *underflow*. In this case
the read method must refill the byte buffer and call decode again, so that
it can fill the remainder of the char buffer.

Listing 7-8. A Simplified InputStreamReader Class

```
public class InputStreamReader extends Reader {
    public static int BUFF_SIZE = 10;
    private ByteBuffer bb = ByteBuffer.allocate(BUFF_SIZE);
    private InputStream is;
    private CharsetDecoder decoder;
    private boolean noMoreInput;

    public InputStreamReader(InputStream is,
                    String charsetname) throws IOException {
        this.is = is;
        decoder = Charset.forName(charsetname).newDecoder();
        bb.position(bb.limit()); //indicates an empty buffer
        noMoreInput = fillByteBuffer();
    }

    public InputStreamReader(InputStream is)
                                        throws IOException {
        this(is, Charset.defaultCharset().name());
    }

    public int read(char cbuf[], int offset, int len)
                                        throws IOException {
        int howmany = len;
        while (true) {
            CharBuffer cb = CharBuffer.wrap(cbuf, offset, len);
            CoderResult result = decoder.decode(bb, cb,
                                                noMoreInput);
            if (result == CoderResult.OVERFLOW)
                return howmany;
```

```
        else if (result == CoderResult.UNDERFLOW
                        && noMoreInput)
            return (cb.position() > 0) ? cb.position() : -1;
        else if (result == CoderResult.UNDERFLOW) {
            // Get more bytes and repeat the loop
            // to fill the remainder of the char buffer.
            noMoreInput = fillByteBuffer();
            offset = cb.position();
            len = howmany - cb.position();
        }
        else
            result.throwException();
    }
}

public void close() throws IOException {
    is.close();
}

private boolean fillByteBuffer() throws IOException {
    bb.compact(); //move leftover bytes to the front
    int pos = bb.position();
    int amtToRead = bb.capacity() - pos;
    int result = is.read(bb.array(), pos, amtToRead);
    int amtActuallyRead = (result < 0) ? 0 : result;
    int newlimit = pos + amtActuallyRead;
    bb.limit(newlimit);
    bb.position(0); //indicates a full buffer
    return (amtActuallyRead < amtToRead);
}
}
```

The Adapter StringReader

The class StringReader is another example of a text stream adapter from the Java library. The job of the class is to create a reader from a string. Each call to its read method returns the next character(s) from the string. A simplified version of its code appears in Listing 7-9.

Listing 7-9. A Simplified StringReader Class

```
public class StringReader extends Reader {
   private String s;
   private int pos = 0;

   public StringReader(String s) throws IOException {
      this.s = s;
   }

   public int read(char[] cbuf, int off, int len)
                                 throws IOException {
      if (pos >= s.length())
         return -1;    // end of stream
      int count=0;
      while (count<len && pos<s.length()) {
         cbuf[off+count] = s.charAt(pos);
         pos++; count++;
      }
      return count;
   }

   public void close() {
      // strings don't need to be closed
   }
}
```

Unlike InputStreamReader, the code for StringReader is short and straightforward. The specified string acts as the input buffer. The read method puts a character from the string into the next slot of cbuf, stopping when len chars have been written ("overflow") or the string is exhausted ("underflow"). In either case, the method returns the number of chars written.

The StringReader class conforms to the adapter pattern, as illustrated by the class diagram of Figure 7-5.

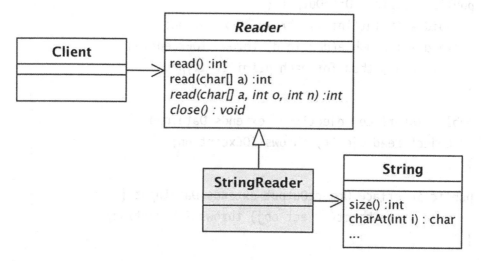

Figure 7-5. *StringReader as an adapter*

Object Streams

The classes InputStream and OutputStream let you read and write byte streams, and Reader and Writer let you read and write character streams. The Java library provides two additional level of read/write. The interfaces DataInput and DataOutput let you read and write primitive values, and the interfaces ObjectInput and ObjectOutput let you read and write objects. Listing 7-10 gives the declaration of these four interfaces.

Listing 7-10. The DataInput, DataOutput, ObjectInput, and ObjectOutput Interfaces

```
public interface DataInput {
   int readInt() throws IOException;
   double readDouble() throws IOException;
   ... // a method for each primitive type
}

public interface DataOutput {
   void writeInt(int i) throws IOException;
   void writeDouble(double d) throws IOException;
   ... // a method for each primitive type
}

public interface ObjectInput extends DataInput {
   Object readObject() throws IOException;
}

public interface ObjectOutput extends DataInput {
   void writeObject(Object obj) throws IOException;
}
```

The Java library classes ObjectInputStream and ObjectOutputStream implement ObjectInput and ObjectOutput, and consequently also DataInput and DataOutput. These two classes are thus able to manage streams that contain a mixture of objects and primitive values.

Listing 7-11 gives code for the class ObjectStreamTest, which demonstrates the use of these classes. The program shows two ways to write a list of strings to an object stream and read them back.

Listing 7-11. The ObjectStreamTest Class

```java
public class ObjectStreamTest {
  public static void main(String[] args) throws Exception {
    List<String>  L = Arrays.asList("a", "b", "c");

    // Write the list to a file, in two ways.
    try (OutputStream os  = new FileOutputStream("sav.dat");
        ObjectOutput oos = new ObjectOutputStream(os)) {
      oos.writeObject(L);     // Write the list.

      oos.writeInt(L.size()); // Write the list size,
      for (String s : L)      // and then its elements.
        oos.writeObject(s);

    }

    // Read the lists from the file.
    try (InputStream is  = new FileInputStream("sav.dat");
        ObjectInput ois = new ObjectInputStream(is)) {

      List<String>  L1 = (List<String>) ois.readObject();

      List<String>  L2 = new ArrayList<>();
      int size = ois.readInt();        // Read the list size.
      for (int i=0; i<size; i++) {   // Read the elements.
        String s = (String) ois.readObject();
        L2.add(s);
      }

      // L, L1, and L2 are equivalent.
      System.out.println(L + ", " + L1 + ", " + L2);
    }
  }
}
```

Reading an object stream is different from reading a byte or text stream. An object stream can contain an arbitrary sequence of objects and primitive values, and the client needs to know exactly what to expect when reading it. For example, in ObjectStreamTest the code to read the stream must know that the file "sav.dat" contains the following: a list of strings, an int, and as many individual strings as the value of the preceding int.

Consequently, a client should never need to read past the end of an object stream. This is very different from byte steams, where the client typically reads bytes until the end-of-stream sentinel value -1 is returned.

As the object returned by readObject is of type Object, the client must cast this object to the appropriate type.

The ObjectStreamTest demo illustrates two ways to write a list to the stream: you can write the entire list as a single object, or you can write the elements individually. Writing the entire list is clearly preferable because it avoids the need to loop through the list elements. The code becomes easier to write and easier to read.

The classes ObjectInputStream and ObjectOutputStream are adapter classes. Figure 7-6 shows the class diagram that illustrates how ObjectInputStream conforms to the adapter pattern. The class diagram for ObjectOutputStream is analogous.

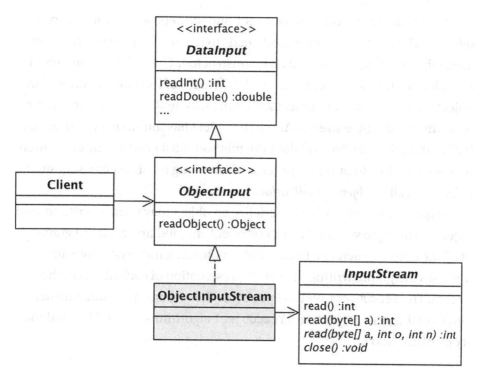

Figure 7-6. *ObjectInputStream as an adapter*

The class ObjectInputStream is implemented similarly to the adapter class InputStreamReader. An ObjectInputStream object holds a reference to the InputStream object it wraps, and uses the methods of that object to implement its methods. The implementation of ObjectOutputStream is similar.

The implementation of the DataInput and DataOutput methods is straightforward. For example, the writeInt method extracts the four bytes from the given int value and writes them to the byte stream. The readInt method reads four bytes from the byte stream and converts them to an int.

The implementation of readObject and writeObject is much more difficult. The writeObject method needs to encode enough information about the object to enable it to be reconstructed. This information includes metadata about the object's class and the values of its state variables. If the object references another object z then the information about z must also be written to the byte stream. And if the object has multiple references to z (either directly or indirectly) then the method must ensure that z is written only once to the stream. This process of encoding an object as a sequence of bytes is called *object serialization*.

In general, the algorithm to serialize an object may need to write several objects to the byte stream. The writeObject method first creates a graph of all the objects reachable from the given object; it then systematically traverses the graph, writing the byte representation of each object to the stream. The readObject method performs the reverse operation. Further details of the writeObject and readObject algorithms are well beyond the scope of this book.

Saving State in the Banking Demo

Object streams are a particularly good way to save the state of a program. Recall that the banking demo currently saves the bank's account information to a file. The class that manages the reading and writing to the file is SavedBankInfo, whose code appeared in Listing 3-14. That class wrote the account information byte by byte; the coding was difficult and tedious.

The use of object streams can dramatically simplify the code for SavedBankInfo. Instead of writing (and reading) each byte of each value of each account to the file, it is now possible to write the entire account map with just a single call to writeObject. Listing 7-12 gives the new code, which is in version 16 of the banking demo.

Listing 7-12. The Version 16 SavedBankInfo Class

```java
public class SavedBankInfo {
   private String fname;
   private Map<Integer,BankAccount> accounts;
   private int nextaccount;

   public SavedBankInfo(String fname) {
      this.fname = fname;
      File f = new File(fname);
      if (!f.exists()) {
         accounts = new HashMap<Integer,BankAccount>();
         nextaccount = 0;
      }
      else {
         try (InputStream is = new FileInputStream(fname);
              ObjectInput ois = new ObjectInputStream(is)) {
            accounts =
               (Map<Integer,BankAccount>) ois.readObject();
            nextaccount = ois.readInt();
         }
         catch (Exception ex) {
            throw new RuntimeException("file read exception");
         }
      }
   }

   public Map<Integer,BankAccount> getAccounts() {
      return accounts;
   }

   public int nextAcctNum() {
      return nextaccount;
   }
```

```
    public void saveMap(Map<Integer,BankAccount> map,
                        int nextaccount) {
        try (OutputStream os = new FileOutputStream(fname);
            ObjectOutput oos = new ObjectOutputStream(os)) {
            oos.writeObject(map);
            oos.writeInt(nextaccount);
        }
        catch (IOException ex) {
            throw new RuntimeException("file write exception");
        }
    }
}
```

The saved file will contain two objects: the account map and the next account number. The constructor reads the map and account number from the saved file if they exist; otherwise it creates an empty map and sets the account number to 0. The method saveMap writes the specified map and number to the saved file, overwriting any previous file contents.

The writeObject method has one additional requirement: The object that it writes and all objects referenced by that object must be *serializable*. That is, they must implement the interface Serializable. Most classes from the Java library are serializable. If you want your classes to be serializable, you must declare them to implement Serializable.

The Serializable interface is unusual in that it has no methods. The point of the interface is to act as an "ok to write" flag. The issue is that a class may contain sensitive information in its private fields (such as passwords, salaries, or bank balances). Serializing that object will make that private information visible to anyone having access to the file, which could have unintended consequences. Thus the programmer is required to "sign off" on the serialization.

Returning to the version 16 banking demo, note that the argument to the writeObject method is the account map. The HashMap and Integer classes are already serializable. The only other components of the map are the bank account classes. You can make them be serializable by having BankAccount implement Serializable, as shown in Listing 7-13.

Listing 7-13. The Version 16 BankAccount Interface

```
public interface BankAccount
        extends Comparable<BankAccount>, Serializable {
    ...
}
```

In addition, any object referenced by a bank account must also be serializable. The AbstractBankAccount class has a reference to OwnerStrategy objects, and so you should also declare the OwnerStrategy interface to be serializable. Currently the only thing that implements OwnerStrategy is the enum Owners. Enums are serializable in Java by default, so technically OwnerStrategy does not need to be explicitly serializable. But it is good practice to declare it anyway, in case you modify the implementation of OwnerStrategy in the future.

Adapters for the Banking Demo

Another use of adapters is to combine information from different classes into a single list, even though the classes might have no common interface. The idea is to create an adapter for each class such that the adapters implement the same interface. The resulting adapted objects can then be placed into a list.

As an example, consider the following scenario related to the banking demo. Suppose that the FBI is investigating money laundering, and wants to see information about foreign-owned accounts having a balance over $10,000. Moreover, the FBI is interested in loans as well as bank accounts, where the "balance" of a loan is considered to be its remaining principal. The FBI wants this information to be stored as a list of FBIAcctInfo objects, where FBIAcctInfo is the interface shown in Listing 7-14.

Listing 7-14. The FBIAcctInfo Interface

```
interface FBIAcctInfo {
   int balance();     // in dollars
   boolean isForeign();
   String acctType(); // "deposit" or "loan"
}
```

For the purposes of this example, version 16 of the banking demo needs to have a class Loan, which contains some rudimentary information about the bank's loans. Listing 7-15 gives its code. The class has methods to return the current status of the loan—its balance, remaining payments, and the monthly payment amount—as well as a method to make the next payment.

Listing 7-15. The Loan Class

```
public class Loan {
   private double balance, monthlyrate, monthlypmt;
   private int pmtsleft;
   private boolean isdomestic;

   public Loan(double amt, double yearlyrate,
               int numyears, boolean isdomestic) {
      this.balance = amt;
      pmtsleft = numyears * 12;
      this.isdomestic = isdomestic;
```

```
      monthlyrate = yearlyrate / 12.0;
      monthlypmt = (amt*monthlyrate) /
                    (1-Math.pow(1+monthlyrate, -pmtsleft));
   }

   public double remainingPrincipal() {
      return balance;
   }

   public int paymentsLeft() {
      return pmtsleft;
   }

   public boolean isDomestic() {
      return isdomestic;
   }

   public double monthlyPayment() {
      return monthlypmt;
   }

   public void makePayment() {
      balance = balance + (balance*monthlyrate) - monthlypmt;
      pmtsleft--;
   }
}
```

To handle the FBI request, the bank needs to combine the bank account and the loan data under the FBIAcctInfo interface. The problem, of course, is that neither BankAccount nor Loan objects implement FBIAcctInfo. BankAccount has an isForeign method, but the corresponding Loan method is isDomestic. In addition, FBIAcctInfo wants its balance method to return a value in dollars, but BankAccount and Loan use different names for the corresponding method and store values in pennies. And neither class has a method corresponding to the acctType method.

The way to address this issue is to create adapter classes for BankAccount and Loan that implement FBIAcctInfo. You can then wrap the BankAccount and Loan objects with these adapters, and place the resulting FBIAcctInfo objects in a list for the FBI to analyze.

The adapter for BankAccount is called BankAccountAdapter and the adapter for Loan is called LoanAdapter. Their code appears in listings 7-16 and 7-17.

Listing 7-16. The BankAccountAdapter Class

```java
public class BankAccountAdapter implements FBIAcctInfo {
    private BankAccount ba;

    public BankAccountAdapter(BankAccount ba) {
        this.ba = ba;
    }

    public int balance() {
        return ba.getBalance() / 100;
    }

    public boolean isForeign() {
        return ba.isForeign();
    }

    public String acctType() {
        return "deposit";
    }
}
```

Listing 7-17. The LoanAdapter Class

```java
public class LoanAdapter implements FBIAcctInfo {
   private Loan loan;

   public LoanAdapter(Loan loan) {
      this.loan = loan;
   }

   public int balance() {
      return (int) (loan.principalRemaining() / 100);
   }

   public boolean isForeign() {
      return !loan.isDomestic();
   }

   public String acctType() {
      return "loan";
   }
}
```

Figure 7-7 shows the class diagram corresponding to these adapters. This figure also shows a class FBIClient, which creates an adapted FBIAcctInfo object for each account and loan and stores them in a list. Then it can process the list as needed; for simplicity, this code just counts the affected accounts. The code appears in Listing 7-18.

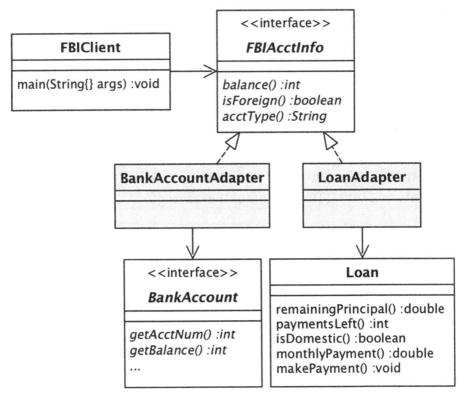

Figure 7-7. *The class diagam of the FBI scenario*

Listing 7-18. The FBIClient Class

```
public class FBIClient {
   public static void main(String[] args) {
      Bank b = getBank();

      // put account info into a single list
      List<FBIAcctInfo> L = new ArrayList<>();
      for (BankAccount ba : b)
         L.add(new BankAccountAdapter(ba));
      for (Loan ln : b.loans())
         L.add(new LoanAdapter(ln));
```

```
    // then process the list
    int count = 0;
    for (FBIAcctInfo a : L)
        if (a.isForeign() && a.balance() > 1000.0)
            count++;
    System.out.println("The count is " + count);
}

private static Bank getBank() {
    SavedBankInfo info = new SavedBankInfo("bank16.info");
    Map<Integer,BankAccount> accounts = info.getAccounts();
    int nextacct = info.nextAcctNum();
    return new Bank(accounts, nextacct);
}
}
```

Summary

A class is called a *wrapper* class if it has a dependency to a class D and implements its methods by calling D's methods to do most (or all) of the work. One common use of a wrapper class is as an *adapter*. An adapter class uses its wrapped class to help it implement a similar interface. For example, the ArrayAsList class of Figure 7-3 implements a list by wrapping an array. The relationship between the adapter class, the class it wraps, and the interface it implements, is called the *adapter pattern*.

The byte stream classes in the Java library illustrate the value of adapters. The classes InputStream, OutputStream, and their subclasses provide ways to read and write bytes between various kinds of inputs and outputs. But byte-level operations are often too low-level to be practical, so Java has classes that support higher-level operations. The classes Reader, Writer, and their subclasses read and write characters, and the interfaces

ObjectInput and ObjectOutput read and write objects and primitive
values. The best way to implement these higher level operations is to use
adapters.

In particular, the class InputStreamReader wraps any InputStream
object and enables it to be read as a sequence of characters. Similarly, the
adapter class ObjectInputStream enables any InputStream object to be
read as a sequence of objects and values. These adapters only need to know
how to encode a character (in the case of InputStreamReader) or an object
(in the case of ObjectInputStream) as a sequence of bytes. Each adapter
class can then let its wrapped InputStream object perform the rest of the
work. The adapter classes OutputStreamWriter and ObjectOutputStream
work similarly for their wrapped ObjectStream object.

CHAPTER 8

Decorators

A *decorator* is a wrapper that implements the same interface as the object it wraps. Decorator methods *enhance* the methods of the wrapped object, in contrast to adapter methods, which *replace* the methods of the wrapped object.

This chapter examines several useful applications of decorators. They can be used to create immutable versions of objects, coordinate the execution of complex tasks, and implement collection streams. The Java library class InputStream uses decorators prominently. The chapter also examines the design issues that the writers of decorator classes must confront.

Decorator Classes

Let's begin with the banking demo. Recall from Chapter 6 that the Bank class has the method iterator, which enables clients to examine its BankAccount objects. For example, the code in Listing 8-1 prints the accounts having a balance of less than $1.

© Edward Sciore 2019
E. Sciore, *Java Program Design*, https://doi.org/10.1007/978-1-4842-4143-1_8

Listing 8-1. A Reasonable Use of the Bank's Iterator Method

```
Iterator<BankAccount> iter = bank.iterator();
while (iter.hasNext()) {
   BankAccount ba = iter.next();
   if (ba.getBalance() < 100)
      System.out.println(ba);
}
```

The problem with this `iterator` method is that a client can also use it to modify `BankAccount` objects, and even delete them. For example, the code in Listing 8-2 deletes all accounts having a balance of less than $1 and doubles the balance of all other accounts.

Listing 8-2. An Unreasonable Use of the Bank's Iterator Method

```
Iterator<BankAccount> iter = bank.iterator();
while (iter.hasNext()) {
   BankAccount ba = iter.next();
   int balance = ba.getBalance();
   if (balance < 100)
      iter.remove();
   else
      ba.deposit(balance);
}
```

Suppose that this is not your intent and that you want the `iterator` method to give read-only access to the bank accounts. Two issues need to be addressed. First, the `iterator` method gives the client complete access to each `BankAccount` object; you want it to deny access to the modification methods of `BankAccount`. Second, iterators have the method `remove`, which deletes the object currently being examined; you want to ensure that clients cannot call this method. The solution to both issues is to use wrapping.

A way to ensure that BankAccount objects are not modifiable is to create a class that wraps BankAccount. The nonmodification methods of the wrapper will call the corresponding methods of the wrapped object and its modification methods will throw an exception. Listing 8-3 gives the code for such a class, called UnmodifiableAccount. To save space, the listing omits the code for the methods getBalance, isForeign, compareTo, hasEnoughCollateral, toString, equals, and fee, as they are similar to the code for getAcctNum.

Listing 8-3. A Proposed UnmodifiableAccount Class

```
public class UnmodifiableAccount implements BankAccount {
   private BankAccount ba;

   public UnmodifiableAccount(BankAccount ba) {
      this.ba = ba;
   }

   public int getAcctNum() {
      return ba.getAcctNum();
   }

   ... // code for the other read-only methods goes here

   public void deposit(int amt) {
      throw new UnsupportedOperationException();
   }

   public void addInterest() {
      throw new UnsupportedOperationException();
   }

   public void setForeign(boolean isforeign) {
      throw new UnsupportedOperationException();
   }
}
```

The same technique can be used to ensure that an iterator is read-only. You create a class that wraps the iterator and throws an exception when the remove method is called. Listing 8-4 gives the code for such a class, named UnmodifiableBankIterator. Note that the next method takes the BankAccount object it receives from the wrapped iterator, wraps it as an UnmodifiableAccount object, and returns the wrapper.

Listing 8-4. The Version 17 UnmodifiableBankIterator Class

```
public class UnmodifiableBankIterator
              implements Iterator<BankAccount> {
   private Iterator<BankAccount> iter;

   public UnmodifiableBankIterator(
                      Iterator<BankAccount> iter) {
      this.iter = iter;
   }

   public boolean hasNext() {
      return iter.hasNext();
   }

   public BankAccount next() {
      BankAccount ba = iter.next();
      return new UnmodifiableAccount(ba);
   }

   public void remove() {
      throw new UnsupportedOperationException();
   }
}
```

Listing 8-5 gives the revised code for the bank's iterator method. The code wraps the iterator in an UnmodifiableBankIterator object before returning it to the client.

Listing 8-5. The Iterator Method of Bank

```
public Iterator<BankAccount> iterator() {
   Iterator<BankAccount> iter = accounts.values().iterator();
   return new UnmodifiableBankIterator(iter);
}
```

Let's pause for a moment to look at how these changes affect the banking demo. The iterator returned by the bank's `iterator` method is an unmodifiable iterator of unmodifiable `BankAccount` objects. However, from the client's point of view nothing has changed. The client still sees an iterator of `BankAccount` objects. Consequently, classes such as `IteratorAccountStats` do not need to be modified.

What makes this feat possible is that the wrapper classes `UnmodifiableAccount` and `UnmodifiableBankIterator` implement the same interface as the objects that they wrap. This feature enables the wrapped objects to be used in place of the unwrapped objects. Such a wrapper is called a *decorator*.

The purpose of a decorator is to change the behavior of one or more methods of a class without changing its interface. The behavioral changes are the "decorations" to the class.

A class can have multiple decorator subclasses. For an example, suppose that the bank wants to be able to flag individual accounts as *suspicious*. A suspicious account changes its behavior in two ways: it writes a message to the console each time the `deposit` method is called, and its `toString` method prepends "##" to the front of the returned string. The class `SuspiciousAccount` implements this behavior. Its code appears in Listing 8-6.

Listing 8-6. A Proposed SuspiciousAccount Class

```
public class SuspiciousAccount implements BankAccount {
   private BankAccount ba;
   public SuspiciousAccount(BankAccount ba) {
      this.ba = ba;
   }

   public int getAcctNum() {
      return ba.getAcctNum();
   }

   ... // other methods go here

   public void deposit(int amt) {
      Date d = new Date();
      String msg = "On " + d + " account #" +
                   ba.getAcctNum() + " deposited " + amt;
      System.out.println(msg);
      ba.deposit(amt);
   }

   public String toString() {
      return "## " + ba.toString();
   }
}
```

Listing 8-6 omits several methods from the BankAccount interface. As in Listing 8-3, the code for these omitted methods are similar to getAcctNum—they simply call the corresponding method of the wrapped object.

One way to make use of the SuspiciousAccount class is to modify Bank to have the method makeSuspicious. The code for the method appears in Listing 8-7. It retrieves the specified bank account, wraps it as a Suspicious Account, and then writes the new BankAccount object to the map, replacing the old one. Note that the accounts map will contain a mixture of suspicious and nonsuspicious accounts, although clients will not be aware of this fact.

Listing 8-7. The Bank's makeSuspicious Method

```
public void makeSuspicious(int acctnum) {
   BankAccount ba = accounts.get(acctnum);
   ba = new SuspiciousAccount(ba);
   accounts.put(acctnum, ba);
}
```

The Decorator Pattern

The classes UnmodifiableAccount in Listing 8-3 and SuspiciousAccount
in Listing 8-6 have a lot of code in common. They both wrap BankAccount
and hold a reference to the wrapped object in a local variable. In addition,
several of their methods do nothing but call the corresponding method of
the wrapped object. You can remove this duplication by creating an abstract
class to hold the common code. This class is called BankAccountWrapper,
and is part of the version 17 banking demo. Its code appears in Listing 8-8.

Listing 8-8. The Version 17 BankAccountWrapper Class

```
public abstract class BankAccountWrapper
                     implements BankAccount {
   protected BankAccount ba;

   protected BankAccountWrapper(BankAccount ba) {
      this.ba = ba;
   }

   public int getAcctNum() {
      return ba.getAcctNum();
   }

   ... //similar code for all the other methods of BankAccount
}
```

BankAccountWrapper implements each BankAccount method by calling the corresponding method of its wrapped object. By itself, this class does nothing. Its value is that it simplifies the writing of other BankAccount wrapper classes. This explains why BankAccountWrapper is an abstract class even though it has no abstract methods. It depends on subclasses to override its methods with interesting behavior.

Version 17 of the banking demo contains the UnmodifiableAccount and SuspiciousAccount classes, rewritten to extend BankAccountWrapper. Their code appears in Listing 8-9 and Listing 8-10. Note that the code is much more straightforward than what originally appeared in listings 8-3 and 8-6.

Listing 8-9. The Version 17 UnmodifiableAccount Class

```
public class UnmodifiableAccount
            extends BankAccountWrapper {

   public UnmodifiableAccount(BankAccount ba) {
      super(ba);
   }

   public void deposit(int amt) {
      throw new UnsupportedOperationException();
   }

   public void addInterest() {
      throw new UnsupportedOperationException();
   }

   public void setForeign(boolean isforeign) {
      throw new UnsupportedOperationException();
   }
}
```

Listing 8-10. The Version 17 SuspiciousAccount Class

```
public class SuspiciousAccount
            extends BankAccountWrapper {

   public SuspiciousAccount(BankAccount ba) {
      super(ba);
   }

   public void deposit(int amt) {
      Date d = new Date();
      String msg = "On " + d + " account #" +
                  ba.getAcctNum() + " deposited " + amt;
      System.out.println(msg);
      ba.deposit(amt);
   }

   public String toString() {
      return "## " + ba.toString();
   }
}
```

A class diagram for the BankAccount classes appears in Figure 8-1. The decorator classes are shaded. Their dependency on BankAccount is held by BankAccountWrapper.

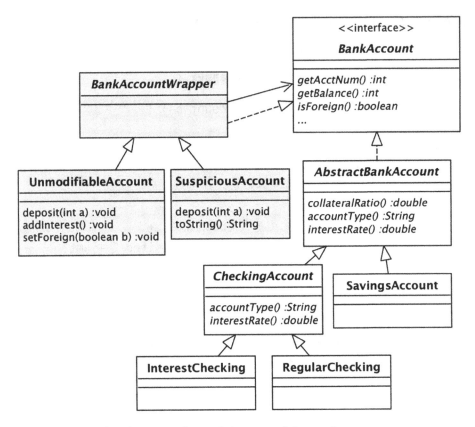

Figure 8-1. *The decorated BankAccount hierarchy*

The decorator classes in this class diagram are organized according to the *decorator pattern.* The decorator pattern asserts that the decorations for an interface form a hierarchy. The root of the hierarchy is an abstract wrapper class that holds a reference to its wrapped class and provides default implementations of the interface methods. The decorator classes are the subclasses of the wrapper class. The nondecorator classes of the interface are called its *base classes.* Figure 8-2 depicts the class diagram for the decorator pattern.

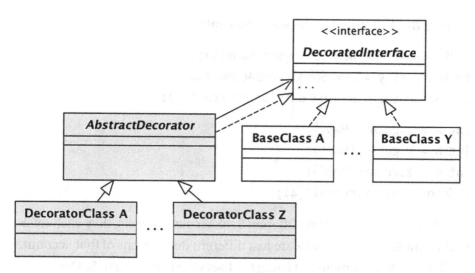

Figure 8-2. *The decorator pattern*

A decorator class, like an adapter, can be thought of as transforming an input object into an output object. The difference is that the output of a decorator has the same type as its input. This feature means that decorators can be composed.

For example, consider the banking demo. The Bank class holds a map of BankAccount objects. Some of them will be undecorated and some will be decorated with SuspiciousAccount. If a client calls the bank's iterator method then all objects in the iterator will be decorated with UnmodifiableAccount. This implies that the suspicious accounts will now have two decorations.

A good way to understand the composition of decorator objects is to examine their representation in memory. Consider the code of Listing 8-11. The first three statements create three different BankAccount objects and bind them to variables x, y, and z.

Listing 8-11. Using Composed Decorators

```
BankAccount x = new SavingsAccount(5);
BankAccount y = new SuspiciousAccount(x);
BankAccount z = new UnmodifiableAccount(y);

int a = x.getAcctNum();
int b = y.getAcctNum();
int c = z.getAcctNum();
x.deposit(4); y.deposit(4);
```

Although x, y, and z are different BankAccount objects, they each refer to account 5. Objects y and z are just different decorations of that account.

The fourth statement in Listing 8-11 sets the variable a to 5. The next statement also sets variable b to 5 because y.getAcctNum calls x.getAcctNum. Similarly, variable c also gets set to 5 because z.getAcctNum calls y.getAcctNum which calls x.getAcctNum.

The call to x.deposit increases x's balance by 4. The call to y.deposit increases x's balance by another 4, because y.deposit calls x.deposit. It also writes a message to the console because y is suspicious. Listing 8-11 deliberately does not call z.deposit because that call would throw an exception due to the fact that z is unmodifiable.

Figure 8-3 depicts the memory contents of these variables after the code has executed. Each variable's rectangle shows the value of its state variables. An AbstractBankAccount object has three state variables: acctnum, balance, and owner. For simplicity, this figure does not show the object that owner refers to. A BankAccountWrapper object has one state variable, ba, which references the object being wrapped.

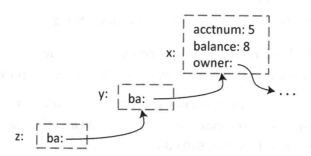

Figure 8-3. *The relationship of three BankAccount objects*

Figure 8-3 illustrates how a decorated object can be thought of as a chain of objects. The head of the chain is the most recent decoration. The tail of the chain is the undecorated version of the object. When a method is called, the method execution starts at the head of the chain and proceeds down the chain.

This situation is a form of recursion. The decorator classes are the recursive classes. A method call can be thought of as recursively traversing the chain of decorators. For example, z.getAcctNum recursively calls y.getAcctNum, which recursively calls x.getAcctNum, which returns its value.

The Chain of Command Pattern

The *chain of command pattern* is a special case of the decorator pattern where the decorators perform tasks instead of calculating values. Each decorator understands some part of the task. A request to perform the task is sent to the first decorator in the chain and is passed down the chain until it encounters a decorator that can perform that task. If no decorator is able to perform the task then the base class performs a default action.

For an example, version 17 of the banking demo uses the chain of command pattern to implement loan authorization. Recall that in earlier versions, the bank authorized a loan only if the specified account had a sufficiently high balance. In version 17 the bank uses two additional criteria, based on the customer's financial history and the bank's previous experience with the customer. These criteria are given in Listing 8-12.

Listing 8-12. Revised Loan Authorization Criteria

- If the bank has had no prior problems with the customer and the loan is less than $2,000 then approve.

- Otherwise if the customer's credit rating is under 500, then deny. If the credit rating is over 700 and the loan amount is less than $10,000, then approve.

- Otherwise if the specified account balance is sufficiently high, then approve, else deny.

These criteria are obviously a simplified version of what a real bank would use. But the point is that loan approval requires the coordination of very different kinds of data—such as customer history, financial creditworthiness, and assets—that are often the responsibility of different departments. You could combine these criteria into a single method but then the entire method would need to be modified if any of the criteria changed. The Single Responsibility rule suggests that a better design is to create a separate class for each kind of criterion. These separate classes can then be implemented as decorators and organized according to the chain of command pattern. Figure 8-4 illustrates this organization. The interface is LoanAuthorizer, which has the method authorizeLoan. The classes GoodCustomerAuthorizer, CreditScoreAuthorizer, and CollateralAuthorizer implement each of the three criteria.

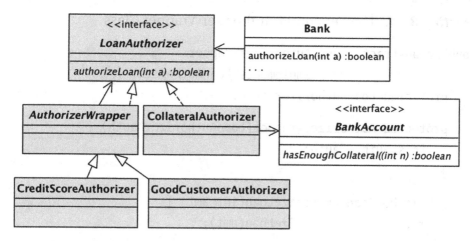

Figure 8-4. *The version 17 LoanAuthorizer hierarchy*

The class CollateralAuthorizer is the base class. It authorizes the loan if the balance of the specified bank account is sufficiently high, and denies the loan otherwise. Its code appears in Listing 8-13. This code is very similar to the loan authorization code from previous versions.

Listing 8-13. The Version 17 CollateralAuthorizer Class

```
public class CollateralAuthorizer implements LoanAuthorizer {
    private BankAccount ba;

    public CollateralAuthorizer(BankAccount ba) {
        this.ba = ba;
    }

    public boolean authorizeLoan(int amt) {
        return ba.hasEnoughCollateral(amt);
    }
}
```

The AuthorizerWrapper class is the standard default wrapper associated with the decorator pattern. Its code appears in Listing 8-14.

Listing 8-14. The Version 17 AuthorizerWrapper Class

```
public abstract class AuthorizerWrapper
                    implements LoanAuthorizer {
   protected LoanAuthorizer auth;

   protected AuthorizerWrapper(LoanAuthorizer auth) {
      this.auth = auth;
   }

   public boolean authorizeLoan(int amt) {
      return auth.authorizeLoan(amt);
   }
}
```

The CreditScoreAuthorizer and GoodCustomerAuthorizer classes are the decorators. Their code appears in Listings 8-15 and 8-16. For these classes to be realistic the banking demo would have to be expanded to include customer information. To keep things simple, the code uses random numbers to mock up the credit rating and customer status.

Listing 8-15. The Version 17 CreditScoreAuthorizer Class

```
public class CreditScoreAuthorizer extends AuthorizerWrapper {
   private int score;

   public CreditScoreAuthorizer(LoanAuthorizer auth) {
      super(auth);
      // For simplicity, mock up the credit score
      // associated with the owner of the bank account.
      Random rnd = new Random();
      this.score = 300 + rnd.nextInt(500);
   }
```

```
    public boolean authorizeLoan(int amt) {
        if (score > 700 && amt < 100000)
            return true;
        else if (score < 500)
            return false;
        else
            return auth.authorizeLoan(amt);
    }
}
```

Listing 8-16. The Version 17 GoodCustomerAuthorizer Class

```
public class GoodCustomerAuthorizer
            extends AuthorizerWrapper {
    private boolean isgood;

    public GoodCustomerAuthorizer(LoanAuthorizer auth) {
        super(auth);
        // For simplicity, mock up the customer status
        // associated with the owner of the bank account.
        Random rnd = new Random();
        isgood = rnd.nextBoolean();
    }

    public boolean authorizeLoan(int amt) {
        if (isgood && amt < 200000)
            return true;
        else
            return auth.authorizeLoan(amt);
    }
}
```

Listing 8-17 gives the code for the authorizeLoan method of class Bank. It gets a LoanAuthorizer object from the static factory method getAuthorizer defined in the LoanAuthorizer interface.

The code for LoanAuthorizer appears in Listing 8-18. Its getAuthorizer method creates a chain of approvers. Outermost is the GoodCustomerAuthorizer decorator, followed by CreditScoreAuthorizer and then CollateralAuthorizer. This ordering implies that a loan authorization will proceed as shown in Listing 8-12.

Listing 8-17. The Bank's Version 17 AuthorizeLoan Method

```
public boolean authorizeLoan(int acctnum, int loanamt) {
    BankAccount ba = accounts.get(acctnum);
    LoanAuthorizer auth = LoanAuthorizer.getAuthorizer(ba);
    return auth.authorizeLoan(loanamt);
}
```

Listing 8-18. The Version 17 LoanAuthorizer Interface

```
public interface LoanAuthorizer {
    boolean authorizeLoan(int amt);

    static LoanAuthorizer getAuthorizer(BankAccount ba) {
        LoanAuthorizer auth = new CollateralAuthorizer(ba);
        auth = new CreditScoreAuthorizer(auth);
        return new GoodCustomerAuthorizer(auth);
    }
}
```

Decorated Iterators

The end of Chapter 6 discussed collection streams and how their *filter* and *map* methods transform one stream to another. You can use decorators to do something similar with iterators. In particular, you can create decorator

classes MapIterator and FilterIterator that transform one iterator
into another one. MapIterator transforms the value of each element in
its component iterator, returning an iterator of those transformed values.
FilterIterator filters its component iterator, returning an iterator
containing the elements that satisfy the given predicate.

Before looking at the code for these classes it will be helpful to examine
how they will be used. The IteratorTest class of Listing 8-19 contains two
examples. The first example converts the strings having length between
2 and 3 to uppercase and prints them. The second example prints the
maximum length of the strings having length between 2 and 3.

Listing 8-19. The IteratorTest Class

```java
public class IteratorTest {
   public static void main(String[] args) {
      Collection<String> c = Arrays.asList("a", "bb",
                                            "ccc", "dddd");

      // Print the strings whose length is between 2 and 3
      // in uppercase.
      Iterator<String> i1, i2, i3, i4;
      i1 = c.iterator();
      i2 = new FilterIterator<String>(i1, s->s.length() > 1);
      i3 = new FilterIterator<String>(i2, s->s.length() < 4);
      i4 = new MapIterator<String,String>(i3,
                                          s->s.toUpperCase());
      while (i4.hasNext()) {
         String s = i4.next();
         System.out.println(s);
      }
```

```
    // Print the maximum length of those strings.
    Iterator<String> j1, j2, j3;
    Iterator<Integer> j4;
    j1 = c.iterator();
    j2 = new FilterIterator<String>(j1, s->s.length() > 1);
    j3 = new FilterIterator<String>(j2, s->s.length() < 4);
    j4 = new MapIterator<String,Integer>(j3, s->s.length());
    int max = -1;
    while (j4.hasNext()) {
        Integer n = j4.next();
        if (n > max)
            max = n;
    }
    System.out.println("The max length is " + max);
  }
}
```

In the first example, the iterator denoted by variable i1 contains the four strings {"a," "bb," "ccc," "dddd"}. The iterator i2 restricts i1 to strings that are more than one character long, that is {"bb," "ccc," "dddd"}. Iterator i3 restricts i2 to strings that are less than four characters long, that is {"bb," "ccc"}. Iterator i4 converts those values to uppercase, that is {"BB," "CCC"}. The code then uses the standard idiom to traverse i4 and print its elements.

The second example is similar. Iterator j4 contains the lengths of those strings whose length is between two and three. The code traverses j4 to find the maximum length and prints it.

It is now time to look at the code for the two iterator classes. The code for MapIterator appears in Listing 8-20. Note how this class makes use of its component iterator. The hasNext method calls the component's hasNext method and returns the value it returned. The next method calls the component's next method, uses the given function to transform that value, and returns the transformed value.

Listing 8-20. The MapIterator Class

```
public class MapIterator<T,R> implements Iterator<R> {
   private Iterator<T> iter;
   private Function<T,R> f;

   public MapIterator(Iterator<T> iter, Function<T,R> f) {
      this.iter = iter;
      this.f = f;
   }

   public boolean hasNext() {
      return iter.hasNext();
   }

   public R next() {
      T t = iter.next();
      return f.apply(t);
   }
}
```

The code for FilterIterator appears in Listing 8-21. This class uses its component iterator a bit more intricately. The issue is that its hasNext method must read ahead through the component iterator in order to determine if there is another value that satisfies the filter. If a satisfying value is found then hasNext stores it in the variable nextvalue, which will be returned when the next method is called.

Listing 8-21. The FilterIterator Class

```
public class FilterIterator<T> implements Iterator<T> {
   private Iterator<T> iter;
   private Predicate<T> pred;
   private T nextvalue;
   private boolean found = false;
```

```
   public FilterIterator(Iterator<T> iter,
                          Predicate<T> pred) {
      this.iter = iter;
      this.pred = pred;
   }

   public boolean hasNext() {
      while (!found && iter.hasNext()) {
         T t = iter.next();
         if (pred.test(t)) {
            nextvalue = t;
            found = true;
         }
      }
      return found;
   }

   public T next() {
      hasNext();  // just to be safe
      if (!found)
         throw new NoSuchElementException();
      found = false;
      return nextvalue;
   }
}
```

These decorated iterators are remarkably efficient. This efficiency stems from the fact that the FilterIterator and MapIterator objects do not pre-calculate their values. Instead, they get their values on demand by querying their component iterators. Note that each decorator class traverses its component iterator once. Consequently, traversing any decorated iterator will traverse its base iterator exactly once, no matter how many decorations it has!

For an example, consider iterator i4 in Listing 8-19. The loop that prints its elements requires just a single pass through the underlying collection of strings. The *sequence diagram* shown in Figure 8-5 can help to clarify this fact. This diagram displays the four communicating iterators of Listing 8-19, one per column. The rows denote a timeline of the method calls between these iterators.

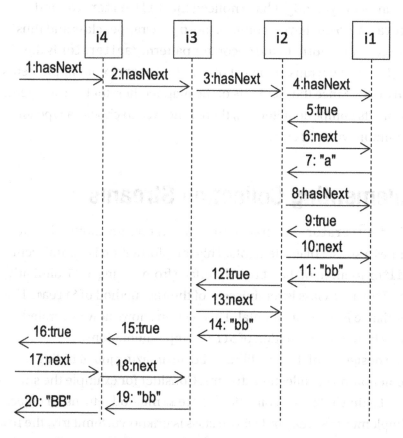

Figure 8-5. *Sequence diagram for Listing 8-19*

This diagram shows the sequence of calls required to retrieve the first value from iterator i4. The main method begins by calling hasNext at step 1 and receives the return value true at step 16. It then calls next at step 17 and receives "BB" at step 20.

The behavior of each iterator can be observed by following the sequence of arrows attached to its column. The behavior of i2 is especially interesting. In order to respond to the hasNext method, it needs to repeatedly call i1.next() until i1 returns a value that satisfies i2's predicate. The diagram shows that the first value returned, "a," did not satisfy the predicate, but the second value "bb" did.

As an aside, you might have noticed that FilterIterator and MapIterator do not have a common abstract wrapper class and thus do not strictly conform to the decorator pattern. MapIterator is the culprit because it wraps an object of type Iterator<T> but implements Iterator<R>. Since the elements of the mapped iterator have a different type from its component iterator, there is no way to choose a type for the common wrapper class.

Implementing Collection Streams

The FilterIterator class transforms an iterator into another iterator that generates a subset of its elements. This transformation is reminiscent of the filter method of the Stream interface from Listing 6-35. Similarly, the MapIterator class is reminiscent of the map method of Stream. This resemblance is not coincidental. This section shows how decorated iterators form the foundation of Stream implementations.

The designers of the Java library did an amazing job of hiding the implementation of collection streams. Consider for example the stream code in Listing 8-22. The collection's stream method returns an object that implements Stream but whose class is unknown. Similarly, the results of the filter and map methods are also objects of unknown classes that implement Stream.

Listing 8-22. Example Stream Code

```
Collection<String> c = Arrays.asList("a", "bb", "ccc");
Stream<String> s = c.stream()
                    .filter(s->s.length() == 2)
                    .map(s->s.toUpperCase());
s.forEach(v -> System.out.println(v)); // prints "BB"
```

The Java library implementation of the Stream classes is to be commended for its encapsulation. However, this encapsulation makes it difficult to study the techniques used to implement streams. Consequently, I have written a stripped-down version of Stream, called SimpleStream. The class SimpleStream contains five of the methods described in Chapter 6: iterator, forEach, filter, map, and reduce. SimpleStream differs from Stream in that it is a class, not an interface. It has a single constructor, whose argument is an iterator.

The class SimpleStreamTest illustrates the use of the SimpleStream class. Its code appears in Listing 8-23. It performs the same two tasks as in Listing 8-19, using streams instead of iterators. The first stream selects the strings having length between two and three, converts them to uppercase, and prints them. The second stream selects the strings having length between two and three, converts each to its length, finds the maximum, and prints it.

Listing 8-23. The SimpleStreamTest Class

```
public class SimpleStreamTest {
  public static void main(String[] args) {
    Collection<String> c = Arrays.asList("a", "bb",
                                        "ccc", "dddd");
```

```
    new SimpleStream<String>(c.iterator())
        .filter(s->s.length() > 1)
        .filter(s->s.length() < 4)
        .map(s->s.toUpperCase())
        .forEach(s->System.out.println(s));

    Integer max =
        new SimpleStream<String>(c.iterator())
            .filter(s->s.length() > 1)
            .filter(s->s.length() < 4)
            .map(s->s.length())
            .reduce(0, (i1, i2)->Math.max(i1, i2));
    System.out.println("The max length is " + max);
  }
}
```

The code for SimpleStream appears in Listing 8-24. Each SimpleStream object wraps an iterator. (In other words, SimpleStream is an adapter class that transforms an iterator to a collection stream.) The filter and map methods decorate the iterator and return a new SimpleStream object that wraps the decorated iterator. The forEach and reduce methods perform their actions by traversing the iterator. The reduce method uses the reduction algorithm of Listing 6-43.

Listing 8-24. The SimpleStream Class

```
public class SimpleStream<T> {
   Iterator<T> iter;

   public SimpleStream(Iterator<T> iter) {
      this.iter = iter;
   }
```

```java
public SimpleStream<T> filter(Predicate<T> pred) {
    Iterator<T> newiter =
                    new FilterIterator<T>(iter, pred);
    return new SimpleStream<T>(newiter);
}

public <R> SimpleStream<R> map(Function<T,R> f) {
    Iterator<R> newiter = new MapIterator<T,R>(iter, f);
    return new SimpleStream<R>(newiter);
}

public void forEach(Consumer<T> cons) {
    while (iter.hasNext()) {
        T t = iter.next();
        cons.accept(t);
    }
}

public T reduce(T identity, BinaryOperator<T> f) {
    T result = identity;
    while (iter.hasNext()) {
        T t = iter.next();
        result = f.apply(result, t);
    }
    return result;
}
}
```

The efficiency of the decorated iterators carries over to the SimpleStream methods. The filter and map methods construct a new decorated iterator and do not perform any traversal. The forEach and reduce methods traverse the wrapped decorated iterator, which will always entail just a single iteration through the underlying collection.

Decorated Input Streams

Decorators also play a prominent role in the Java byte-stream classes (which, you should recall, are completely unrelated to the collection streams of the previous section). Consider again the abstract class InputStream. This class was discussed in Chapter 3, along with its subclasses FileInputStream, PipedInputStream, and ByteArrayInputStream. This chapter examines some of the decorator subclasses of InputStream.

The class FilterInputStream is the abstract InputStream wrapper. Three of its decorator subclasses are BufferedInputStream, ProgressMonitorInputStream, and CipherInputStream. Figure 8-6 gives the corresponding class diagram. Note how it conforms to the decorator pattern. The following subsections discuss these FilterInputStream subclasses.

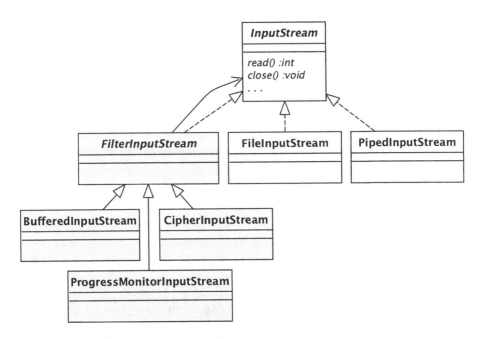

Figure 8-6. *The InputStream decorator classes*

Buffered Input Streams

Listing 8-25 gives the code for a class InputStreamEfficiency that illustrates three ways to read a file. Each of these ways is implemented by a method that returns the number of milliseconds it took to read the file.

Listing 8-25. The InputStreamEfficiency Class

```
public class InputStreamEfficiency {
   public static void main(String[] args) throws IOException {
      String src = "mobydick.txt";
      long t1 = readFileUnbuffered(src);
      long t2 = readFileArrayBuffer(src);
      long t3 = readFileDecoratorBuffer(src);
      System.out.println("Unbuffered time: " + t1);
      System.out.println("Array Buffer time: " + t2);
      System.out.println("Decorator Buffer time: " + t3);
   }
   ... // code for the three methods goes here
}
```

The code for the method readFileUnbuffered appears in Listing 8-26. The method reads the input stream according to the standard idiom, using the no-arg read method to read each byte individually. Unfortunately, this idiom is a very inefficient way to read bytes from a file. The issue is that each call to read results in a call to the operating system, and OS calls are time consuming.

Listing 8-26. The readFileUnbuffered Method

```
public static long readFileUnbuffered(String src)
                 throws IOException {
  long begintime = System.currentTimeMillis();
```

```
    try (InputStream is = new FileInputStream(src)) {
        int x = is.read();
        while (x >= 0) {
            byte b = (byte) x;
            // process b ...
            x = is.read();
        }
    }
    return System.currentTimeMillis() - begintime;
}
```

The readFileArrayBuffer method addresses this issue by reading the bytes of its underlying stream an array at a time. This technique is called *buffering* and the array is called a *buffer*. The code for the method appears in Listing 8-27. It has two nested loops. The outer loop calls the 1-arg read method to fill its array with bytes, repeating until the underlying stream has been completely read. The inner loop processes each byte in the array. This use of buffering results in a remarkable increase in efficiency. On my computer and using a 100-byte array, this method is about 100 times faster than readFileUnbuffered.

Listing 8-27. The readFileArrayBuffer Method

```
public static long readFileArrayBuffer(String src)
                    throws IOException {
    long begintime = System.currentTimeMillis();
    try (InputStream is = new FileInputStream(src)) {
        byte[] a = new byte[100];
        int howmany = is.read(a);
        while (howmany > 0) {
            for (int pos=0; pos<howmany; pos++) {
```

```
        byte b = a[pos];
        // process b ...
    }
    howmany = is.read(a);
  }
}
return System.currentTimeMillis() - begintime;
}
```

Although buffering can significantly improve execution time, it also adds complexity to the code. In particular, the readFileArrayBuffer method needs two nested loops to read bytes from the input stream and its code needs to be carefully crafted to ensure that the buffer is managed correctly.

The readFileDecoratorBuffer method in Listing 8-28 uses the decorator class BufferedInputStream from the Java library to perform the buffering automatically. A BufferedInputStream object stores an array of bytes internally. It initially fills the array with bytes from its component stream by using a single call to read. When a client calls a read method, the BufferedInputStream object extracts the next byte(s) from the array. If the array runs out of bytes then the object automatically refills it.

The interesting feature of Listing 8-28 is that it uses the standard idiom to read its input stream. The code is simple, but also efficient. The BufferedInputStream decorator performs the buffering without the client's knowledge. The running time of this method on my computer is comparable to that of readFileArrayBuffer.

Listing 8-28. The readFileDecoratorBuffer Method

```
public static long readFileDecoratorBuffer(String src)
                  throws IOException {
   long begintime = System.currentTimeMillis();
   try (InputStream  is = new FileInputStream(src);
      InputStream bis = new BufferedInputStream(is)) {
      int x = bis.read();
      while (x >= 0) {
         byte b = (byte) x;
         // process b ...
         x = bis.read();
      }
   }
   return System.currentTimeMillis() - begintime;
}
```

Progress Monitoring

Another InputStream decorator subclass is ProgressMonitorInputStream.
This decorator does not affect how the bytes are read. Instead, its
"decoration" is to display a window containing a progress bar. Listing
8-29 gives code for the class ProgressMonitorFileRead, which uses a
ProgressMonitorInputStream to decorate a FileInputStream.

Listing 8-29. The ProgressMonitorFileRead Class

```
public class ProgressMonitorFileRead {
   public static void main(String[] args) throws IOException {
      String src = "mobydick.txt";
      String msg = "reading " + src;
```

```
try (InputStream  is = new FileInputStream(src);
     InputStream pis = new ProgressMonitorInputStream(
                           null, msg, is)) {
   int x = pis.read();
   while (x >= 0) {
     byte b = (byte) x;
     // process b ...
     x = pis.read();
   }
 }
}
}
```

The ProgressMonitorInputStream constructor has three arguments. The first is a pointer to the parent window of the progress monitor window. The value is null in Listing 8-29 because the program is not running in a GUI environment. The second argument is the label to be displayed with the progress bar. In this example the label is "reading mobydick.txt." The third is a reference to the input stream being decorated. Figure 8-7 displays a screenshot of the progress monitor window from my computer.

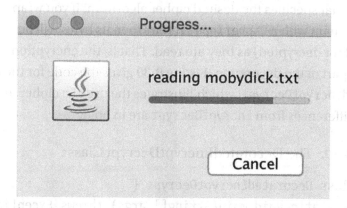

Figure 8-7. *A progress monitor window*

The `ProgressMonitorInputStream` decorator is responsible for monitoring the progress of reading its wrapped input stream and displaying a progress bar if warranted. Its constructor calls the `available` method of the wrapped stream, which returns its best guess as to the total number of bytes remaining in the stream. Each call to `read` repeats the call to `available` and compares its current value to the initial value. If that ratio is sufficiently high, it redisplays the progress window.

Cipher Input Streams

Consider the program `EncryptDecrypt` from Listing 3-12. Its `encrypt` method implemented a simple Caesar cipher: It read each byte of its input stream, added a fixed offset, and wrote the resulting byte to the output stream.

There are two reasons why this program is unsatisfactory. First, Caesar ciphers are easy to crack; any practical situation would require a more sophisticated algorithm. Second, the programmer must write the encryption code explicitly, and code for sophisticated cipher algorithms can be difficult to write. The Java library class `CipherInputStream` solves both of these problems.

`CipherInputStream` is a decorator class. Its constructor has an argument that specifies the desired cipher algorithm. If you wrap an input stream with a `CipherInputStream` then its bytes will be encrypted (or decrypted) as they are read. That is, the encryption occurs as part of the decoration. Listing 8-30 gives the code for the class `DecoratedEncryptDecrypt`, which illustrates the use of a cipher input stream. Differences from `EncryptDecrypt` are in bold.

Listing 8-30. The DecoratedEncryptDecrypt Class

```
public class DecoratedEncryptDecrypt {
    public static void main(String[] args) throws Exception {
        KeyGenerator kg = KeyGenerator.getInstance("DES");
        kg.init(56); // DES uses 56-bit keys
```

```
    SecretKey key = kg.generateKey();

    encrypt("mobydick.txt",  "encrypted.txt", key,
            Cipher.ENCRYPT_MODE);
    encrypt("encrypted.txt", "decrypted.txt", key,
            Cipher.DECRYPT_MODE);
}

private static void encrypt(String source, String output,
        SecretKey key, int mode) throws Exception {
    Cipher c = Cipher.getInstance("DES");
    c.init(mode, key);
    try (InputStream  is = new FileInputStream(source);
        InputStream cis = new CipherInputStream(is, c);
        OutputStream os = new FileOutputStream(output)) {

        int x = cis.read();
        while (x >= 0) {
            byte b = (byte) x;
            os.write(b);
            x = cis.read();
        }
    }
}
}
```

The CipherInputStream constructor requires a Cipher object, which embodies the encryption algorithm. Different cipher algorithms require different specifications. The class SecretKey creates the 56-byte key required by the DES algorithm.

Note that the encrypt method once again uses the standard idiom to read the file. The CiphierInputStream decorator automatically transforms its input bytes by either encrypting or decrypting them, depending on the value of the mode parameter.

Decorator Transparency

Another way that a decorator class can enhance the functionality of its component object is to implement new methods. For example, the decorator classes PushbackInputStream and PushbackReader implement the method unread. This method puts a specified byte (or character) onto the input stream so that the next call to read will return it before continuing with the rest of the stream.

As an example, Listing 8-31 gives the code for a method openAndSkip, which opens a text file and skips over any leading whitespace. The problem with writing such a method is that the only way to know that you have finished reading the whitespace is to read a non-whitespace character. You need the pushback reader to put that non-whitespace character back on the stream for you.

Listing 8-31. A Method to Open a File, Skipping Initial Whitespace

```java
public Reader openAndSkip(String f) throws IOException {
   Reader r = new FileReader(f);
   PushbackReader pr = new PushbackReader(r);
   skipWhitespace(pr);
   return pr;
}

private void skipWhitespace(PushbackReader pr) {
   int x = pr.read();
   while (x >= 0) {
      char c = (char) x;
      if (!Character.isWhitespace(c)) {
         pr.unread(c); // put c back on the input stream
         return;
      }
```

```
    x = pr.read();
  }
}
```

The unread method is not defined in Reader. Consequently, the variable pr in Listing 8-31 must have the type PushbackReader. (If it had the type Reader, then its call to unread would not compile.) The helper method skipWhitespace is therefore not transparent because it needs to know that the reader being passed to it is a pushback reader.

For another example of decorator classes that implement new methods, consider again BufferedInputStream and BufferedReader. These classes implement two methods for rereading portions of a stream: the method mark, which marks a location in the stream; and the method reset, which repositions the stream at the marked location.

For an example use of these methods, consider the following task: given a text file and an integer N, write a program DoubledChars that finds a character that appears twice in the file separated by N characters. For example, if N=0 then the program is looking for doubled characters in the text, as in "...aa..."; if N=1 then the program is looking for doubled characters with one character in between, as in "...aba...".

The code for DoubledChars appears in Listing 8-32. The main method reads the characters from the file, passing each one to the check method. The check method reads the next N+1 characters. If the last character read matches the given one then the method prints that segment of the file. Note how the check method marks the position of the stream when it is called and resets the stream to that position when it returns.

Listing 8-32. The DoubledChars Class

```
public class DoubledChars {
    public static final int N = 1;

    public static void main(String[] args) throws IOException {
```

```
    try (Reader  r = new FileReader("mobydick.txt");
        Reader br = new BufferedReader(r)) {
        int x = br.read();   // For each char,
        while (x >= 0) {
            char c = (char) x;
            check(br, c);     // check the N+1st char after it.
            x = br.read();
        }
    }
}

private static void check(Reader r, char c)
                    throws IOException {
    char[] a = new char[N+1];
    r.mark(N+1);
    int howmany = r.read(a);
    if (howmany == N+1 && a[N] == c) {
        System.out.print(c); System.out.println(a);
    }
    r.reset();
    }
}
```

Many Reader classes (such as FileReader) are only able to read their characters once, and so they cannot implement mark and reset. However, the decorator class BufferedReader can use its buffer to get around this limitation. A call to its mark method sets the "mark location" to be the current position in the buffer and a call to reset sets the buffer position back to the saved mark location. Consequently, when characters are reread following a reset, they will be taken from the buffer and not the underlying reader. The argument to the mark method specifies the maximum size of the buffer array. Without this limit, the buffer array could become too large and generate unintended memory exceptions.

Note that the argument to the check method in Listing 8-32 has the type Reader and not BufferedReader. That is, the check method is transparent. This transparency is possible because mark and reset are defined by Reader.

But how can that be, given that some readers (such as file readers) do not support mark and reset? The answer is that all readers must have mark and reset methods; it is just that many of those methods throw an exception if called. This possibility of throwing an exception is the price the Java designers paid for achieving transparency.

The Java library has the method markSupported to help clients avoid these exceptions. If a class can implement the mark and reset methods then a call to markSupported returns true. If a class cannot implement them then markSupported returns false and the mark and reset methods throw exceptions. A client can call markSupported if it has any doubts about whether a reader supports the methods.

For example, Listing 8-33 gives a variation of Listing 8-32 in which the main method is replaced by a method printDoubleChars that takes a Reader as an argument. Since printDoubleChars does not know what kind of reader it has, it calls markSupported. If markSupported returns false then the method wraps the reader in a BufferedReader object before proceeding.

Listing 8-33. A Variant of the DoubledChars Class

```
public class DoubledChars {
    public static final int N = 1;

    public static void printDoubledChars(Reader r)
                    throws IOException {
        if (!r.markSupported())
            r = new BufferedReader(r);
        int x = r.read();  // For each char,
```

```
    while (x >= 0) {
        char c = (char) x;
        check(r, c);      // check the N+1st char after it.
        x = r.read();
    }
  }
  // ... the check method is unchanged
}
```

Let's stop to review the design implications of PushbackReader and BufferedReader. Although both decorator classes implement new methods, the Java library treats them very differently. The PushbackReader method unread is not recognized by Reader, and clients that use the method must do so non-transparently. On the other hand, the BufferedReader methods mark and reset are part of Reader, and clients can call the methods transparently. The downside to this transparency is that a client must be careful to avoid generating exceptions.

These two design decisions can be summarized as a choice between *transparency* and *safety*. There is no general rule that a designer can use to make this choice; you have to consider each situation individually.

The Java library usually opts for safety. A big reason why the library chose transparency for mark and reset is that those methods are also supported by some of the nondecorator base classes, such as ByteArrayInputStream, CharArrayReader, and StringReader. Each of these classes store the stream in an underlying array. In effect, their values are already buffered, so mark and reset are easily implemented. Since mark and reset are supported by multiple classes, the designers likely decided that they deserved inclusion in the InputStream API.

A final aspect of transparency concerns the order in which the decorators of an object are composed. In a fully transparent design each decorator class is independent of every other decorator class, and so the order in which they are composed should not affect the correctness of the code. In practice however, a decorator class may have requirements that cause certain orderings to fail. For example, suppose that you want to create an input stream that supports the mark, reset, and unread methods. Consider the following two statements:

```
InputStream bis = new BufferedInputStream(is);
PushbackInputStream pis = new PushbackInputStream(bis);
```

The class PushbackInputStream does not support mark and reset, even if its underlying input stream does. Thus variable pis will support unread but not mark and reset. On the other hand, if you interchange the declarations of bis and pis then bis will support mark and reset but not unread. In fact, there is no way for an input stream (or reader) to support mark, reset, and unread.

For another example, suppose that you want to add a progress monitor to a buffered input stream. You write the following statements:

```
InputStream  bis = new BufferedInputStream(is);
InputStream pmis = new ProgressMonitorInputStream(bis);
```

The class ProgressMonitorInputStream, unlike PushbackInputStream, supports mark and reset when its underlying input stream does. Thus variable pmis supports mark and reset. Interchanging the declarations of bis and pmis does not change the functionality of the decorated input stream.

On the other hand, suppose that you want to add a progress monitor to a cipher input stream. In this case, the following ordering works.

```
InputStream pmis = new ProgressMonitorInputStream(is);
InputStream  cis = new CipherInputStream(pmis, cipher);
```

However, the following ordering, which interchanges the declarations of pmis and cis, will not work.

```
InputStream  cis = new CipherInputStream(is, cipher);
InputStream pmis = new ProgressMonitorInputStream(cis);
```

The problem is that `ProgressMonitorInputStream` calls the `available` method of its underlying stream, which tells it how many bytes remain. But `CipherInputStream` cannot accurately know how many characters will result from its encoding, so its `available` method always returns 0. Thus, `pmis` believes that the reading has finished and will not display the monitor window.

The lesson here is that decorator transparency is an elusive goal. At first glance the enhancements provided by the input stream decorators seem to be independent of each other, but they interact in subtle ways. If a programmer is not aware of these interactions then "mysterious" bugs are likely to occur. The more that a designer can approach decorator transparency, the easier it will be for the users of these classes.

Summary

A *decorator class* is a wrapper that implements the same interface as the class that it wraps. The purpose of this wrapping is to alter the functionality of the wrapped object, either by enhancing the behavior of its existing methods or providing new ones. Decorators embrace the spirit of the Open/Closed rule—by decorating a class, you can change how the class works without having to make any modifications to it.

The *decorator pattern* indicates how to organize the decorators for a given interface. All decorators should have a common abstract superclass to manage the wrapping and provide default implementations of the interface methods. Each decorator class will extend this common superclass and provide implementations of the methods that it wishes to enhance. The *chain of command pattern* is a special instance of the decorator pattern in which the decorators perform tasks instead of calculate values.

When designing decorator classes, you must consider the issue of transparency. Ideally, a client should be able to use an `InputStream` or `Reader` object without knowing its class, and should be able to compose decorators without having to consider their possible interactions. A designer must recognize the possibility of conflict between different decorators so as to better analyze the tradeoffs involved.

CHAPTER 9

Composites

Chapter 8 examined decorators, which are wrappers that implement the same interface as the object they wrap. This chapter examines *composite* objects. A composite object is similar to a decorator except that it wraps *multiple* objects, each of which implements the same interface as itself. This seemingly small distinction makes a big difference in the structure of a composite and how it is used. Composite objects correspond to trees and composite methods tend to involve tree traversals.

This chapter presents three examples of composites: predicates, graphical user interfaces (GUIs), and cookbook recipes. These examples share a common class design known as the *composite pattern*. They also have some functional differences that illustrate the different choices a designer faces.

Predicates as Composites

A *predicate* is a mathematical expression that evaluates to true or false. Given two predicates, you can create another, larger predicate by applying the operator and or or to them. This larger predicate is called a *composite* and the two smaller predicates are its *components*. You can continue this process for as long as you like, building up larger and larger composite predicates. A noncomposite predicate is called a *basic* predicate.

© Edward Sciore 2019
E. Sciore, *Java Program Design*, https://doi.org/10.1007/978-1-4842-4143-1_9

For example, Listing 9-1 displays a composite predicate that is composed of three basic predicates. It returns true if n is less than 20 and divisible by 2 or 3.

Listing 9-1. A Composite Predicate

```
n<20 and (n%2=0 or n%3=0)
```

A composite predicate can be represented as a tree whose internal nodes are the operators {and, or} and whose leaves are basic predicates. Figure 9-1 depicts the predicate tree for Listing 9-1.

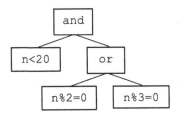

Figure 9-1. *The predicate tree for Listing 9-1*

A Java predicate is an object that implements the interface Predicate, as discussed in Chapter 6. A basic predicate is typically created via a lambda expression. For example, Listing 9-2 gives Java statements to implement the three basic predicates in Listing 9-1.

Listing 9-2. Basic Predicates in Java

```
Predicate<Integer> pred1 = n -> n < 20;
Predicate<Integer> pred2 = n -> n%2 == 0;
Predicate<Integer> pred3 = n -> n%3 == 0;
```

One way to support composite predicates in Java is to create a class for each operator. Call these classes AndPredicate and OrPredicate. Each class wraps two component predicates and implements Predicate. The test method for AndPredicate returns true if both components return true, and the test method for OrPredicate returns true if at least one component returns true. For coding convenience I will also create the class CompositePredicate to be the common superclass of AndPredicate and OrPredicate that manages their wrapped objects. Listing 9-3 gives the code for CompositePredicate and Listing 9-4 gives the code for AndPredicate. The code for OrPredicate is similar and is omitted.

Listing 9-3. The CompositePredicate Class

```
public abstract class CompositePredicate<T>
                        implements Predicate<T> {
    protected Predicate<T> p1, p2;

    protected CompositePredicate(Predicate<T> p1,
                                  Predicate<T> p2) {
        this.p1 = p1;
        this.p2 = p2;
    }

    public abstract boolean test(T t);
}
```

Listing 9-4. The AndPredicate Class

```
public class AndPredicate<T> extends CompositePredicate<T> {
    public AndPredicate(Predicate<T> p1, Predicate<T> p2) {
        super(p1, p2);
    }

    public boolean test(T t) {
        return p1.test(t) && p2.test(t);
    }
}
```

Figure 9-2 contains a class diagram that shows the relationship between these Predicate classes. The three "BasicPredicate" classes correspond to the anonymous classes created for pred1, pred2, and pred3 in Listing 9-2.

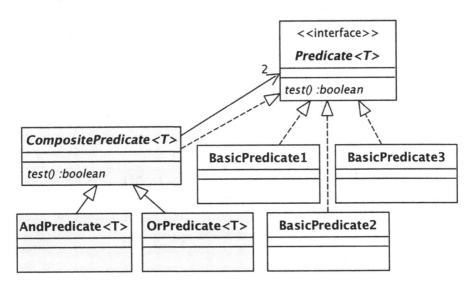

Figure 9-2. *The class diagram for Predicate*

The class diagram looks very much like the decorator pattern. The difference is that the wrapper class CompositePredicate wraps two objects instead of one. To highlight this difference, the dependency arrow is annotated with the optional cardinality label "2."

The class CompositePredicateTest in Listing 9-5 illustrates the use of composite predicates in Java. This code begins by creating the basic predicates pred1, pred2, and pred3 as in Listing 9-2. It then implements the composite predicate of Listing 9-1 in three different ways.

Listing 9-5. The CompositePredicateTest Class

```
public class CompositePredicateTest {
    public static void main(String[] args) {
        Predicate<Integer> pred1 = n -> n < 20;
```

```
Predicate<Integer> pred2 = n -> n%2 == 0;
Predicate<Integer> pred3 = n -> n%3 == 0;

// First: use AndPredicate and OrPredicate objects
Predicate<Integer> pred4 =
                new OrPredicate<Integer>(pred2, pred3);
Predicate<Integer> pred5 =
                new AndPredicate<Integer>(pred1, pred4);
printUsing(pred5);

// Second: use the 'or' and 'and' methods separately
Predicate<Integer> pred6 = pred2.or(pred3);
Predicate<Integer> pred7 = pred1.and(pred6);
printUsing(pred7);

// Third: compose the 'or' and 'and' methods
Predicate<Integer> pred8 = pred1.and(pred2.or(pred3));
printUsing(pred8);
    }

    private static void printUsing(Predicate<Integer> p) {
        for (int i=1; i<100; i++)
            if (p.test(i))
                System.out.print(i + " ");
        System.out.println();
    }
}
```

The first way uses the AndPredicate and OrPredicate classes. Predicate pred4 is an OrPredicate object and predicate pred5 is an AndPredicate object. The diagram of Figure 9-3 depicts these five Predicate objects in memory. The diagram is similar to the memory diagram of Figure 8-3, in that each object is represented by a rectangle and the values of its global variables are shown within its rectangle. Note how the object references form a tree that corresponds exactly to the predicate tree of Figure 9-1.

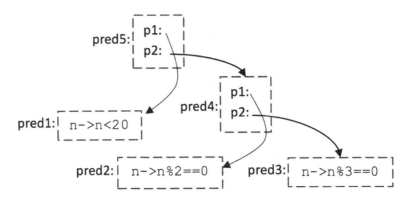

Figure 9-3. *The memory representation of a composite predicate*

After creating the predicate pred5, the code of Listing 9-5 passes pred5 to its printUsing method, which calls the predicate's test method on the integers from 1 to 100. Figure 9-4 depicts a sequence diagram that traces the execution of the expression pred5.test(9). Step 2 calls the test method of pred5's first component, pred1, which returns true. Step 4 then calls test on its second component, pred4. In order to determine its response, pred4 calls test on its two components. Component pred2 returns false but pred3 returns true; thus pred4 can return true. Since both components of pred5 have now returned true, pred5 returns true.

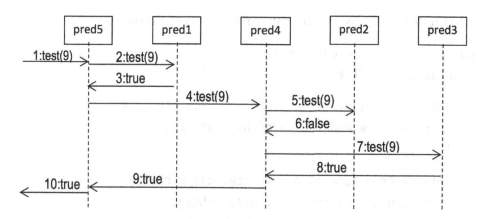

Figure 9-4. *A sequence diagram for the expression pred5.test(9)*

Note how the call to test(9) gets passed from the root of the predicate tree down to its leaves. In fact, this sequence of method calls corresponds to a postorder traversal of the tree.

The classes AndPredicate and OrPredicate are not part of the Java library. Instead, the Predicate interface has the default methods and and or, which make it possible to create composite predicates without having to create the composite objects yourself.

The use of these methods is illustrated in the second and third parts of Listing 9-5. The variable pred6 returns true if either pred2 or pred3 is true, and is functionally equivalent to pred4. Similarly, the variable pred7 is functionally equivalent to pred5. The calls to the and and or methods can also be composed, as shown by variable pred8.

Listing 9-6 shows how the and and or methods can be implemented. The and method creates and returns an AndPredicate object that wraps two objects: the current object and the object passed into the method. The implementation of the or method is similar.

Listing 9-6. A Reasonable Implementation of Predicate

```
public interface Predicate<T> {
   boolean test(T t);

   default Predicate<T> and(Predicate<T> other) {
      return new AndPredicate(this, other);
   }

   default Predicate<T> or(Predicate<T> other) {
      return new OrPredicate(this, other);
   }
}
```

The actual Java library implementation of these methods is slightly different from Listing 9-6, and appears in Listing 9-7. The lambda expressions define anonymous inner classes that are equivalent to AndPredicate and OrPredicate. This code is quite elegant, as it eliminates the need for explicit AndPredicate and OrPredicate classes.

Listing 9-7. The Actual Implementation of Predicate

```
public interface Predicate<T> {
   boolean test(T t);

   default Predicate<T> and(Predicate<T> other) {
      return t -> test(t) && other.test(t);
   }

   default Predicate<T> or(Predicate<T> other) {
      return t -> test(t) || other.test(t);
   }
}
```

Composite Objects in JavaFX

For a second example of composite objects, consider a library for building GUI applications. When you create an application window, you often structure its contents as a composite object. For an example, Figure 9-5 depicts a window that I created using the JavaFX library.

Figure 9-5. *A JavaFX window*

In JavaFX, a window's content is constructed of *nodes*. The JavaFX library has classes to implement several types of node. This example window uses two types of node: *controls* and *panes*.

A *control* is a node that can be manipulated by the user. All controls in JavaFX extend the abstract class Control. The controls in the example window belong to the classes Label, ChoiceBox, CheckBox, and Button.

A *pane* is a node that can contain other nodes, called its *children*. Each pane is responsible for determining where its child nodes are placed on the screen. This is called the pane's *layout strategy*.

The JavaFX library has several pane classes, each with its own layout strategy. They all extend the class Pane. The example window uses two of them: HBox and VBox. An HBox pane lays out its children horizontally. A VBox pane lays out its children vertically.

The window of Figure 9-5 has nine nodes: five controls and four panes. Figure 9-6 depicts their layout.

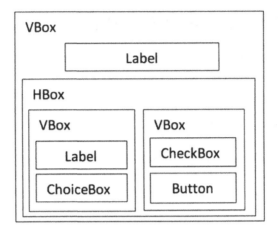

Figure 9-6. *The nodes of Figure 9-5*

An alternative way to depict the structure of a window is to use a tree whose interior nodes are the panes and whose leaf nodes are the controls. This tree is called the window's *node hierarchy*. Figure 9-7 depicts the node hierarchy corresponding to Figure 9-6. The labels on these nodes correspond to the variable names in the JavaFX class AccountCreationWindow, which is the code that implements the window.

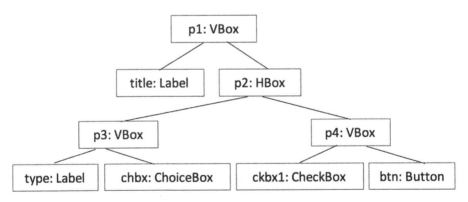

Figure 9-7. *The node hierarchy of Figure 9-6*

Listing 9-8 gives the code for AccountCreationWindow. As this code is
your first introduction to a JavaFX program, it is worth examining in detail.
JavaFX programs extend the library class Application and follow the
template pattern. The template class is Application, which has the public
method launch and the abstract strategy method start. The strategy class
that implements start is AccountCreationWindow.

Listing 9-8. The AccountCreationWindow Class

```
public class AccountCreationWindow extends Application {
    public void start(Stage stage) {
        Pane root = createNodeHierarchy();
        stage.setScene(new Scene(root));
        stage.setTitle("Bank Account Demo");
        stage.show();
    }

    public static void main(String[] args) {
        Application.launch(args);
    }

    private Pane createNodeHierarchy() {
        // see Listing 9-9
    }
}
```

This technique is very similar to the way that Thread uses the template
pattern (as you may recall from the end of Chapter 3). The difference is
that unlike Thread, a client cannot create an Application object by simply
calling the Application constructor. Instead, the static factory method
launch is responsible for creating the Application object and running it
in a new thread. The advantage of using a factory method is that it hides
the application thread from the client, thereby shielding the thread from
improper use.

The launch method also creates a Stage object, which manages the window's frame. For example, the Stage method setTitle specifies the string to be displayed in the window's title bar. The launch method then calls the application's start method, passing the Stage object as the argument.

The start method of Listing 9-8 calls createNodeHierarchy to create the node hierarchy. It passes the root of that hierarchy to a new Scene object, and then sends that object to the stage via the setScene method.

Most of the code in AccountCreationWindow is devoted to creating the node hierarchy. The code for the createNodeHierarchy method appears in Listing 9-9.

Listing 9-9. The createNodeHierarchy Method

```
private Pane createNodeHierarchy() {
    VBox p3 = new VBox(8);
    p3.setAlignment(Pos.CENTER);
    p3.setPadding(new Insets(10));
    p3.setBackground(
          new Background(
                new BackgroundFill(Color.SKYBLUE,
                      new CornerRadii(20), new Insets(0))));
    Label type = new Label("Select Account Type:");
    ChoiceBox<String> chbx  = new ChoiceBox<>();
    chbx.getItems().addAll("Savings", "Checking",
                           "Interest Checking");
    p3.getChildren().addAll(type, chbx);

    VBox p4 = new VBox(8);
    p4.setAlignment(Pos.CENTER);
    p4.setPadding(new Insets(10));
    CheckBox ckbx = new CheckBox("foreign owned?");
    Button btn  = new Button("CREATE ACCT");
    p4.getChildren().addAll(ckbx, btn);
```

```
HBox p2 = new HBox(8);
p2.setAlignment(Pos.CENTER);
p2.setPadding(new Insets(10));
p2.getChildren().addAll(p3, p4);

VBox p1 = new VBox(8);
p1.setAlignment(Pos.CENTER);
p1.setPadding(new Insets(10));
Label title = new Label("Create a New Bank Account");
double size = title.getFont().getSize();
title.setFont(new Font(size*2));
title.setTextFill(Color.GREEN);
p1.getChildren().addAll(title, p2);

btn.setOnAction(event -> {
    String foreign = ckbx.isSelected() ? "Foreign " : "";
    String acct = chbx.getValue();
    title.setText(foreign + acct + " Account Created");
});
    return p1;
}
```

The controls behave as follows. A Label object displays a string. The string's initial value is specified in the constructor, but its value can be changed at any time by calling the setText method. A CheckBox object displays a check box and a descriptive string. Its isSelected method returns true if the box is currently selected and false otherwise. A ChoiceBox object allows a user to select from a list of objects. The getItems method returns that list, and the getValue method returns the object chosen.

A `Button` object has a label and performs an action when fired. Its constructor specifies the label. The method `setOnAction` specifies its action. The argument to `setOnAction` is an `EventHandler` object. Chapter 10 will examine event handlers in more detail. For now, it suffices to know that this event handler is specified by a lambda expression whose body contains the code to execute when the button is clicked.

The lambda expression in Listing 9-9 calls the check box's `isSelected` and the choice box's `getValue` methods to obtain the type of the new account and its foreign ownership status. It then constructs a message describing these choices and sets the text of the title label to that message. In particular, if a user chooses the type "Checking," checks "is foreign," and clicks the button, the title label will display "Foreign Checking Account Created."

You might be disappointed that clicking the button does not actually create an account. The problem is that the window cannot create an account without having a reference to a `Bank` object. Chapter 11 will discuss the proper way to connect banking information to a window, so you will need to wait until then.

Panes behave as follows. Each `Pane` object has the method `getChildren`, which returns the list of its child nodes. A client can modify the contents of the list at any time. Its `setPadding` method specifies the number of pixels in the margin around the pane.

A pane's `setBackground` method specifies its background. Pane `p3` of `AccountCreationWindow` demonstrates its use. The `BackgroundFill` object specifies a solid-colored background. (Another possibility is to use a `BackgroundImage` object, which specifies an image as the background.) The three arguments to `BackgroundFill` specify the color, the roundedness of the corners, and the size of the margin around the background.

The constructors shown for `VBox` and `HBox` take one argument, which is the number of pixels between their children. Their `setAlignment` method specifies how the children should be aligned. Since not all `Pane` subclasses support this method, it must be defined nontransparently in `VBox` and in `HBox`.

Figure 9-8 shows the class diagram for the JavaFX Node classes described in this section. This diagram deliberately omits a lot of JavaFX classes, which makes it appear far simpler than it is in reality. This simplicity makes it easier to understand the design principles underlying JavaFX. A full discussion of the JavaFX node classes is outside the scope of this book.

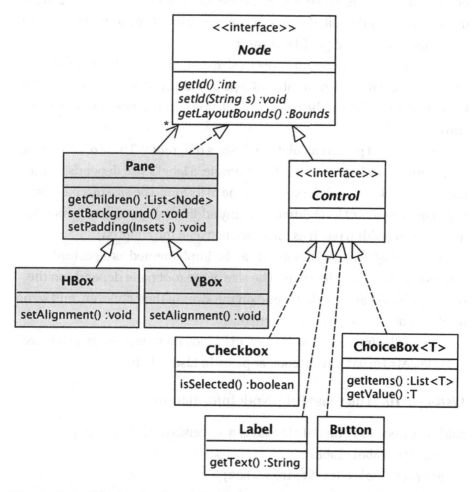

Figure 9-8. *The Node class hierarchy*

Note how this class diagram is similar to the Predicate class diagram of Figure 9-2. The base classes are the subclasses of Control. The wrapper class is Pane and its subclasses are the recursive classes. The dependency arrow from Pane to Node has the label "*" to indicate that a pane can wrap an arbitrary number of nodes.

The Node interface declares many methods; the class diagram of Figure 9-8 shows just three of them. Every node holds a string that can be used as its id. By default, the id is the empty string. The method setId sets the id and the method getId returns it.

Every node also needs to know its size and location. The method getLayoutBounds returns a value of type Bounds. A Bounds object contains the height and width of the node, as well as the coordinates of its top left corner.

Controls and panes calculate their sizes differently. The size of a control is determined by its properties. For example, a label's size depends on the text to be displayed and the size and type of its font. The size of a pane is based on the sizes of its children plus any additional space determined by the layout algorithm (such as the space between the children).

The getLayoutBounds method can be implemented as a postorder traversal of the node hierarchy. The size of the root pane depends on the sizes of its children, which depend on the sizes of their children, and so on until the Control objects are reached.

For an illustration of the getLayoutBounds method, consider the class PrintNodeInformation. Its code appears in Listing 9-10.

Listing 9-10. The Class PrintNodeInformation

```
public class PrintNodeInformation extends Application {
    private Label label;
    private ChoiceBox<String> chbx;
    private Button btn;
    private Pane p1, p2;
```

```java
public void start(Stage stage) {
    createNodeHierarchy();
    stage.setScene(new Scene(p1));
    stage.setTitle("Bank Account Demo");
    stage.show();

    System.out.println("NODE\tWID HT");
    printNodeSize(label);
    printNodeSize(chbx);
    printNodeSize(p2);
    printNodeSize(btn);
    printNodeSize(p1);
}

public static void main(String[] args) {
    Application.launch(args);
}

private void printNodeSize(Node n) {
    Bounds b = n.getLayoutBounds();
    int w = (int) b.getWidth();
    int h = (int) b.getHeight();
    System.out.println(n.getId() + "\t" + w + " " + h );
}

private void createNodeHierarchy() {
    p2 = new VBox(10);
    p2.setId("p2");
    label = new Label("Select Account Type:");
    label.setId("label");
    chbx = new ChoiceBox<>();
    chbx.setId("chbox");
    chbx.getItems().addAll("Savings", "Checking",
                           "Interest Checking");
```

```
        p2.getChildren().addAll(label, chbx);

        p1 = new HBox(10);
        p1.setId("p1");
        btn = new Button("CREATE ACCT");
        btn.setId("button");
        p1.setPadding(new Insets(10));
        p1.getChildren().addAll(p2, btn);
    }
}
```

This code is a stripped-down version of AccountCreationWindow, containing only two panes and three controls. It creates the window shown in Figure 9-9.

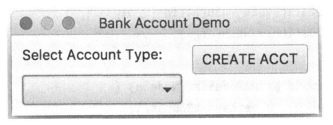

Figure 9-9. *The window created by PrintNodeInformation*

The start method calls the method printNodeSize for each node in the window. The printNodeSize method prints the id, height, and width of the given node, based on the value returned by getLayoutBounds. The output of the program appears in Listing 9-11.

Listing 9-11. The Output of PrintNodeInformation

```
NODE     WID HT
label    132 17
chbox    149 27
p2       149 54
button   108 27
p1       287 74
```

Let's make sense of this output. First consider pane p2 and its children label and chbox. These controls calculate their own sizes. The program output asserts that chbox is a bit higher and wider than label, which is borne out by the screenshot. Pane p2 is a VBox, which means that its width should be the same as its widest child, which in this case is chbox. The height of p2 is the sum of the heights of its children plus 10 pixels to account for the space between them. These values are verified by the program output.

Now consider pane p1 and its children p2 and btn. Pane p1 has 10-pixel margins on all four sides. Thus its height and width will be an additional 20 pixels larger than the values calculated for its children. Pane p1 is an HBox, so its height will be the maximum height of its children (which in this case is the height of p2) plus 20 pixels for the margins. The width of p1 is the sum of the widths of its children plus 10 pixels for the space between them plus 20 pixels for the margins. These values are also verified by the program output.

The Composite Pattern

You have so far seen two examples of composite objects: Java predicates and JavaFX nodes. Although these objects come from wildly different domains, their class diagrams—as pictured in Figures 9-2 and 9-8—are remarkably similar. This similarity is known as the *composite pattern*.

The composite pattern expresses the preferred way to create tree-structured objects. Its class diagram appears in Figure 9-10. A tree consists of objects of type Component. These components are either of type CompositeComponent or BaseComponent. A BaseComponent object has no children and will be a leaf of its tree. A CompositeComponent object can have any number of children (thus the "*" label on its dependency arrow) and will be in the interior of the tree.

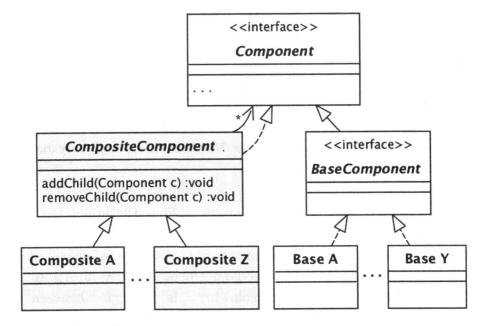

Figure 9-10. *The composite pattern*

The Component interface specifies the methods that all components will have; these methods are not shown in the diagram. CompositeComponent is an abstract class that contains methods to modify a composite object's list of children.

The class diagram of the composite pattern is similar to that of the decorator pattern. Their only difference is that a decorator class wraps only one object, whereas a composite class can wrap multiple objects. Consequently, decorators form a chain and composites form a tree.

This difference has a profound impact on how decorators and composites are used. A decorator chain has a single endpoint, which is treated as the primary object of the chain. The remaining objects on the chain are "decorators" that enhance the behavior of this primary object. On the other hand, a composite tree has multiple leaves, none of which is primary. Instead, its primary object is the root of the tree. The root treats its children as "assistants," relying on them to help compute the answer to its methods. That is why composite methods are often implemented as tree traversals.

The class CompositeComponent in Figure 9-10 contains two methods for managing the children of a composite object. This design is one out of many possible designs. For example, the JavaFX Pane class has the single method getChildren to manage its children.

Moreover, the Predicate hierarchy has no child-management methods. When a composite Predicate object is created, its children are assigned by the constructor and there is no way to change those children afterwards. Such a design is called *static*. Composite designs that have methods to add and remove children are called *dynamic*.

A designer of a dynamic composite can decide to place the child-management methods either in the composite interface or in the abstract wrapper class. The choice shown in Figures 9-8 and 9-10 is to place the methods in the wrapper class. This decision causes the methods to be nontransparent. For example, consider the getChildren method in JavaFX. This method is defined in Pane, which means that it cannot be called by variables of type Node. Note that variables p1, p2, p3, and p4 in Listing 9-9 belong to classes VBox and HBox, and not Node.

The alternative design is to move the modification methods to the Component interface. This design achieves transparency, but at the cost of safety. With such a design, a client could add a child to a base object even though doing so would have no legitimate meaning.

Such a design is occasionally adopted, but usually as a last resort. One such example occurs in the Java Swing library, which is a precursor to JavaFX. In order to support legacy software, the control classes in Swing were specified to be subclasses of Container, which is the class that defines the add method. Consequently, the following code is legal Java:

```
JButton b1 = new JButton("push me");
JButton b2 = new JButton("where am I?");
b1.add(b2);
```

The add method places button b2 in the list of b1's children. But since b1 (justifiably) ignores this list, b2 will never be displayed. This sort of bug can be quite difficult to uncover.

A Cookbook Example

For a third example of the composite pattern, consider the task of writing a program to manage the recipes in a cookbook. A recipe consists of a list of ingredients and some directions. An ingredient can be a "basic food" such as carrot, apple, or milk; alternatively, it can be the result of another recipe. Figure 9-11 displays an example recipe.

	Recipe for Salad
Ingredients:	1 head of lettuce
	6 pieces of bacon
	1 recipe of salad dressing
Directions:	Chop lettuce, add bacon. Pour dressing over it.

Figure 9-11. *An example recipe*

The first order of business is to design the recipe classes. Since a recipe can include other recipes as well as basic foods, the composite pattern is indicated. Figure 9-12 gives a reasonable class diagram. It contains a class for basic foods and a class for recipes. Both classes implement the FoodItem interface. The Recipe class also has a dependency on FoodItem, which denotes its list of ingredients.

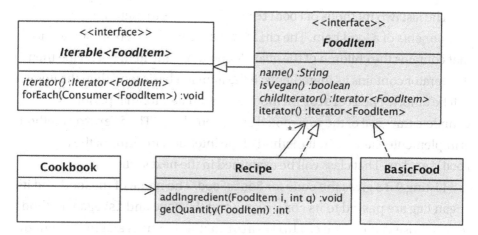

Figure 9-12. *The Cookbook class diagram*

The FoodItem interface appears in Listing 9-12. It declares the three abstract methods that BasicFood and Recipe must implement. The first two methods denote properties of the food item: the method name returns the name of the item and the method isVegan returns true if the food contains no animal products. Each basic food has an explicit flag indicating whether it is vegan; a recipe is vegan if all of its ingredients are vegan.

Listing 9-12. The FoodItem Interface

```
public interface FoodItem extends Iterable<FoodItem> {
    String name();
    boolean isVegan();
    Iterator<FoodItem> childIterator();

    default Iterator<FoodItem> iterator() {
        return new FoodIterator(this);
    }
}
```

The last two methods of FoodItem enable clients to examine the components of a food item. The childIterator method returns an iterator that contains the children of the given food item. If the item is a recipe then the iterator contains its ingredients; if the item is a basic food then the iterator will be empty. The iterator method returns an iterator that performs a complete traversal of the tree rooted at a given object. The iterator method is implemented as a default method of the interface, in terms of the class FoodIterator. That class will be examined in the next section.

Listing 9-13 gives the code for BasicFood. The name of the food and its vegan flag are passed to its constructor and the name and isVegan methods return those values. The childIterator method returns an empty iterator because basic foods do not have children.

Listing 9-13. The BasicFood Class

```java
public class BasicFood implements FoodItem {
   private String name;
   private boolean isvegan;

   public BasicFood(String name, boolean isvegan) {
      this.name = name;
      this.isvegan = isvegan;
   }

   public String name() {
      return name;
   }

   public boolean isVegan() {
      return isvegan;
   }

   public Iterator<FoodItem> childIterator() {
      return Collections.emptyIterator();
   }
```

```
public String toString() {
    String veg = isvegan ? " (vegan)" : "";
    return name + veg;
}
}
```

Listing 9-14 gives the code for Recipe. A Recipe object is a composite whose children are the ingredients used in the recipe. The ingredients are held in a map. The key of the map is the FoodItem object and its value is the associated quantity. The method addIngredient adds the specified ingredient to the map. I chose to put this method in Recipe (and not FoodItem) because I preferred safety over transparency. The isVegan method computes its value by checking the recipe's ingredients. If it finds an ingredient that is not vegan then it returns false; otherwise it returns true. Note how the recursion causes this method to perform a tree traversal though the recipe's ingredient hierarchy. Finally, the childIterator method returns the iterator associated with the map's keys.

Listing 9-14. The Recipe Class

```
public class Recipe implements FoodItem {
    private String name;
    private Map<FoodItem,Integer> ingredients = new HashMap<>();
    private String directions;

    public Recipe(String name, String directions) {
        this.name = name;
        this.directions = directions;
    }

    public void addIngredient(FoodItem item, int qty) {
        ingredients.put(item, qty);
    }
```

```
public String name() {
    return name;
}

public boolean isVegan() {
    Iterator<FoodItem> iter = childIterator();
    while (iter.hasNext())
        if (!iter.next().isVegan())
            return false;
    return true;
}

public Iterator<FoodItem> childIterator() {
    return ingredients.keySet().iterator();
}

public int getQuantity(FoodItem item) {
    return ingredients.get(item);
}

public String toString() {
    String veg = isVegan() ? " (vegan)" : "";
    String result = "Recipe for " + name + veg + "\n";
    result += "Ingredients:";
    for (FoodItem item : ingredients.keySet()) {
        int qty = ingredients.get(item);
        result += "\t" + qty + " " + item.name() + "\n";
    }
    return result + "Directions: " + directions + "\n";
}
}
```

Listing 9-15 shows the code for a method addRecipes that illustrates recipe creation. To create a recipe you first call the Recipe constructor, passing in the recipe's name and directions. Then you call the addIngredient method for each ingredient. Note that the ingredient can be either a BasicFood object or a Recipe object. The code assumes a global variable cbook, which maps a String object to its associated Recipe object.

Listing 9-15. The addRecipes Method

```
private static void addRecipes() {
    Recipe dressing = new Recipe("dressing", "Mix well.");
    dressing.addIngredient(new BasicFood("oil", true), 4);
    dressing.addIngredient(new BasicFood("vinegar", true), 2);
    cbook.put("dressing", dressing);

    Recipe salad = new Recipe("salad",
            "Chop lettuce, add bacon. Pour dressing over it.");
    salad.addIngredient(new BasicFood("lettuce", true), 1);
    salad.addIngredient(new BasicFood("bacon", false), 6);
    salad.addIngredient(dressing, 1);
    cbook.put("salad", salad);
}
```

Traversing a Composite Object

A composite object typically has methods that traverse the object's components. Examples are the method test in Predicate, the method getLayoutBounds in Node, and the method isVegan in FoodItem. These methods are called *internal* tree traversals because the traversal occurs inside the methods without the knowledge or control of the client. The concept is analogous to the concept of internal iteration discussed in Chapter 6. These internal tree traversals, like internal iterators, are task specific.

341

This section is concerned with the question of whether the clients of a composite should be able to perform customized tree traversals, and if so, how. The Predicate interface, for example, was designed so that customized traversals are not possible. The designers omitted any method that would enable a client to examine the structure of a predicate, meaning that there is no way to determine the base predicates of a given Predicate object or even to tell if it is composite. The only way to traverse a Predicate object is to call its test method.

On the other hand, a JavaFX client can perform customized traversals of a Pane object by using its getchildren method. The class NodeTraversal in Listing 9-16 provides an example. The class first constructs the same JavaFX window as in Figure 9-9. It then calls two methods that traverse the window's hierarchy: printAllNodes, which prints the height and width of each node; and getWidestControl, which returns the node corresponding to the widest control.

Listing 9-16. The NodeTraversal Class

```
public class NodeTraversal extends Application {
    ...
    public void start(Stage stage) {
        createNodeHierarchy(); // as in Listing 9-9 with root p1
        stage.setScene(new Scene(p1));
        stage.setTitle("Bank Account Demo");
        stage.show();
        System.out.println("NODE\tWID HT");
        printAllNodes(p1);
        Node n = getWidestControl(p1);
        System.out.println("The widest control is "+ n.getId());
    }
    ...
```

```
private void printAllNodes(Node n) {
    // see listing 9-17
}

private Node getWidestControl(Node n) {
    // see listing 9-18
}
}
```

Listing 9-17 gives the code for printAllNodes. Its argument is a node n, and it prints every node in the composite hierarchy rooted at n. It does so by performing a preorder traversal of n. That is, it first prints the size of n; then, if n is a pane, it calls printAllNodes recursively on each of n's children.

Listing 9-17. Printing the Components of a Node

```
private void printAllNodes(Node n) {
    // first print the node
    printNodeSize(n);    // same as in Listing 9-10

    // then print its children, if any
    if (n instanceof Pane) {
        Pane p = (Pane) n;
        for (Node child : p.getChildren())
            printAllNodes(child);
    }
}
```

Listing 9-18 gives the code for getWidestControl. The structure of this method is similar to printAllNodes. If the argument n is a control then it is clearly the only control in its tree and thus the widest. If n is a pane then the code calls getWidestControl recursively on its children and chooses the widest of the returned objects.

Listing 9-18. Calculating a Node's Widest Control

```
private Node getWidestControl(Node n) {
   if (n instanceof Control)
      return n;
   Node widest = null;
   double maxwidth = -1;
   Pane p = (Pane) n;
   for (Node child : p.getChildren()) {
      Node max = getWidestControl(child);
      double w = max.getLayoutBounds().getWidth();
      if (w > maxwidth) {
         widest = max;
         maxwidth = w;
      }
   }
   return widest;
}
```

Although the getChildren method can be used in this way for customized traversals of Node objects, it is somewhat unsuited for that purpose. The method is defined in Pane, which means that it cannot be used transparently. The result is that the code in listings 9-17 and 9-18 require if-statements and awkward type casts.

The traversal methods childIterator and iterator in the cookbook example are defined in the FoodItem interface, and are thus better suited to the writing of customized tree traversals. The Cookbook code in Listing 9-19 illustrates the use of these methods. Its main method creates some Recipe objects and saves them in a map keyed by their name. It then calls methods that perform traversals of the recipes.

Listing 9-19. The Cookbook Class

```
public class Cookbook {
    private static Map<String,Recipe> cbook = new HashMap<>();

    public static void main(String[] args) {
        addRecipes(); // from Listing 9-15
        System.out.println("\n---VEGAN RECIPES---");
        printRecipes(r->r.isVegan());
        System.out.println("\n---RECIPES USING 4+ ITEMS---");
        printRecipes(r -> foodsUsed1(r)>=4);
        printRecipes(r -> foodsUsed2(r)>=4);
        printRecipes(r -> foodsUsed3(r)>=4);
        System.out.println("\n---RECIPES COMPRISING SALAD---");
        printRecipesUsedIn1(cbook.get("salad"));
        printRecipesUsedIn2(cbook.get("salad"));
        System.out.println("\n---SHOPPING LIST FOR SALAD---");
        printShoppingList(cbook.get("salad"));
    }
    ... // the remaining methods are in listings 9-20 to 9-26
}
```

Listing 9-20 shows the printRecipes method. For each recipe in the cookbook, it prints the recipe if it satisfies the given predicate. The Cookbook class calls printRecipes four times, each with a different predicate. The first predicate calls the recipe's isVegan method, which performs an internal tree traversal. The remaining three predicates call variations of the method foodsUsed, which use an external tree traversal to count the basic foods used in a recipe. The code for those methods appears in Listings 9-21 to 9-23.

345

Listing 9-20. The printRecipes Method

```
private static void printRecipes(Predicate<Recipe> pred) {
   for (Recipe r : cbook.values())
      if (pred.test(r))
         System.out.println(r);
}
```

The code for method foodsUsed1 appears in Listing 9-21. It calls the childIterator method to explicitly examine the ingredients of the specified food item. If the ingredient is a basic food then it increments the count. If an ingredient is a recipe then it recursively calls foodsUsed1 on that recipe. Note how the transparency of the childIterator method simplifies the code compared with the methods in the JavaFX example.

Listing 9-21. The foodsUsed1 Method

```
private static int foodsUsed1(FoodItem r) {
   int count = 0;
   if (r instanceof BasicFood)
      count = 1;
   else {
      Iterator<FoodItem> iter = r.childIterator();
      while (iter.hasNext())
         count += foodsUsed1(iter.next());
   }
   return count;
}
```

The method foodsUsed2 uses the iterator method to examine the entire composite tree rooted at the specified recipe. This code is simpler than foodsUsed1 because the code can perform a single loop through the iterator with no need for recursion. Its code appears in Listing 9-22.

Listing 9-22. The foodsUsed2 Method

```
private static int foodsUsed2(FoodItem r) {
   int count = 0;
   Iterator<FoodItem> iter = r.iterator();
   while (iter.hasNext())
      if (iter.next() instanceof BasicFood)
         count++;
   return count;
}
```

The method foodsUsed3 is essentially the same as foodsUsed2. The difference is that the iterator method is called implicitly, via the for-each loop.

Listing 9-23. The foodsUsed3 Method

```
private static int foodsUsed3(FoodItem r) {
   int count = 0;
   for (FoodItem item : r)
      if (item instanceof BasicFood)
         count++;
   return count;
}
```

The two printRecipesUsedIn methods in the Cookbook class print the name of all the recipes needed to make a given recipe. For example, the recipes required to make a salad are "salad" and "dressing." The code for both methods takes advantage of the fact that FoodItem is an iterable. The method printRecipesUsedIn1 uses the iterator method to loop through the recipe's composite tree, printing the name of any food item that is a recipe. Its code appears in Listing 9-24.

Listing 9-24. The printRecipesUsedIn1 Method

```
private static void printRecipesUsedIn1(Recipe r) {
   for (FoodItem item : r) {
      if (item instanceof Recipe)
         System.out.println(item.name());
   }
}
```

The code for printRecipesUsedIn2 appears in Listing 9-25. It uses the method forEach and the visitor pattern.

Listing 9-25. The printRecipesUsedIn2 Method

```
private static void printRecipesUsedIn2(Recipe r) {
   r.forEach(item -> {
      if (item instanceof Recipe) {
         System.out.println(item.name());
   }});
}
```

Listing 9-26 gives the code for printShoppingList. This method prints the name and quantity needed for each basic item used in a recipe. The second argument to the method is the number of portions of the recipe that will be made. One complexity to the code is that the quantity of each item in the recipe must be multiplied by the number of portions of its recipe that are being made.

This method is unlike the others because its code needs to know the structure of the composite tree. In particular, the code needs to know which recipe an ingredient belongs to and how many portions of that recipe will be made. The code therefore must use the childIterator to manually traverse the ingredients of a recipe and perform the recursion for subrecipes. The iterator method is not useful here.

Listing 9-26. The printShoppingList Method

```
private static void printShoppingList(Recipe r, int howmany) {
   Iterator<FoodItem> iter = r.childIterator();
   while (iter.hasNext()) {
      FoodItem item = iter.next();
      int amt = r.getQuantity(item) * howmany;
      if (item instanceof BasicFood)
         System.out.println(item.name() + " " + amt);
      else
         printShoppingList((Recipe) item, amt);
   }
}
```

The final topic of this section concerns how to implement the iterator method. Recall from Listing 9-12 that the code for this method was declared in the FoodItem interface as follows:

```
default Iterator<FoodItem> iterator() {
   return new FoodIterator(this);
}
```

Listing 9-27 gives the code for the FoodIterator class. It implements Iterator<FoodItem>. The argument to its constructor is a food item f. Successive calls to next will return every item in the composite hierarchy rooted at f, beginning with f itself.

Listing 9-27. The FoodIterator Class

```
public class FoodIterator implements Iterator<FoodItem> {
   private Stack<Iterator<FoodItem>> s = new Stack<>();

   public FoodIterator(FoodItem f) {
      Collection<FoodItem> c = Collections.singleton(f);
      s.push(c.iterator());
   }
```

```
public boolean hasNext() {
    return !s.isEmpty();
}

public FoodItem next() {
    FoodItem food = s.peek().next(); // return this value
    if (!s.peek().hasNext())
        s.pop();        // pop the iterator when it is empty
    Iterator<FoodItem> iter = food.childIterator();
    if (iter.hasNext())
        s.push(iter); // push the child iterator if non-empty
    return food;
}
}
```

The next method essentially performs a nonrecursive tree traversal using a stack of iterators. Each call to next removes an item from the topmost iterator. If that iterator has no more elements then it is popped from the stack. If the retrieved item has children then its child iterator gets pushed onto the stack. The hasNext method returns true if the stack is not empty. The constructor primes the stack by adding an iterator containing the root of the composite hierarchy.

Summary

A *composite object* has a hierarchical structure. Each object in the hierarchy implements the same interface, called the *composite interface*. The *composite pattern* describes the preferred way to organize the classes of a composite object. These classes form two categories: *base classes*, whose objects are the leaves of the composite hierarchy, and *recursive classes*, whose objects form the interior of the hierarchy. Each recursive object wraps one or more objects that implement the composite interface. These wrapped objects are called its *children*.

Syntactically, a composite object is very similar to a decorator object; the only difference is that a composite can have multiple children whereas a decorator can have just one. This difference, however, completely changes their purpose. A decorator is a chain, where the recursive objects serve to enhance the methods of the base object at the end of the chain. A composite is a tree, whose nonroot objects combine to execute the methods of the root. A composite method is often implemented as a tree traversal.

When designing classes that conform to the composite pattern, you need to consider the transparency of their methods. A method that modifies a composite's list of children should not be defined in the composite interface, as it will allow clients to perform meaningless (and potentially dangerous) operations on base objects. It is better to define such methods in the wrapper class and use them nontransparently. On the other hand, it is possible to design methods for the composite interface that enable clients to transparently traverse the composite hierarchy. This chapter presented two such methods: `childIterator`, which returns an iterator containing the object's children, and `iterator`, which returns an iterator containing the entire composite hierarchy. Implementing the `iterator` method also lets the composite interface extend `Iterable`, which means that clients can use the `forEach` method and the for-each loop to examine composite objects.

CHAPTER 10

Observers

The state of a program changes over time, as new objects get created and existing objects are modified. The program may respond to some of these *change events*. For example, a large deposit to a foreign-owned bank account might initiate a process that checks for illegal activity. The program may also respond to certain *input events* such as mouse actions and keyboard entries. For example, a mouse click on a button is normally responded to, but a mouse click on a label is often ignored.

The use of *observers* is a general-purpose technique for managing a program's responses to events. An object can maintain a list of observers and notify them when a notable event occurs. This chapter introduces the *observer pattern*, which is the preferred way to incorporate observers into your code. The chapter gives practical examples of its use and examines various design issues and tradeoffs.

Observers and Observables

Consider the banking demo. Suppose that the bank wants to perform some actions whenever a new account gets created. For example, the marketing department wants to send a "welcome to the bank" information packet to the account owner and the auditing department wants to do background checks on new foreign-owned accounts.

© Edward Sciore 2019
E. Sciore, *Java Program Design*, https://doi.org/10.1007/978-1-4842-4143-1_10

To implement this capability, the Bank class will need a reference to each object that wants to be informed about a new account, so that its newAccount method can notify those objects. The code in Listing 10-1 is a straightforward implementation of this idea, in which the Bank class holds a reference to a MarketingRep and an Auditor object.

Listing 10-1. Adding Observers to the Bank Class

```java
public class Bank implements Iterable<BankAccount> {
    private Map<Integer,BankAccount> accounts;
    private int nextacct;
    private MarketingRep rep;
    private Auditor aud;

    public Bank(Map<Integer,BankAccount> accounts, int n,
                MarketingRep r, Auditor a) {
        this.accounts = accounts;
        nextacct = n;
        rep = r; aud = a;
    }

    public int newAccount(int type, boolean isforeign) {
        int acctnum = nextacct++;
        BankAccount ba =
                    AccountFactory.createAccount(type, acctnum);
        ba.setForeign(isforeign);
        accounts.put(acctnum, ba);
        rep.update(acctnum, isforeign);
        aud.update(acctnum, isforeign);
        return acctnum;
    }
    ...
}
```

The `MarketingRep` and `Auditor` classes are called *observer* classes, and their objects are called *observers*. The Bank class is known as the *observable* class. It notifies its observers when a new account is created. By convention, the notification method is named "update" to denote that the observable is telling its observers that an update has occurred.

The observable-observer relationship is analogous to the relationship between publishers and their subscribers. When a publisher has new material to distribute, it notifies its subscribers. Consequently, the use of observers in a program is also known as the *publish-subscribe* technique.

The Twitter application is a well-known example of publish-subscribe. A Twitter user has a list of followers. When someone tweets (i.e., publishes) a message, that message is sent to each follower (subscriber) on the list. The publish-subscribe technique is also used by message boards and listservs. If someone sends a message to a listserv, then all subscribers to the listserv receive the message.

The problem with the Bank code in Listing 10-1 is that the bank knows exactly which objects are observing it. In other words, the observable class is tightly coupled to its observer classes. This tight coupling will make it necessary to modify Bank each time the observers change.

For example, suppose that the bank decides to use multiple marketing agents, say one for foreign accounts and another for domestic accounts. The bank will then have two `MarketingRep` objects observing it. Or suppose that the bank decides to add an observer that logs information about each new account to a file. In this case, Bank would need to hold an additional observer object, this time of type `AccountLogger`.

The proper way to address this problem is to note that the bank doesn't really care how many observer objects it has, nor does it care what their classes are. It is sufficient for the bank to simply hold a list of observers. When a new account gets created, it can notify each object in the list.

For this idea to work, the observer classes must implement a common interface. Call this interface BankObserver. It will have a single method, named update, as shown in Listing 10-2.

Listing 10-2. The BankObserver Interface

```
public interface BankObserver {
    void update(int acctnum, boolean isforeign);
}
```

The Bank code would then look like Listing 10-3. Note how this design has drastically reduced the coupling between the observable and its observers.

Listing 10-3. An Improved Bank Class

```
public class Bank implements Iterable<BankAccount> {
    private Map<Integer,BankAccount> accounts;
    private int nextacct;
    private List<BankObserver> observers;

    public Bank(Map<Integer,BankAccount> accounts,
                int n, List<BankObserver> L) {
        this.accounts = accounts;
        nextacct = n;
        observers = L;
    }

    public int newAccount(int type, boolean isforeign) {
        int acctnum = nextacct++;
        BankAccount ba =
                AccountFactory.createAccount(type, acctnum);
        ba.setForeign(isforeign);
        accounts.put(acctnum, ba);
```

```
observers.forEach(obs->obs.update(acctnum, isforeign));
   return acctnum;
   }
   ...
}
```

The list provided to the Bank constructor can contain any number of observers, and these observers can belong to any of the classes that implement BankObserver. For a concrete example, consider a simple version of the Auditor class that writes the account number of each new foreign-owned account to the console. Its code might look like Listing 10-4.

Listing 10-4. The Auditor Class

```
public class Auditor implements BankObserver {
   public void update(int acctnum, boolean isforeign) {
      if (isforeign)
         System.out.println("New foreign acct" + acctnum);
   }
}
```

The class diagram of Figure 10-1 depicts this relationship between the Bank class and its observers.

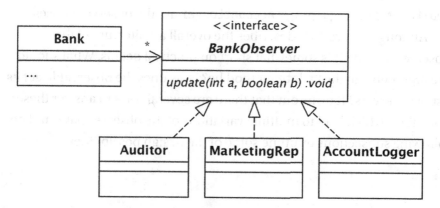

Figure 10-1. *The Bank class and its observers*

The Observer Pattern

This relationship between Bank and its observers is an example of the *observer pattern*. The basic idea is that an observable object holds a list of observers. When the observable decides to publicize a change to its state, it notifies its observers. This idea is expressed in the class diagram of Figure 10-2.

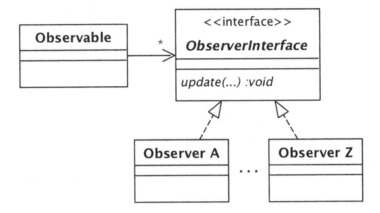

Figure 10-2. *The observer pattern*

This class diagram is very similar to the diagram of Figure 10-1. The Bank class is the observable, BankObserver is the observer interface, and Auditor, MarketingRep, and AccountLogger are the observer classes.

Although Figure 10-2 describes the overall architecture of the observer pattern, it is somewhat short on practical details. What should the arguments to the update method be? How does the observable get its list of observers? It turns out that there are several ways to answer these questions, which lead to multiple variations of the observer pattern. The following subsections examine some of the design possibilities.

Push vs. pull

The first issue is to consider the arguments to the update method. In the BankObserver interface of Listing 10-2, update has two arguments, which are the values of the newly created bank account that are of interest to its observers. In a more realistic program, the method might need to have many more arguments. For example, a realistic Auditor class would want to know the owner's account number, foreign status, and tax id number; whereas the MarketingRep class would want the owner's account number, name, and address.

This design technique is called *push*, because the observable "pushes" the values to its observers. The difficulty with the push technique is that the update method must send all values that could possibly be needed by any observer. If the observers require many different values then the update method becomes unwieldy. Moreover, the observable has to guess what values any future observer might need, which can cause the observable to push many unnecessary values "just in case."

Another design technique, called *pull*, alleviates these problems. In the pull technique, the update method contains a reference to the observable. Each observer can then use that reference to "pull" the values it wants from the observable.

Listing 10-5 shows the code for BankObserver, revised to use the pull technique. Its update method passes a reference to the Bank object. It also passes the account number of the new account so that the observer can pull the information from the proper account.

Listing 10-5. Revising the BankObserver Interface to Use Pull

```
public interface BankObserver {
    void update(Bank b, int acctnum);
}
```

Listing 10-6 shows the revised code for the Auditor observer. Note how its update method pulls the foreign-status flag from the supplied Bank reference.

Listing 10-6. The Revised Auditor Class

```
public class Auditor implements BankObserver {
   public void update(Bank b, int acctnum) {
      boolean isforeign = b.isForeign(acctnum);
      if (isforeign)
         System.out.println("New foreign acct" + acctnum);
   }
}
```

The pull technique has a certain elegance, in that the observable provides each observer with tools that enable it to extract the information it needs. One problem with the pull technique is that the observer must go back to the observable to retrieve the desired values, and this time lag can potentially affect correctness.

For example, suppose that a user creates a new domestic account, but soon afterward calls the setForeign method to change it to a foreign owner. If an observer pulls the account information from the bank after setForeign was executed then it will incorrectly assume that the account was created as a foreign account.

Another problem is that the pull technique can only be used when the observable keeps the information the observer wants. For example, suppose that a bank observer wants to be notified each time the deposit method is executed, so it can investigate unusually large deposits. If the bank does not save the amount of each deposit, then pull is not viable. Instead, the bank will need to push the deposit amount via its update method.

Hybrid push-pull designs can be used to balance the tradeoffs between push and pull. For example, the update method could push some values as well as a reference to the observable. Or the update method could push a reference to a relevant object that the observers could then pull from.

Listing 10-7 gives an example of this latter interface. In it, the observable pushes a reference to the new BankAccount object, from which the observers can pull the information they need.

Listing 10-7. A Hybrid Push-Pull BankObserver Interface

```
public interface BankObserver {
   void update(BankAccount ba);
}
```

Managing the Observer List

The second issue that needs to be examined is how an observable gets its list of observers. In Listing 10-3, the list was passed to the observable via its constructor and remained unchanged throughout the life of the program. However, such a design cannot handle situations in which observers come and go dynamically.

For example, suppose you want an observer to log all bank transactions that occur outside of normal banking hours. One option is for the observer to be continually active. Upon each event notification, the observer checks the current time. If the bank is closed then it logs the event.

The problem is that banking activity is typically heaviest during business hours, which means that the observer will spend a lot of time ignoring most of the notifications it gets. A better idea is to add the observer to the observer list when the bank closes for the evening and remove it when the bank reopens in the morning.

To accommodate this need, observables must provide methods to explicitly add and remove observers from the observer list. These methods are typically called addObserver and removeObserver. With these changes, the Bank code would look like Listing 10-8.

Listing 10-8. Another Revision to the Bank Class

```
public class Bank implements Iterable<BankAccount> {
   private Map<Integer,BankAccount> accounts;
   private int nextacct;
   private List<BankObserver> observers = new ArrayList<>();

   public Bank(Map<Integer,BankAccount> accounts, int n) {
      this.accounts = accounts;
      nextacct = n;
   }

   public void addObserver(BankObserver obs) {
      observers.add(obs);
   }

   public void removeObserver(BankObserver obs) {
      observers.remove(obs);
   }
   ...
}
```

This technique of dynamically adding an observer to an observable list is a form of dependency injection. The observable has a dependency on each observer, and this dependency is injected into the observable through its addObserver method. This form of dependency injection is known as *method injection* (as opposed to the *constructor injection* of Listing 10-3).

There are two ways to perform method injection. The first way is for another class (such as BankProgram) to add the observers to the list; the other way is for each observer to add itself. The BankProgram code of Listing 10-9 illustrates the first form of method injection.

Listing 10-9. One Way to perform Method Injection

```
public class BankProgram {
    public static void main(String[] args) {
        ...
        Bank bank = new Bank(accounts, nextacct);
        BankObserver auditor = new Auditor();
        bank.addObserver(auditor);

        ...
    }
}
```

One advantage to this form of method injection is that the observer object can be expressed as a lambda expression, thereby eliminating the need for an explicit observer class. This idea is shown in Listing 10-10, assuming the BankObserver interface of Listing 10-7.

Listing 10-10. Revising BankProgram to Use a Lambda Expression

```
public class BankProgram {
    public static void main(String[] args) {
        ...
        Bank bank = new Bank(accounts, nextacct);
        bank.addObserver(ba -> {
            if (ba.isForeign())
                System.out.println("New foreign acct: "
                            + ba.getAcctNum());
        });
        ...
    }
}
```

Listing 10-11 illustrates the second form of method injection. The
Auditor observer receives a reference to the observable Bank object via its
constructor, and adds itself to the bank's observer list.

Listing 10-11. A Second Way to Perform Method Injection

```
public class BankProgram {
    public static void main(String[] args) {
        ...
        Bank bank = new Bank(accounts, nextacct);
        BankObserver auditor = new Auditor(bank);
        ...
    }
}

public class Auditor implements BankObserver {
    public Auditor(Bank b) {
        b.addObserver(this);
    }
    ...
}
```

This technique results in a very interesting relationship between an
observable and its observers. The observable calls the update method of
its observers, yet knows nothing about them. The observers, on the other
hand, know which object is calling them. This situation is completely
backwards from typical method calls, in which the caller of a method
knows who it is calling, and the callee does not know who calls it.

The Generic Observer Pattern in Java

The Java library contains the interface Observer and the class Observable, which are intended to simplify the implementation of the observer pattern. Observer is an all-purpose observer interface, whose code appears in Listing 10-12. Its update method has two arguments, which support hybrid push-pull designs.

Listing 10-12. The Observer Interface

```
interface Observer {
  public void update(Observable obs, Object obj);
}
```

The first argument to update is a reference to the observable making the call, for use by the pull technique. The second argument is an object that contains the values sent by the push technique. If the observable wants to push multiple values then it embeds them in a single object. If the observable wants to push no values then it sends null as the second argument.

Observable is an abstract class that implements the list of observers and its associated methods. An observable extends this abstract class in order to inherit this functionality. Its code appears in Listing 10-13.

Listing 10-13. The Observable Class

```
public abstract class Observable {
  private List<Observer> observers = new ArrayList<>();
  private boolean changed = false;

  public void addObserver(Observer obs) {
    observers.add(obs);
  }
```

```java
public void removeObserver(Observer obs) {
    observers.remove(obs);
}

public void notifyObservers(Object obj) {
    if (changed)
        for (Observer obs : observers)
            obs.update(this, obj);
    changed = false;
}

public void notifyObservers() {
    notifyObservers(null);
}

public void setChanged() {
    changed = true;
}
    ...
}
```

Note the two different notifyObservers methods. The one-argument version passes the argument to the observer as the second argument to update. The zero-argument version sends null as the second argument to update.

Note also that the notifyObservers methods do nothing until the client first calls setChanged. The purpose of setChanged is to support programs that perform notification periodically, instead of immediately after each change. In such programs, the code doing the periodic notification can call notifyObservers at any time, confident that it will have no effect unless setChanged has been called since the previous notification.

Listing 10-14 shows how to rewrite the banking demo using the Observer and Observable classes and the push technique. The listing contains the relevant code for Bank (the observable) and Auditor (the observer). Note how Bank no longer needs code to manage its observer list and associated methods, because its superclass Observable handles them.

Listing 10-14. Rewriting Bank and Auditor Using Observable and Observer

```
public class Bank extends Observable
                  implements Iterable<BankAccount> {
   ...
   public int newAccount(int type, boolean isforeign) {
      int acctnum = nextacct++;
      BankAccount ba =
                  AccountFactory.createAccount(type, acctnum);
      ba.setForeign(isforeign);
      accounts.put(acctnum, ba);
      setChanged();
      ObserverInfo info =
                  new ObserverInfo(acctnum, isforeign);
      notifyObservers(info);
      return acctnum;
   }
   ...
}

public class Auditor implements Observer {
   public Auditor(Bank bank) {
      bank.addObserver(this);
   }

   public void update(Observable obs, Object obj) {
      ObserverInfo info = (ObserverInfo) obj;
      if (info.isForeign())
```

```
        System.out.println("New foreign account: "
                      + info.getAcctNum());
  }
}
```

The second argument to the update method is an object of type
ObserverInfo. This class embeds the account number and the foreign-
status flag in a single object. Its code appears in Listing 10-15.

Listing 10-15. The ObserverInfo Class

```
public class ObserverInfo {
    private int acctnum;
    private boolean isforeign;

    public ObserverInfo(int a, boolean f) {
        acctnum = a;
        isforeign = f;
    }

    public int getAcctNum() {
        return acctnum;
    }

    public boolean isForeign() {
        return isforeign;
    }
}
```

Although Observable and Observer implement the basics of the
observer pattern, their general-purpose nature has some drawbacks.
Observable is an abstract class, not an interface, which implies that the
observable is unable to extend any other class. The update method is "one
size fits all," in that an application has to squeeze its pushed data in and

out of an object such as ObserverInfo. Because of these drawbacks, and the fact that it's rather simple to write the code that they provide, it is often better to skip the use of Observable and Observer.

Events

The previous sections have focused on how the Bank class can notify its observers when a new bank account is created. The creation of a new account is an example of an *event*. In general, an observable may wish to notify its observers about multiple types of event. For example, the version 18 Bank class has four event types. These types correspond to the four methods that affect its bank accounts, namely newAccount, deposit, setForeign, and addInterest. The version 18 bank demo defines these four event types as constants of the enum BankEvent. See Listing 10-16.

Listing 10-16. The Version 18 BankEvent Enum

```
public enum BankEvent {
   NEW, DEPOSIT, SETFOREIGN, INTEREST;
}
```

The question is how an observable such as Bank can manage notifications for four different events. There are two issues: how many observer lists the observable should keep, and how many update methods the observer interface should have. It is also possible to create a separate observer interface for each event.

Consider the observer lists. Keeping a single list is simpler, but would mean that every observer would be notified for every event. It is usually better if the observable can keep an observer list for each event, so that its observers can register for only the events that they care about.

Now consider update methods. One option is for the observer interface to have an update method for each event. The advantage is that you can design each method so that its arguments are customized for its event. The disadvantage is that an observer would have to provide an implementation for every method, even if it is interested in just one of them.

The alternative is for the interface to have a single update method. The first argument of the method could identify the event, and the remaining arguments would communicate enough information to satisfy all observers. The downside is that it might be difficult to pack all of that information into a single set of argument values.

For the version 18 bank demo, I chose to use a single update method. Listing 10-17 gives the version 18 BankObserver interface. The update method has three arguments: the event, the affected bank account, and an integer denoting the deposit amount. Not all arguments apply to each event. For example, DEPOSIT observers will use all of the arguments; the NEW and SETFOREIGN observers will use only the event and bank account; and the INTEREST observers will use only the event.

Listing 10-17. The Version 18 BankObserver Interface

```
public interface BankObserver {
    void update(BankEvent e, BankAccount ba, int depositamt);
}
```

The version 18 Bank class has an observer list for each of the four event types. For convenience, it bundles those lists into a single map keyed on the event type. Its addObserver method adds an observer to the specified list. The removeObserver method would be similar, but its code was omitted for convenience. Bank also has a notifyObservers method that notifies the observers on the specified list.

Bank has four methods that generate events: newAccount, deposit, setForeign, and addInterest. Version 18 modifies these methods to call the notifyObservers method. Listing 10-18 gives the relevant portion of the code. Note that the third argument to notifyObservers is 0 for all but the deposit method because DEPOSIT is the only event where that value is relevant. The other events ignore that value.

Listing 10-18. The Version 18 Bank Class

```
public class Bank implements Iterable<BankAccount> {
   private Map<Integer,BankAccount> accounts;
   private int nextacct;
   private Map<BankEvent,List<BankObserver>> observers
                              = new HashMap<>();

   public Bank(Map<Integer,BankAccount> accounts, int n) {
      this.accounts = accounts;
      nextacct = n;
      for (BankEvent e : BankEvent.values())
         observers.put(e, new ArrayList<BankObserver>());
   }

   public void addObserver(BankEvent e, BankObserver obs) {
      observers.get(e).add(obs);
   }

   public void notifyObservers(BankEvent e, BankAccount ba,
                              int depositamt) {
      for (BankObserver obs : observers.get(e))
         obs.update(e, ba, depositamt);
   }
```

```
public int newAccount(int type, boolean isforeign) {
    int acctnum = nextacct++;
    BankAccount ba =
                AccountFactory.createAccount(type, acctnum);
    ba.setForeign(isforeign);
    accounts.put(acctnum, ba);
    notifyObservers(BankEvent.NEW, ba, 0);
    return acctnum;
}

public void setForeign(int acctnum, boolean isforeign) {
    BankAccount ba = accounts.get(acctnum);
    ba.setForeign(isforeign);
    notifyObservers(BankEvent.SETFOREIGN, ba, 0);
}

public void deposit(int acctnum, int amt) {
    BankAccount ba = accounts.get(acctnum);
    ba.deposit(amt);
    notifyObservers(BankEvent.DEPOSIT, ba, amt);
}

public void addInterest() {
    forEach(ba->ba.addInterest());
    notifyObservers(BankEvent.INTEREST, null, 0);
}
...
}
```

The version 18 code for class Auditor appears in Listing 10-19. The class is an observer of two events: NEW and SETFOREIGN. Because it observes two events, it checks the first argument of its update method to determine which event occurred.

Listing 10-19. The Version 18 Auditor Class

```
public class Auditor implements BankObserver {
   public Auditor(Bank bank) {
      bank.addObserver(BankEvent.NEW, this);
      bank.addObserver(BankEvent.SETFOREIGN, this);
   }

   public void update(BankEvent e, BankAccount ba,
                      depositamt amt) {
      if (ba.isForeign()) {
         if (e == BankEvent.NEW)
            System.out.println("New foreign account: "
                  + ba.getAcctNum());
         else
            System.out.println("Modified foreign account: "
                  + ba.getAcctNum());
      }
   }
}
```

The version 18 BankProgram code appears in Listing 10-20. The
class creates two observers: an instance of Auditor and a lambda
expression that observes DEPOSIT events. This observer calls the bank's
makeSuspicious method if it detects a deposit greater than $100,000.

Listing 10-20. The Version 18 BankProgram Class

```
public class BankProgram {
   public static void main(String[] args) {
      SavedBankInfo info = new SavedBankInfo("bank18.info");
      Map<Integer,BankAccount> accounts = info.getAccounts();
      int nextacct = info.nextAcctNum();
      Bank bank = new Bank(accounts, nextacct);
```

```
Auditor aud = new Auditor(bank);
bank.addObserver(BankEvent.DEPOSIT,
      (event,ba,amt) -> {
         if (amt > 10000000)
            bank.makeSuspicious(ba.getAcctNum());
      });
   ...
}
}
```

Observers in JavaFX

Events and event observers play an important role in GUI applications. In JavaFX, a user's interaction with a screen causes a sequence of *input events* to occur. The JavaFX library specifies several types of input event. Each event type is an object in a class that extends the class Event. Three such classes are MouseEvent, KeyEvent, and ActionEvent. Listing 10-21 shows some common event types for these classes.

Listing 10-21. Four Common JavaFX Event Types

```
MouseEvent.MOUSE_CLICKED
MouseEvent.MOUSE_ENTERED
KeyEvent.KEY_TYPED
ActionEvent.ACTION
```

An event type indicates the kind of event that was generated. The *target* of an event is the node that is responsible for handling it. For example, if the user mouse-clicks at a particular location on the screen, then the topmost node at that location will be the target of a MOUSE_CLICKED event.

Every JavaFX Node object is an observable. A node keeps a separate observer list for each event type. That is, a node will have a list for mouse-click observers, mouse-enter observers, key-typed observers, and so on.

In JavaFX, event observers are called *event handlers*. Each node has the method addEventHandler, which adds an observer to the node's observer list for a given event type. This method takes two arguments: the event type of interest, and the reference to the event handler.

An event handler belongs to a class that implements the interface EventHandler. The interface has a single method, named handle. Its code appears in Listing 10-22.

Listing 10-22. The EventHandler Interface

```
public interface EventHandler {
   void handle(Event e);
}
```

Listing 10-23 gives the code for the event handler class ColorLabelHandler, whose handle method changes the text of a specified label to have a specified color.

Listing 10-23. The ColorLabelHandler Class

```
public class ColorLabelHandler
            implements EventHandler<Event> {
   private Label lbl;
   private Color color;

   public ColorLabelHandler(Label lbl, Color color) {
      this.lbl = lbl;
      this.color = color;
   }
```

```
public void handle(Event e) {
   lbl.setTextFill(color);
}
}
```

For an example use of event handlers, consider again the AccountCreationWindow program from Listing 9-8 and 9-9. Figure 10-3 displays its initial screen.

Figure 10-3. *The initial AccountCreationWindow screen*

Listing 10-24 revises the program to have four event handlers:

- A MOUSE_ENTERED handler on the title label that turns its text red when the mouse enters the region of the label.

- A MOUSE_EXITED handler on the title label that turns its text back to green when the mouse exits the region of the label. The combination of these two handlers produces a "rollover" effect, where the label temporarily turns red as the mouse rolls over it.

- A MOUSE_CLICKED handler on the outermost pane that resets the screen by unchecking the check box, setting the value of the choice box to null, and changing the text of the title label back to "Create a new bank account."

- A `MOUSE_CLICKED` handler on the button that uses the values of the check box and choice box to change the text of the title label.

Listing 10-24. A Revised AccountCreationWindow Class

```
public class AccountCreationWindow extends Application {
   public void start(Stage stage) {
      ...
      Label title = ... // the label across the top
      title.addEventHandler(MouseEvent.MOUSE_ENTERED,
                  new ColorLabelHandler(title, Color.RED));
      title.addEventHandler(MouseEvent.MOUSE_EXITED,
                  e -> title.setTextFill(Color.GREEN));

      Pane p1 = ... // the outermost pane
      p1.addEventHandler(MouseEvent.MOUSE_CLICKED,
         e -> {
            ckbx.setSelected(false);
            chbx.setValue(null);
            title.setText("Create a New Bank Account");
         });

      Button btn = ... // the CREATE ACCT button
      btn.addEventHandler(MouseEvent.MOUSE_CLICKED,
         e -> {
            String foreign = ckbx.isSelected() ?
                           "Foreign " : "";
            String acct = chbx.getValue();
```

```
                title.setText(foreign + pref + acct
                                    + " Account Created");
                stage.sizeToScreen();
            });
        ...
    }
}
```

The first handler uses the `ColorLabelHandler` class from Listing 10-23. Its `handle` method will be executed when the mouse enters the region of the title label. The second handler uses a lambda expression to define the `handle` method. One of the features of a lambda expression (or an inner class) is that it can reference variables (such as `title`) from its surrounding context. This avoids the need to pass those values into the constructor, as is done in `ColorLabelHandler`.

The third handler observes mouse clicks on pane p1, and the fourth handler observes mouse clicks on the button. Both of these handlers define their `handle` method via a lambda expression.

A common way to specify a button handler is to replace the event type `MouseEvent.MOUSE_CLICKED` with `ActionEvent.ACTION`. An `ACTION` event signifies a "submit" request from the user. Buttons support several kinds of submit request, such as a mouse-clicking on the button, touching the button via a touch screen, and pressing the space key when the button has the focus. Using an `ACTION` event for a button handler is usually better than using a `MOUSE_CLICKED` event, because a single `ACTION` event handler will support all these requests.

The `Button` class also has a method `setOnAction`, which further simplifies the specification of a button handler. For example, the button handler in Listing 9-9 used `setOnAction` instead of `addEventHandler`. The following two statements have the same effect.

```
btn.addEventHandler(ActionEvent.ACTION, h);
btn.setOnAction(h);
```

JavaFX Properties

The state of a JavaFX node is represented by various *properties*. For example, two properties of the class ChoiceBox are items, which denotes the list of items the choice box should display, and value, which denotes the currently selected item. For each of a node's properties, the node has a method that returns a reference to that property. The name of the method is the property name followed by "Property." For example, ChoiceBox has methods itemsProperty and valueProperty.

Formally, a property is an object that implements the interface Property. Three of its methods are shown in Listing 10-25. Based on these methods, you can rightfully infer that a Property object is both a wrapper and an observable. The methods getValue and setValue get and set the wrapped value, and the method addListener adds a listener to its observer list. These two aspects of a property are examined in the following subsections.

Listing 10-25. Methods of the Property Interface

```
public interface Property<T> {
    T getValue();
    void setValue(T t);
    void addListener(ChangeListener<T> listener);
    ...
}
```

Properties as Wrappers

A property's getValue and setValue methods are rarely used because each node has substitute convenience methods. In particular, if a node has a property named p, then it has convenience methods getP and setP. For an example, Listing 10-26 shows the beginning of the createNodeHierarchy method from Listing 9-9. The calls to the getP and setP methods are in bold.

Listing 10-26. The Beginning of the AccountCreationWindow Class

```
private Pane createNodeHierarchy() {
    VBox p3 = new VBox(8);
    p3.setAlignment(Pos.CENTER);
    p3.setPadding(new Insets(10));
    p3.setBackground(...);
    Label type = new Label("Select Account Type:");
    ChoiceBox<String> chbx  = new ChoiceBox<>();
    chbx.getItems().addAll("Savings", "Checking",
                            "Interest Checking");

    ...
}
```

These methods are all convenience methods, and result from the fact that class VBox has properties alignment, padding, and background, and ChoiceBox has the property items. To demonstrate this point, Listing 10-27 gives an alternative version of the code that doesn't use these convenience methods.

Listing 10-27. Revising Listing 10-26 to Use Explicit Property Objects

```
private Pane createNodeHierarchy() {
    VBox p3 = new VBox(8);
    Property<Pos> alignprop = p3.alignmentProperty();
    alignprop.setValue(Pos.CENTER);
    Property<Insets> padprop = p3.paddingProperty();
    padprop.setValue(new Insets(10));
    Property<Background> bgprop = p3.backgroundProperty();
    bgprop.setValue(...);
    Label type = new Label("Select Account Type:");
    ChoiceBox<String> chbx  = new ChoiceBox<>();
```

```
Property<String> itemsprop = chbx.itemsProperty();
itemsprop.getValue().addAll("Savings", "Checking",
                                "Interest Checking");
    ...
}
```

Properties as Observables

A property is an observable, and maintains a list of observers. When its wrapped object changes state, the property notifies its observers. A property observer is called a *change listener*, and implements the interface ChangeListener as shown in Listing 10-28.

Listing 10-28. The ChangeListener Interface

```
public interface ChangeListener<T> {
    void changed(Property<T> obs, T oldval, T newval);
}
```

The interface consists of one method, named changed. Note that changed is a hybrid push-pull observer method. The second and third arguments push the old and new values to the observer. The first argument is the observable itself, from which the observer can pull additional information. (Technically, this first argument is of type ObservableValue, which is a more general interface than Property. But for simplicity I am ignoring that issue.)

The easiest way to create a change listener is to use a lambda expression. For example, Listing 10-29 gives the code for a listener that you can add to the AccountCreationWindow class. This listener observes the check box ckbx. Executing its code causes the label's text to turn green if the box becomes selected, and red if the box becomes unselected.

Listing 10-29. A Check Box Change Listener

```
ChangeListener<Boolean> checkboxcolor =
    (obs, oldval, newval) -> {
        Color c = newval ? Color.GREEN : Color.RED;
        ckbx.setTextFill(c);
    };
```

To get the change listener to execute, you must add it to the property's observer list by calling the property's addListener method, as shown in Listing 10-30. The result is that the check box label will change color from red to green and back again as it is selected and unselected.

Listing 10-30. Attaching a Change Listener to a Property

```
ChangeListener<Boolean> checkboxcolor = ... // Listing 10-29
Property<Boolean> p = ckbx.selectedProperty();
p.addListener(checkboxcolor);
```

Listings 10-29 and 10-30 required three statements to create a listener and add it to the observer list of the desired property. I wrote it this way to show you what needs to occur, step by step. In reality, most JavaFX programmers would write the entire code as a single statement, as shown in Listing 10-31.

Listing 10-31. Revising the Check Box Change Listener

```
ckbx.selectedProperty().addListener(
    (obs, oldval, newval) -> {
        Color c = newval ? Color.GREEN : Color.RED;
        ckbx.setTextFill(c);
    });
```

Change listeners can also be used to synchronize the behavior of JavaFX controls. Consider again the initial screen of AccountCreationWindow shown in Figure 10-3. Note that the choice box is unselected. If a user clicked the CREATE ACCT button at this point, a runtime error would occur if the code actually tried to create an account.

To eliminate the possibility of error, you can design the screen so that the button is initially disabled and becomes enabled only when an account type is selected. This design calls for adding a change listener to the choice box. Its code is shown in Listing 10-32.

Listing 10-32. Adding Change Listener for the Choice Box

```
public class AccountCreationWindow extends Application {
    public void start(Stage stage) {

        ...

        chbx.valueProperty().addListener(
            (obj, oldval, newval) ->
                            btn.setDisable(newval==null));

        ...

    }
}
```

The variable chbx references the choice box. The change listener disables the button if the new value of the choice box becomes null, and enables it otherwise. The result is that the enabled/disabled status of the button is synchronized with the selected/unselected status of the choice box.

Event listeners and change listeners can interact. Recall from Listing 10-24 that the outermost pane p1 of AccountCreationWindow has an event listener that sets the value of the choice box to null when the pane is clicked. This change will cause the change listener of the choice box to fire, which will then disable the button. That is, selecting an item from the choice box enables the button, and clicking on the outer pane disables the button. A user can repeatedly enable and disable the button by selecting an account type from the choice box and then clicking on the outer pane. Try it.

JavaFX Bindings

JavaFX supports the notion of a computed property, which is called a *binding*. Bindings implement the interface Binding, two of whose methods are shown in Listing 10-33. Note that the primary difference between a binding and a property is that a binding does not have a setValue method. Bindings do not have setValue because their values are computed and cannot be set manually.

Listing 10-33. The Binding Interface

```
public interface Binding<T> {
    public T getValue();
    public void addListener(ChangeListener<T> listener);
    ...
}
```

Bindings can be created in several ways, but easiest is to use the methods associated with the type of property you have. For example, properties that wrap objects extend the class ObjectProperty and inherit the method isNull. Listing 10-34 shows how to create a binding for the value property of a choice box.

Listing 10-34. An example Binding

```
ChoiceBox chbx = ...
ObjectProperty<String> valprop = chbx.valueProperty();
Binding<Boolean> nullvalbinding = valprop.isNull();
```

The variable `nullvalbinding` references a `Binding` object that wraps a boolean. The value of this boolean is computed from the choice box's `value` property–in particular, if `value` wraps a null then the boolean will be true and otherwise false.

When a `Binding` object is created, it adds itself to the observer list of its property. Consequently, a change to the property value will notify the binding, which can then change its value correspondingly. To help you visualize the situation, look at the diagram of Figure 10-4, which depicts a memory diagram of the three variables of Listing 10-34.

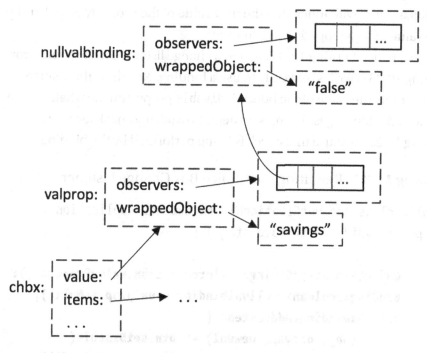

Figure 10-4. *The relationship between a binding and its property*

The chbk object represents the choice box. It has a reference to each of its properties. The diagram shows only the reference to value and hints at the reference to items. The valprop object represents the value property. It has a reference to its wrapped object (which is the string "savings") and to its observer list. The diagram shows that the list has at least one observer, which is the binding nullvalbinding. Note that the binding has a similar structure to a property. Its wrapped object is a boolean that has the value false.

When the chbx node changes its wrapped object, say by executing the code valueProperty().setValue(null), the value property will send a change notification to its observers. When the binding receives the notification, it will notice that the new value of the property is null and set the value of its wrapped object to true.

The code of Listing 10-32 created a change listener for the choice box. Listing 10-35 rewrites that code to use a binding. Note how the change listener sets the value of the button's disable property to be whatever the value of the binding is. There is no need to explicitly check for null as in Listing 10-32, because that check is being performed by the binding.

Listing 10-35. Rewriting the Choice Box Change Listener

```
public class AccountCreationWindow extends Application {
    public void start(Stage stage) {
        ...
        ObjectProperty<String> valprop = chbx.valueProperty();
        Binding<Boolean> nullvalbinding = valprop.isNull();
        nullvalbinding.addListener(
              (obj, oldval, newval) -> btn.setDisable(
                                  nullvalbinding.getValue()));
        ...
    }
}
```

The code of Listing 10-35 is somewhat difficult to read (and to write!). To simplify things, Property objects have the method bind, which performs the binding for you. Listing 10-36 is equivalent to the code of Listing 10-35.

Listing 10-36. Using the Bind Method to Create an Implicit Change Listener

```
public class AccountCreationWindow extends Application {
   public void start(Stage stage) {
      ...
      btn.disableProperty()
         .bind(chbx.valueProperty().isNull());
      ...
   }
}
```

The bind method has one argument, which is a binding (or property). Here, the method's argument is the binding created by the isNull method. The bind method adds a change listener to that binding so that when its wrapped value changes, the value of the button's disable property changes to match it. The behavior is exactly the same as in Listing 10-35.

The code of Listing 10-36 is extraordinarily beautiful. The bind method and the isNull method both create change listeners, and these listeners interact via the observer pattern (twice!) to enable the two controls to synchronize their values. And all this occurs behind the scenes, without the client's knowledge. It is a wonderful example of the usefulness and applicability of the observer pattern.

Summary

An *observer* is an object whose job is to respond to one of more *events*. An *observable* is an object that recognizes when certain events occur, and keeps a list of observers interested in those events. When an event occurs it informs its observers.

The *observer pattern* specifies this general relationship between observers and observables. But the pattern leaves multiple design issues unaddressed. One issue concerns the update method: what values should an observable push to its observers, and what values should the observers pull from the observable? A second issue concerns how the observable handles multiple types of events: should it treat each event independently, with separate update methods and observer lists, or can it combine event processing somehow? There is no best solution to these issues. A designer must consider the various possibilities for a given situation, and weigh their tradeoffs.

The observer pattern is especially useful for the design of GUI applications. In fact, JavaFX is so infused with the observer pattern that it is practically impossible to design a JavaFX application without making extensive use of observers and observables. And even if an application does not explicitly use observers, the class libraries used by the application almost certainly do.

JavaFX nodes support two kinds of observer: *event handlers* and *change listeners*. An event handler responds to input events, such as mouse clicks and key presses. Each event handler belongs to the observer list of some node. A change listener responds to changes in the state of a node. Each change listener belongs to the observer list of some property of a node. By designing event handlers and change listeners appropriately, a JavaFX screen can be given remarkably sophisticated behavior.

CHAPTER 11

Model, View, and Controller

This last chapter of the book takes up the issue of how to separate a program's computation-related responsibilities from its presentation-related ones. You may recall that Chapter 1 first addressed this issue when it created version 2 of the banking demo. Version 2 contained the new classes BankClient, which embodied the presentational responsibilities, and Bank, which embodied the computational ones.

It turns out that Chapter 1 didn't go far enough. This chapter argues that programs should also *isolate* the computation classes from the presentation classes, and for this you need classes to mediate between them. The computation, presentation, and mediator classes are called *model*, *view*, and *controller*. This chapter introduces the *MVC pattern*, which is the preferred way to organize these classes in a program. The chapter also discusses the advantages of using the MVC pattern and gives several examples.

© Edward Sciore 2019
E. Sciore, *Java Program Design*, https://doi.org/10.1007/978-1-4842-4143-1_11

The MVC Design Rule

A program has two general areas of interest. The first is how it interacts with the user, requesting inputs and presenting outputs. The second is how it computes the outputs from the inputs. Experience has shown that well-designed programs keep the code for these two areas separate from each other. The input/output portion is called the *view*. The computation portion is called the *model*.

This idea is expressed by the design rule "Separate the model from the view." In an object-oriented environment, this rule implies that there should be classes devoted to computing the results, and classes devoted to presenting the results and requesting input. Moreover, there should not be a class that does both.

The view and model have different concerns. The view needs to be a visually attractive interface that is easy to learn and use. The model should be functional and efficient. As these concerns have nothing in common, it follows that the view and model should be designed independently of each other. Consequently, the model should know nothing about how the view displays its results and the view should know nothing about the meaning of the values it displays.

In order to maintain this isolation, a program must have code that connects the model with the view. This code is called the *controller*. The controller understands the overall functionality of the program and mediates between the view and the model. It knows which methods of the model correspond to each view request and what values from the model to display in the view.

These ideas are codified in the following *Model-View-Controller* design rule, otherwise known as the *MVC* rule. This rule, which is a special case of the Single Responsibility rule, asserts that a class should not combine model, view, or controller responsibilities.

The Model-View-Controller Rule

A program should be designed so that its model, view,
and controller code belong to distinct classes.

For example, consider the version 18 banking demo. The Bank class is part of the model, as are the classes and interfaces it depends on. As these classes contain no view or controller code, they satisfy the MVC rule. On the other hand, the BankClient and InputCommands classes do not satisfy the MVC rule because each of them combines view and controller code. This situation is illustrated in Listings 11-1 and 11-2.

Listing 11-1 shows the portion of InputCommands that defines the constant DEPOSIT. The lambda expression contains view code (the calls to the scanner and System.out.print) as well as controller code (the call to bank.deposit).

Listing 11-1. A Fragment of the Version 18 InputCommands Enum

```
public enum InputCommands implements InputCommand {
   ...
   DEPOSIT("deposit", (sc, bank, current)->{
      System.out.print("Enter deposit amt: ");
      int amt = sc.nextInt();
      bank.deposit(current, amt);
      return current;
   }),
   ...
}
```

Listing 11-2 shows the beginning of the BankClient class and two of its methods. To its credit, the class contains mostly view code. The only issue is that two of its variables, bank and current, refer to the model. Although the class does not use these variables in any significant way, they do not belong in the view.

Listing 11-2. A Fragment of the Version 18 BankClient Class

```
public class BankClient {
    private Scanner scanner;
    private boolean done = false;
    private Bank bank;
    private int current = 0;
    ...

    private void processCommand(int cnum) {
        InputCommand cmd = commands[cnum];
        current = cmd.execute(scanner, bank, current);
        if (current < 0)
            done = true;
    }
}
```

The version 19 banking demo rectifies the problems with these classes by moving their controller code to the new class InputController. Listing 11-3 gives some of its code.

Listing 11-3. The Version 19 InputController Class

```
public class InputController {
    private Bank bank;
    private int current = 0;
```

```java
    public InputController(Bank bank) {
        this.bank = bank;
    }

    public String newCmd(int type, boolean isforeign) {
        int acctnum = bank.newAccount(type, isforeign);
        current = acctnum;
        return "Your new account number is " + acctnum;
    }

    public String selectCmd(int acctnum) {
        current = acctnum;
        int balance = bank.getBalance(current);
        return "Your balance is " + balance;
    }

    public String depositCmd(int amt) {
        bank.deposit(current, amt);
        return "Amount deposited";
    }
    ...
}
```

The controller has a method for each input command. The view will call these methods, supplying the appropriate argument values. The controller is responsible for performing the necessary actions on the model. It is also responsible for constructing a string describing the result and returning it to the view. The controller also manages the variable current, which holds the current account.

Listings 11-4 and 11-5 give the version 19 code for BankClient and InputCommands. These classes constitute the view. They use the scanner for input and System.out for output. BankClient passes the controller to InputCommands, and InputCommands delegates all model-related activity to the controller.

Listing 11-4. The Version 19 BankClient Class

```java
public class BankClient {
    private Scanner scanner;
    private InputController controller;
    private InputCommand[] commands = InputCommands.values();

    public BankClient(Scanner scanner, InputController cont) {
        this.scanner = scanner;
        this.controller = cont;
    }

    public void run() {
        String usermessage = constructMessage();
        String response = "";
        while (!response.equals("Goodbye!")) {
            System.out.print(usermessage);
            int cnum = scanner.nextInt();
            InputCommand cmd = commands[cnum];
            response = cmd.execute(scanner, controller);
            System.out.println(response);
        }
    }
    ...
}
```

Listing 11-5. The Version 19 InputCommands Enum

```java
public enum InputCommands implements InputCommand {
    QUIT("quit", (sc, controller)->{
        sc.close();
        return "Goodbye!";
    }),
```

```
NEW("new", (sc, controller)->{
   printMessage();
   int type = sc.nextInt();
   boolean isforeign = requestForeign(sc);
   return controller.newCmd(type, isforeign);
}),
SELECT("select", (sc, controller)->{
   System.out.print("Enter acct#: ");
   int num = sc.nextInt();
   return controller.selectCmd(num);
}),
DEPOSIT("deposit", (sc, controller)->{
   System.out.print("Enter deposit amt: ");
   int amt = sc.nextInt();
   return controller.depositCmd(amt);
}),
...
}
```

The main class BankProgram must be revised to accommodate the view and controller classes. Its code appears in Listing 11-6. This class is best understood as belonging to neither the model, controller, nor view. Instead, its job is to create and configure the model, controller, and view classes. The bold code in Listing 11-6 highlights the order in which these classes are created. BankProgram first creates the model object (which is of type Bank). It then creates the controller, passing it a reference to the model. Finally, it creates the view, passing it a reference to the controller.

Listing 11-6. The Version 19 BankProgram Class

```
public class BankProgram {
   public static void main(String[] args) {
      SavedBankInfo info = new SavedBankInfo("bank19.info");
```

```
    Map<Integer,BankAccount> accounts = info.getAccounts();
    int nextacct = info.nextAcctNum();
    Bank bank = new Bank(accounts, nextacct);
    ...
    InputController controller = new InputController(bank);
    Scanner scanner = new Scanner(System.in);
    BankClient client = new BankClient(scanner, controller);
    client.run();
    info.saveMap(accounts, bank.nextAcctNum());
  }
}
```

Figure 11-1 shows a class diagram depicting the relationship between these model, view, and controller classes. Note that even though the view and the model consist of multiple classes, there is one class that acts as the "primary" class for the purposes of configuration. This situation is generally true for all MVC designs.

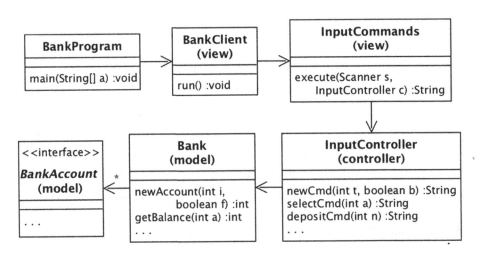

Figure 11-1. *A class diagram for the MVC-based banking demo*

Theoretically, the distinction between a model and a view is clear cut: something belongs in the model if its functionality is independent of how it is presented, and something belongs in the view if it is irrelevant to the model. In practice, however, making these distinctions can require careful analysis. The banking demo provides some examples.

One example is the notion of the current account. I argued earlier that it should not be part of the view. But should it be part of the controller or the model? The answer depends on whether the current account is relevant to only the particular view or is inherent to the model. The key for me was to realize that each session of the bank client could have a different current account, and I didn't want the model to be responsible for managing session-specific data. This indicated to me that the current account belongs in the controller and not the model.

For another example, consider the numbers that BankClient assigns to input choices. Input commands are assigned a number from 0–7, account types a number from 1–3, and the ownership specification is 1 for "domestic" and 2 for "foreign." The view is responsible for assigning numbers for the commands and the domestic/foreign selections, but the model decides the account type numbers. Why?

The criterion is whether the meaning of an input value is relevant to the model. If the model doesn't care then the view should be responsible for determining the meaning of the values. This is the case for the command and ownership numbers, since the model never sees them. The account types, on the other hand, are manipulated by the model and thus must be decided by the model.

Multiple Views for a Model

One advantage of separating model from view is that you can create different programs that use the same model. For example, the banking model could be used by a program for customers (e.g., online banking), another program for bank employees, and another for bank executives. To write each program, it suffices to write the view plus a controller that hooks the view into the existing model.

The separation between model and view also makes it easier to modify a view so that it has a different user interface. For example, BankClient could be modified to use command names instead of numbers, or to support voice commands, or to have a GUI-based interface. This last option will be considered later in the chapter.

The version 18 banking demo has four programs that use the banking model: BankProgram, FBIClient, IteratorStatProgram, and StreamStatProgram. The last three programs do not satisfy the MVC rule. They are all quite simple—they have no input, and their output just prints the result of some test queries. Does it make sense to rewrite their code to use MVC? The simplest of the programs is StreamStatProgram, which has the associated class StreamAccountStats. These classes were initially discussed in Chapter 6. Let's rewrite them and see what happens.

Listing 11-7 gives the first two methods of StreamAccountStats. It is primarily model code; the only issue is that the methods call System.out. println.

Listing 11-7. The Original StreamAccountStats Class

```java
public class StreamAccountStats {
   private Bank bank;

   public StreamAccountStats(Bank b) {
      bank = b;
   }

   public void printAccounts6(Predicate<BankAccount> pred) {
      Stream<BankAccount> s = bank.stream();
      s = s.filter(pred);
      s.forEach(ba->System.out.println(ba));
   }
}
```

```java
public void printAccounts7(Predicate<BankAccount> pred) {
    bank.stream()
        .filter(pred)
        .forEach(ba->System.out.println(ba));
}
...
}
```

Listing 11-8 shows the version 19 revision, which is called StreamStatModel. The two printAccounts methods have changed. The prefix "print" in their name has been renamed "get" to reflect that their return type is now String instead of void. In addition, their use of the forEach method must be modified to use reduce, so that it can create a single string from the individual calls to ba.toString.

Listing 11-8. The Revised StreamStatModel Class

```java
public class StreamStatModel {
    private Bank bank;

    public StreamStatModel(Bank b) {
        bank = b;
    }

    public String getAccounts6(Predicate<BankAccount> pred) {
        Stream<BankAccount> s = bank.stream();
        s = s.filter(pred);
        Stream<String> t = s.map(ba->ba.toString());
        return t.reduce("", (s1,s2)->s1 + s2 + "\n");
    }
```

```
public String getAccounts7(Predicate<BankAccount> pred) {
    return bank.stream()
              .filter(pred)
              .map(ba->ba.toString())
              .reduce("", (s1,s2)->s1 + s2 + "\n");
}
    ...
}
```

The original code for StreamStatProgram appears in Listing 11-9. It contains both view and controller code. The controller code consists of calling the model methods. The view code consists of printing their results.

Listing 11-9. The Original StreamStatProgram Class

```
public class StreamStatProgram {
    public static void main(String[] args) {
        ...
        StreamAccountStats stats = ...

        Predicate<BankAccount> pred = ba -> ba.fee() == 0;
        ...
        System.out.println("Here are the domestic accounts.");
        stats.printAccounts6(pred);
        System.out.println("Here are the domestic accounts
                            again.");
        stats.printAccounts7(pred);
    }
}
```

Version 19 of the banking demo contains the view class StreamStatView. Its code, shown in Listing 11-10, calls controller methods instead of model methods. Note that the view is not aware of the predicate because the predicate refers to the model.

Listing 11-10. The Version 19 StreamStatView Class

```java
public class StreamStatView {
   StreamStatController c;

   public StreamStatView(StreamStatController c) {
      this.c = c;
   }

   public void run() {
      ...
      System.out.println("Here are the domestic accounts.");
      System.out.println(c.getAccounts6());
      System.out.println("Here are the domestic accounts
                        again.");
      System.out.println(c.getAccounts7());
   }
}
```

The `StreamStatController` class appears in Listing 11-11. It implements each of the three view methods in terms of the model. It also creates the predicate.

Listing 11-11. The Version 19 StreamStatController Class

```java
public class StreamStatController {
   private StreamStatModel model;
   Predicate<BankAccount> pred = ba -> ba.fee() == 0;

   public StreamStatController (StreamStatModel model) {
      this.model = model;
   }
```

```
    public String getAccounts6() {
        return model.getAccounts6(pred);
    }

    public String getAccounts7() {
        return model.getAccounts7(pred);
    }
    ...
}
```

Finally, Listing 11-12 gives the code for the version 19 StreamStatProgram class. The class configures the model, view, and controller, and then calls the view's run method.

Listing 11-12. The Version 19 StreamStatProgram Class

```
public class StreamStatProgram {
    public static void main(String[] args) {
        SavedBankInfo info = new SavedBankInfo("bank19.info");
        Map<Integer,BankAccount> accounts = info.getAccounts();
        int nextacct = info.nextAcctNum();
        Bank bank = new Bank(accounts, nextacct);
        StreamStatModel m = new StreamStatModel(bank);
        StreamStatController c = new StreamStatController(m);
        StreamStatView v = new StreamStatView(c);
        v.run();
    }
}
```

Compare the MVC versions of the StreamStatProgram classes to their original code. You may be surprised at how much cleaner and better organized the MVC version is. Although it contains more code than the original version, each individual class is short and easily modified. The moral is that even for small programs, an MVC design is worth considering.

MVC in Excel

Excel is an example of a commercial program that follows the MVC design rule. The model consists of the cells of the spreadsheet. Each of the spreadsheet's charts is a view of the model. Figure 11-2 shows a screenshot depicting a chart and its underlying cells.

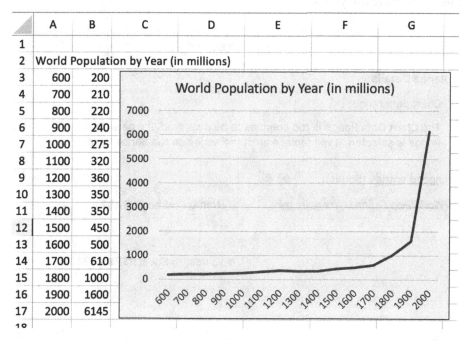

Figure 11-2. *A spreadsheet's model and view*

Excel maintains a strict separation between the model and the views. The cells don't know about the charts. Each chart is an "object" that sits on top of the cells.

The creation of an Excel chart has two aspects. The first aspect is what the chart looks like. Excel has tools to specify different chart types, colors, labels, and so on. These tools correspond to view methods; they let you make the chart look attractive, independent of whatever data it represents.

403

The second aspect is what data the chart displays. Excel has a tool called "Select Data" for specifying the chart's underlying cells. This tool corresponds to the controller. Figure 11-3 gives a screenshot of the controller window for Figure 11-2. The "Name" text field specifies the cell that contains the chart title; "Y values" specifies the cells containing the population values; and "Horizontal (Category) axis labels" specifies the cells containing the years.

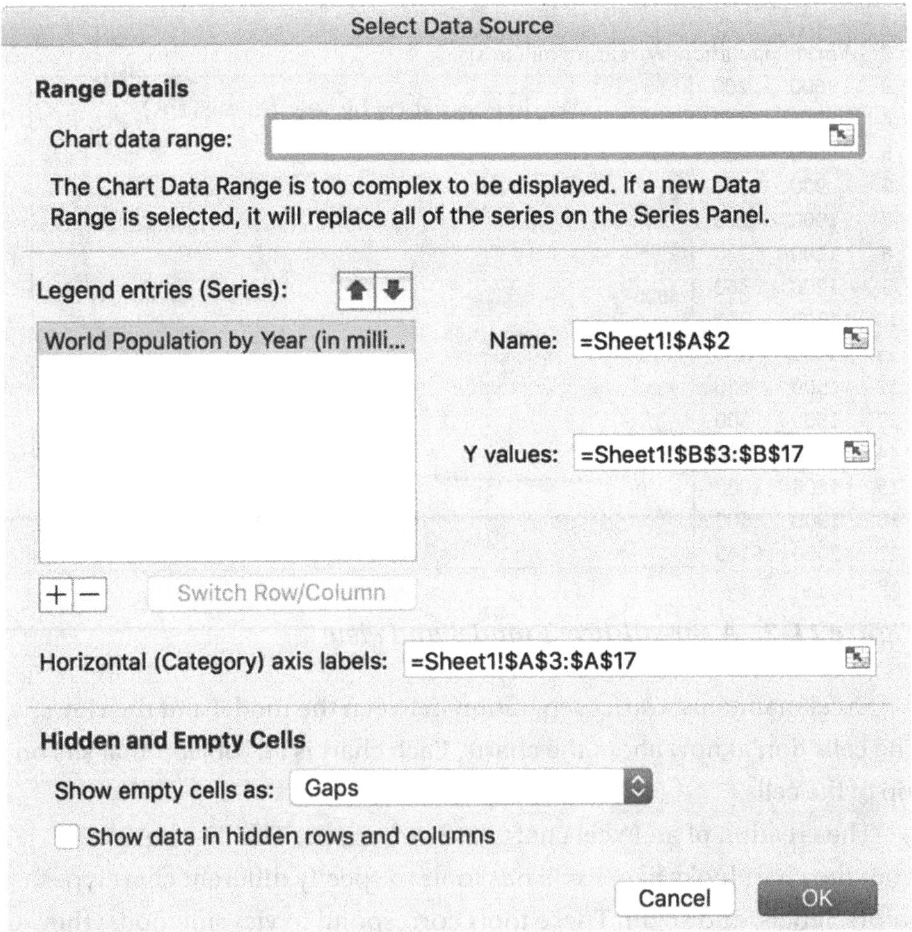

Figure 11-3. *A chart's controller*

Separating the model and view provides a lot of flexibility. A range of cells can be the model for many different charts, and a chart can be the a view for many different cell ranges. The controller links them together.

JavaFX Views and Controllers

Consider again the AccountCreationWindow class that appeared in Figure 10-3. This class displays JavaFX controls that let a user choose the type of bank account to create. However, the class is not connected to the bank model. Clicking the CREATE ACCT button has no effect except to change the text of the title label. In other words, this program is purely view code, which is entirely appropriate because JavaFX is for creating views.

How to create the controller that would connect the view to the bank model? Before attacking this question, let's begin with a simple JavaFX example that illustrates the issues. The program Count1 displays a window containing two buttons and a label, as shown in Figure 11-4. The label displays the value of the variable count. The two buttons increment and decrement the count.

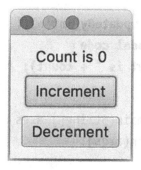

Figure 11-4. *The initial screen of the Count1 program*

Listing 11-13 gives the code for Count1. This code does not satisfy the MVC design rule. The model consists of the variable count. The updateBy method updates the count (an operation on the model), but also changes the text of the label (an operation on the view).

Listing 11-13. The Count1 Class

```
public class Count1 extends Application {
   private static int count = 0;
   private static Label lbl = new Label("Count is 0");

   public void start(Stage stage) {
      Button inc = new Button("Increment");
      Button dec = new Button("Decrement");
      VBox p = new VBox(8);
      p.setAlignment(Pos.CENTER);
      p.setPadding(new Insets(10));
      p.getChildren().addAll(lbl, inc, dec);

      inc.setOnAction(e -> updateBy(1));
      dec.setOnAction(e -> updateBy(-1));

      stage.setScene(new Scene(p));
      stage.show();
   }

   private static void updateBy(int n) {
      count += n; // model code
      lbl.setText("Count is " + count); // view code
   }

   public static void main(String[] args) {
      Application.launch(args);
   }
}
```

Version 2 of the counting demo separates the code into model, view, and controller classes. The main class Count2 is responsible for creating these classes and connecting them to each other. Its code appears in Listing 11-14.

Listing 11-14. The Count2 Class

```
public class Count2 extends Application {
    public void start(Stage stage) {
        CountModel model = new CountModel();
        CountController controller = new CountController(model);
        CountView view = new CountView(controller);

        Scene scene = new Scene(view.getRoot());
        stage.setScene(scene);
        stage.show();
    }

    public static void main(String[] args) {
        Application.launch(args);
    }
}
```

The structure of this class is similar to the structure of the Version 19 BankProgram and StreamStatProgram classes. First the model is created. Then the controller is created, passing in the model. Then the view is created, passing in the controller.

The class calls the view method getRoot, which returns the root of its node hierarchy. This root is passed into the Scene constructor, and then to the stage (via its setScene method).

The model consists of a single class named CountModel, whose code appears in Listing 11-15. The class has a variable count that holds the current count, and methods getCount and updateBy that get and update the count.

Listing 11-15. The CountModel Class

```java
public class CountModel {
    private int count = 0;

    public void updateBy(int n) {
        count += n;
    }

    public int getCount() {
        return count;
    }
}
```

The view consists of a single class, called CountView. Its code appears in Listing 11-16.

Listing 11-16. The CountView Class

```java
class CountView {
    private Pane root;

    public CountView(CountController cont) {
        root = createNodeHierarchy(cont);
    }

    public Pane getRoot() {
        return root;
    }

    private Pane createNodeHierarchy(CountController cont) {
        Button inc = new Button("Increment");
        Button dec = new Button("Decrement");
        Label  lbl = new Label("Count is 0");
```

```
VBox p = new VBox(8);
p.setAlignment(Pos.CENTER);
p.setPadding(new Insets(10));
p.getChildren().addAll(lbl, inc, dec);

inc.setOnAction(e -> {
    String s = cont.incrementButtonPressed();
    lbl.setText(s);
});
dec.setOnAction(e ->
        lbl.setText(cont.decrementButtonPressed()));

    return p;
  }
}
```

Most of the view code is devoted to the mundane task of creating the node hierarchy. More interesting is how the view uses its two button handlers to interact with the controller. The increment button handler calls the controller's incrementButtonPressed method. This method does what it needs to do (which in this case is to tell the model to increment the count), and then returns a string for the view to display in its label. Similarly, the decrement button handler calls the controller's decrementButtonPressed method, and displays its return value.

Note that the two handlers have the same structure. I wrote their code differently from each other simply to illustrate different coding styles.

The controller class is named *CountController*. Its code appears in Listing 11-17. The controller is responsible for translating events on the view into actions on the model, and translating return values from the model to displayable strings on the view.

409

Listing 11-17. The CountController Class

```
class CountController {
   private CountModel model;

   public CountController(CountModel model) {
      this.model = model;
   }

   public String incrementButtonPressed() {
      model.updateBy(1);
      return "Count is " + model.getCount();
   }
   public String decrementButtonPressed() {
      model.updateBy(-1);
      return "Count is " + model.getCount();
   }
}
```

Note how the controller mediates between the model and the view, which enables the view to be unaware of the model. The view knows "hey, my button got pushed," but it doesn't know what to do about it. So the view delegates that job to the controller. Moreover, the view agrees to display whatever value the controller returns.

In 2003, an Apple engineer sang a wonderful song about MVC at the Apple developer's conference, and his performance was recorded for posterity. You can find the video by searching YouTube for "MVC song." As you watch the performance, you'll probably get drawn in by the catchy melody. But pay special attention to the lyrics, which succinctly convey the true beauty of MVC.

Extending the MVC Architecture

This chapter has thus far presented three examples of MVC programs: BankProgram (Listing 11-6), StreamStatProgram (Listing 11-12), and Count2 (Listing 11-14). Each of these programs has a similar architecture, in which the view talks to the controller who talks to the model. This architecture is simple and straightforward.

Although this architecture handles single-view programs fine, it fails miserably with programs that have multiple views. For an example, consider version 3 of the counting demo, which adds a second view to the version 2 demo. Figure 11-5 shows a screenshot of the program after a few button clicks.

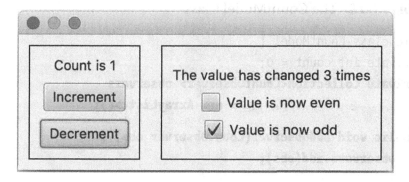

Figure 11-5. *A screenshot of the Count3 program*

The two views each have a pane within the window. The second view is a "watcher" view. It keeps track of how many times the count was changed, and displays whether the count is even or odd. But how can the watcher view know when the model has changed? The answer is to use the observer pattern! The model needs to broadcast changes made by the counting view so that the watcher view can observe them. The model therefore needs to be modified to be an observable.

Define an observer interface, called `CountObserver`. This interface will have one observer method, `update`, which pushes the new count to its observers. Its code appears in Listing 11-18.

Listing 11-18. The CountObserver Interface

```java
public interface CountObserver {
   public void update(int count);
}
```

The class `CountModel` needs to manage an observer list. Its `updateBy` method will broadcast the new count to the observers on the list. Listing 11-19 shows the resulting changes to the class.

Listing 11-19. The CountModel Class

```java
public class CountModel {
   private int count = 0;
   private Collection<CountObserver> observers
                        = new ArrayList<>();

   public void addObserver(CountObserver obs) {
      observers.add(obs);
   }

   private void notifyObservers(int count) {
      for (CountObserver obs : observers)
         obs.update(count);
   }

   public void updateBy(int n) {
      count += n;
      notifyObservers(count);
   }
```

```
public int getCount() {
   return count;
}
}
```

The watcher's controller will be the model observer. When the controller receives a notification from the model, it will determine the changes that need to be made to its view and pass those changes to the view. Unfortunately, this behavior is not currently possible because the watcher controller does not know who its view is! To address this problem, the watcher view and its controller need to be modified: the controller needs a reference to the view, and the view needs to have a method that the controller can call.

By giving the controller a reference to its view, the watcher view and its controller will have references to each other. The view gets its reference via constructor injection. But the controller cannot, because the view has not yet been created when the controller is created. The solution is for the controller to get its reference to the view via method injection. It defines a method setView. When the view is created, it can call the controller's setView method, passing the controller a reference to itself.

The watcher view defines the method updateDisplay for the controller to call. The method has three arguments, corresponding to three values that the controller will want to pass to the view: the new message for its label, and the desired values of the two checkboxes.

Listing 11-20 gives the code for the controller. Note that the controller is responsible for keeping track of the number of times the model changes, because I decided that this value is not relevant to the model. If you feel otherwise, you should change the model so that it keeps that information.

Listing 11-20. The WatcherController Class

```
public class WatcherController
                    implements CountObserver {
   private WatcherView view;
   private int howmany = 0;

   public WatcherController(CountModel model) {
      model.addObserver(this);
   }

   // called by the view
   public void setView(WatcherView view) {
      this.view = view;
   }

   // called by the model
   public void update(int count) {
      howmany++;
      boolean isEven = (count%2 == 0);
      boolean isOdd = !isEven;
      String msg = "The count has changed "
                    + howmany + " times";
      view.updateDisplay(msg, isEven, isOdd);
   }
}
```

Listing 11-21 gives the code for the watcher view. Its constructor calls the controller's setView method, thereby establishing the two-way connection between the view and controller. The updateDisplay method sets the value of the view's three controls. Note that the view has no idea what these values mean.

Listing 11-21. The WatcherView Class

```
class WatcherView {
   private Label lbl
            = new Label("The count has not yet changed");
   private CheckBox iseven
            = new CheckBox("Value is now even");
   private CheckBox isodd = new CheckBox("Value is now odd");
   private Pane root;

   public WatcherView(WatcherController controller) {
      root = createNodeHierarchy();
      controller.setView(this);
   }

   public Pane root() {
      return root;
   }

   public void updateDisplay(String s, boolean even,
                                       boolean odd) {
      lbl.setText(s);
      iseven.setSelected(even);
      isodd.setSelected(odd);
   }

   private Pane createNodeHierarchy() {
      iseven.setSelected(true);
      isodd.setSelected(false);

      VBox p = new VBox(8);
      p.setAlignment(Pos.CENTER);
      p.setPadding(new Insets(10));
```

415

```
        p.getChildren().addAll(lbl, iseven, isodd);
        return p;
    }
}
```

The main program, Count3, configures the two views into a single window. In order to deal with the multiple views, the code places the node hierarchies of the two views into a single HBox pane. Listing 11-22 gives the code. The statements that combine the views are in bold.

Listing 11-22. The Count3 Class

```
public class Count3 extends Application {
    public void start(Stage stage) {
        CountModel model = new CountModel();

        // the first view
        CountController ccontroller
                        = new CountController(model);
        CountView cview   = new CountView(ccontroller);

        // the second view
        WatcherController wcontroller
                        = new WatcherController(model);
        WatcherView wview = new WatcherView(wcontroller);

        // Display the views in a single two-pane window.
        HBox p = new HBox();
        BorderStroke bs = new BorderStroke(Color.BLACK,
                                BorderStrokeStyle.SOLID,
                                null, null, new Insets(10));
        Border b = new Border(bs);
        Pane root1 = cview.root(); Pane root2 = wview.root();
        root1.setBorder(b); root2.setBorder(b);
```

```
    p.getChildren().addAll(root1, root2);
    stage.setScene(new Scene(p));
    stage.show();
  }

  public static void main(String[] args) {
    Application.launch(args);
  }
}
```

The MVC Pattern

Although WatcherController needs to be a model observer, CountController does not. Since it is the only view that can change the model, it knows exactly when and how the model will change. At least for now, that is. But what if the program happens to add another view that can change the model? Then the value displayed by CountView can wind up being incorrect. This kind of bug can be very difficult to detect. If we want CountView to always display the current count, regardless of what other views exist, then CountController also needs to be a model observer.

To be a model observer, CountController must implement the update method. Its code for update will construct a message describing the new count and send it to the view. Consequently, the button handler methods incrementButtonPressed and decrementButtonPressed should now be void, as they are no longer responsible for constructing the message. In addition, the controller needs a reference to the view. It therefore implements the method setView using the same technique as WatcherController. Listing 11-23 gives the revised code.

Listing 11-23. The Revised CountController Class

```
class CountController implements CountObserver {
   private CountModel model;
   private CountView view;

   public CountController(CountModel model) {
      this.model = model;
      model.addObserver(this);
   }

   // Methods called by the view
   public void setView(CountView view) {
      this.view = view;
   }
   public void incrementButtonPressed() {
      model.updateBy(1);
   }
   public void decrementButtonPressed() {
      model.updateBy(-1);
   }

   // Method called by the model
   public void update(int count) {
      view.setLabel("Count is " + count);
   }
}
```

The class CountView needs to be modified to correspond to the changes in its controller. The view constructor calls the controller's method setView, and the view implements the method setLabel for the controller to call. The code appears in Listing 11-24.

Listing 11-24. The revised CountView Class

```
class CountView {
    private Label lbl = new Label("Count is 0");
    private Pane root;
    public CountView(CountController controller) {
        root = createNodeHierarchy(controller);
        controller.setView(this);
    }

    public Pane root() {
        return root;
    }

    public void setLabel(String s) {
        lbl.setText(s);
    }

    private Pane createNodeHierarchy(CountController cont) {
        Button inc = new Button("Increment");
        Button dec = new Button("Decrement");

        ... // create the node hierarchy, having root p

        inc.setOnAction(e -> cont.incrementButtonPressed());
        dec.setOnAction(e -> cont.decrementButtonPressed());

        return p;
    }
}
```

To understand the effect of these changes, consider what now happens to the count view and count controller when the Increment button is clicked.

- The view calls the controller's incrementButtonPressed method.

- That method calls the model's updateBy method.

- That method updates the count and calls notifyObservers, which calls the controller's update method.

- That method formats the string for the view to display, and calls the view's setLabel method.

- That method modifies the text of its label to be the current count.

This sequence of method calls has the same effect as in the Count2 controller. The difference is that the controller calls a pair of void methods instead of a single method that returns a value. This added complexity is necessary to guarantee that the count will be updated in all views, no matter which view does the updating.

The insight that controllers should be observers is the basis for the *MVC Design Pattern*. This pattern asserts that an application should be structured similarly to Count3. In particular: the model should be an observable and all controllers should be model observers; the controllers talk directly to the model; and each view/controller pair can talk directly to each other. This pattern is expressed by the class diagram of Figure 11-6.

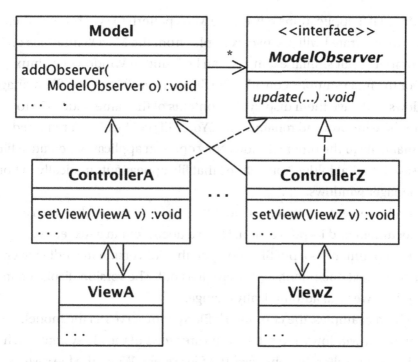

Figure 11-6. *The MVC pattern*

Communication using the MVC pattern works as follows:

- An action on a view (such as a button click) gets communicated to its controller.

- The controller translates that action to a method call on the model.

- If that method call is a request for data, then the model returns the requested data directly to the controller, which forwards it to its view.

- If that method call causes the model to change, the model notifies its observers.

- Each controller, being a model observer, decides if the update is relevant to its view. If so, it calls the appropriate view methods.

421

Many GUI applications rely on the MVC pattern to synchronize their views. To illustrate I will use two examples from the MacOS interface on my computer, but similar examples can be found in Windows or Linux.

For the first example, consider the file manager. Open two file manager windows and have them display the contents of the same folder. Go to one of the windows and rename a file. You will see the file get renamed automatically in the other window. Now open an application, create a file, and save it to that folder. You will see that file appear automatically in both file manager windows.

For the second example, consider the correspondence between a text document and its pdf version. Open a document in a text editor. Save the document as a pdf file and open the pdf version in a pdf viewer. Change the text document, and resave it as pdf. The version displayed in your pdf viewer will automatically change.

In both examples, the computer's file system serves as the model. File manager windows and pdf viewers are views of the file system. Each view has a controller that observes the file system. When the file system changes, it notifies its observers. When a file manager controller is notified, it determines if the changes affect the files being displayed, and if so, updates its view. When a pdf controller is notified, it determines if the changes affect the file that it is displaying, and if so, tells the view to reload the new contents of the file.

MVC and the Banking Demo

The time has finally come to develop a JavaFX-based interface to the banking demo. The interface will have one window that contains three views: a view for creating a new account; a view for managing a selected account; and a view that displays all account information. Figure 11-7 displays a screenshot of the three views.

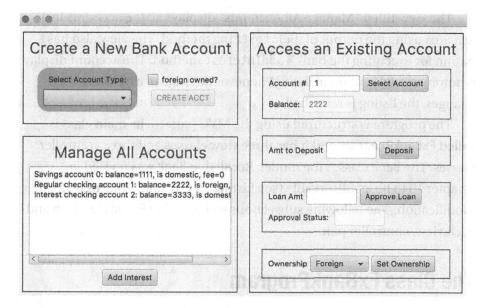

Figure 11-7. *The JavaFX interface to the banking demo*

You have already encountered the view titled "Create a New Bank Account." The user selects the desired account type, specifies whether the account is domestic or foreign-owned, and clicks the button. A new account is created.

In the view titled "Access an Existing Account," the user specifies the current account by entering the account number in the text field of the top pane and clicking the "Select Account" button. The account balance then appears in the text field below it and the domestic/foreign choice box in the bottom pane is set to the corresponding value of the account. After selecting an account, the user can make a deposit to it, request a loan authorization, or change its ownership status. Throughout, the account balance is always kept up to date. When a deposit occurs or interest is accrued, the balance is updated.

The view titled "Manage All Accounts" displays all the accounts in a text area using the output of their toString method. The view also has a button for executing the bank's addInterest method. The account display is automatically kept up to date. Whenever the state of a bank account changes, the listing is refreshed.

The program is structured using the MVC pattern. Its main class is called FxBankProgram, and it has three view classes and three controller classes. The Bank class is the model. Recall that Bank was revised in Chapter 10 to be an observable (see Listing 10-18), and requires no further modification. The following subsections will examine FxBankProgram and each view/controller pair.

The Class FxBankProgram

This class configures the views into a single JavaFX window. Listing 11-25 gives the code. The JavaFX Application class has the two methods init and stop in addition to start. The launch method first calls init, then start, and then stop. The purpose of init is to initialize values needed by the application. Here, init creates the node hierarchies for each of the three views and saves their roots in the variables root1, root2, and root3. It also creates the model and the three controllers. The stop method saves the status of the bank.

Listing 11-25. The FxBankProgram Class

```java
public class FxBankProgram extends Application {
    private SavedBankInfo info =
            new SavedBankInfo("bank19.info");
    private Map<Integer,BankAccount> accounts =
            info.getAccounts();
    Bank bank = new Bank(accounts, info.nextAcctNum());
    private Pane root1, root2, root3;
```

```java
public void start(Stage stage) {
    VBox left = new VBox();
    left.getChildren().addAll(root1, root2);
    HBox all = new HBox(left, root3);

    stage.setScene(new Scene(all));
    stage.show();
}

public void init() {
    Auditor aud = new Auditor(bank);
    bank.addObserver(BankEvent.DEPOSIT,
            (event,ba,amt) -> {
                if (amt > 10000000)
                    bank.makeSuspicious(ba.getAcctNum());
            });

    CreationController c1 = new CreationController(bank);
    AllController c2 = new AllController(bank);
    InfoController c3 = new InfoController(bank);
    CreationView v1 = new CreationView(c1);
    AllView v2 = new AllView(c2);
    InfoView v3 = new InfoView(c3);

    BorderStroke bs = new BorderStroke(Color.BLACK,
                            BorderStrokeStyle.SOLID,
                            null, null, new Insets(10));
    Border b = new Border(bs);
    root1 = v1.root(); root2 = v2.root(); root3 = v3.root();
    root1.setBorder(b); root2.setBorder(b);
                    root3.setBorder(b);
}
```

```
    public void stop() {
        info.saveMap(accounts, bank.nextAcctNum());
    }

    public static void main(String[] args) {
        Application.launch(args);
    }
}
```

The Create Account View

The "create account" view class is called CreationView. Its code appears in Listing 11-26. The code is similar to the AccountCreationWindow class from Chapters 9 and 10, except that it now has a controller to talk to.

Listing 11-26. The CreationView Class

```
public class CreationView {
    private Pane root;
    private Label title = new Label("Create a New Bank Acct");

    public CreationView(CreationController controller) {
        controller.setView(this);
        root = createNodeHierarchy(controller);
    }

    public Pane root() {
        return root;
    }

    public void setTitle(String msg) {
        title.setText(msg);
    }
```

```
private Pane createNodeHierarchy(CreationController cont) {
    ... // Create the hierarchy as in Listing 9-9. Root is p1.

    btn.addEventHandler(ActionEvent.ACTION, e -> {
        cont.buttonPressed(chbx.getSelectionModel()
                                     .getSelectedIndex(),
                             ckbx.isSelected());
        String foreign = ckbx.isSelected() ? "Foreign " : "";
        String acct = chbx.getValue();
        title.setText(foreign + acct + " Account Created");
    });
    return p1;
  }
}
```

The view talks to its controller via the button handler. The handler calls the controller's buttonPressed method, passing it the values of the choice box and the check box. After an account has been created, the controller will call the view's setTitle method, passing it the message to be displayed.

The controller is called CreationController. Its code appears in Listing 11-27. Its buttonPressed method calls the bank's newAccount method to create the account.

Listing 11-27. The CreationController Class

```
public class CreationController implements BankObserver {
    private Bank bank;
    private CreationView view;

    public CreationController(Bank bank) {
        this.bank = bank;
        bank.addObserver(BankEvent.NEW, this);
    }
```

427

```
   // methods called by the view
   void setView(CreationView view) {
      this.view = view;
   }
   public void buttonPressed(int type, boolean isforeign) {
      bank.newAccount(type+1, isforeign);
   }

   // method called by the model
   public void update(BankEvent e, BankAccount ba, int amt) {
      view.setTitle("Account " + ba.getAcctNum()
                                  + " created");
   }
}
```

The controller, like all controllers that follow the MVC pattern, is a model observer. Recall from Chapter 10 that Bank supports four events. The controller registers itself with the bank as an observer of NEW events. When the controller receives an update notification, it constructs a message for the view to display and calls the view's setTitle method.

The Account Information View

The "account information" view class is called InfoView. Its code appears in Listing 11-28.

Listing 11-28. The InfoView Class

```
public class InfoView {
   private Pane root;
   private TextField balfld = createTextField(true);
   private ChoiceBox<String> forbx = new ChoiceBox<>();
```

```java
public InfoView(InfoController controller) {
    controller.setView(this);
    root = createNodeHierarchy(controller);
}

public Pane root() {
    return root;
}

public void setBalance(String s) {
    balfld.setText(s);
}

public void setForeign(boolean b) {
    String s = b ? "Foreign" : "Domestic";
    forbx.setValue(s);
}

private Pane createNodeHierarchy(InfoController cont) {
    ... // Create the hierarchy, with p1 as the root.

    depbtn.setOnAction(e ->
            controller.depositButton(depfld.getText()));
    loanbtn.setOnAction(e ->
            respfld.setText(controller.loanButton(
                                    loanfld.getText())));
    forbtn.setOnAction(e ->
            controller.foreignButton(forbx.getValue()));
    selectbtn.setOnAction(e ->
            controller.selectButton(selectfld.getText()));

    return p1;
}
}
```

The view has four buttons, and the handler for each one calls a different controller method. Note that the values sent to the controller methods are strings even if the values denote numbers. The controller is responsible for translating a value to its proper type because it understands how the value is to be used.

The loan authorization button is different from the others in that it requests a value from the model. Thus its controller method is not void. The view displays the return value in its "loan response" text field.

The view's controller is called InfoController. Its code appears in Listing 11-29. It has a method for each button of the view; each method performs the necessary actions on the model for its button. For example, the depositButton method calls the bank's deposit method. The selectButton method retrieves the BankAccount object for the current account, and tells the view to set the displayed value of the balance text field and ownership choice box.

Listing 11-29. The InfoController Class

```
public class InfoController implements BankObserver {
    private Bank bank;
    private int current = 0;
    private InfoView view;

    public InfoController(Bank bank) {
        this.bank = bank;
        bank.addObserver(BankEvent.DEPOSIT, this);
        bank.addObserver(BankEvent.INTEREST, this);
        bank.addObserver(BankEvent.SETFOREIGN, this);
    }

    // methods called by the view
    public void setView(InfoView view) {
        this.view = view;
    }
```

```java
   public void depositButton(String s) {
      int amt = Integer.parseInt(s);
      bank.deposit(current, amt);
   }
   public String loanButton(String s) {
      int loanamt = Integer.parseInt(s);
      boolean result = bank.authorizeLoan(current, loanamt);
      return result ? "APPROVED" : "DENIED";
   }
   public void foreignButton(String s) {
      boolean b = s.equals("Foreign") ? true : false;
      bank.setForeign(current, b);
   }
   public void selectButton(String s) {
      current = Integer.parseInt(s);
      view.setBalance(
                Integer.toString(bank.getBalance(current)));
      String owner = bank.getAccount(current).isForeign() ?
                                       "Foreign" : "Domestic";
      view.setForeign(bank.isForeign(current));
   }

   // method called by the model
   public void update(BankEvent e, BankAccount ba, int amt) {
      if (e == BankEvent.SETFOREIGN &&
            ba.getAcctNum() == current)
         view.setForeign(ba.isForeign());
      else if (e == BankEvent.INTEREST ||
            ba.getAcctNum() == current)
         view.setBalance(
                Integer.toString(bank.getBalance(current)));
   }
}
```

431

The controller registers itself as the observer of three bank events: DEPOSIT, INTEREST, and SETFOREIGN. Its update method checks its first argument to determine which event caused the update. For an INTEREST event, the controller gets the balance of the current account and sends it to the view's setBalance method. For a DEPOSIT or SETFOREIGN event, the controller checks to see if the affected account is the current account. If so, it gets the balance (or ownership) of the current account and sends it to the view.

The All Accounts View

The "all accounts" view class is called AllView. Listing 11-30 gives its code. The handler for the Add Interest button simply calls the controller's interestButton method. When the controller decides to refresh the display of accounts, it calls the view's setAccounts method.

Listing 11-30. The AllView Class

```
public class AllView {
   private Pane root;
   TextArea accts = new TextArea();

   public AllView(AllController controller) {
      controller.setView(this);
      root = createNodeHierarchy(controller);
   }

   public Pane root() {
      return root;
   }

   public void setAccounts(String s) {
      accts.setText(s);
   }
```

```
private Pane createNodeHierarchy(AllController cont) {
    accts.setPrefColumnCount(22);
    accts.setPrefRowCount(9);

    Button intbtn = new Button("Add Interest");
    intbtn.setOnAction(e -> cont.interestButton());

    VBox p1 = new VBox(8);
    p1.setAlignment(Pos.TOP_CENTER);
    p1.setPadding(new Insets(10));
    Label title = new Label("Manage All Accounts");
    double size = title.getFont().getSize();
    title.setFont(new Font(size*2));
    title.setTextFill(Color.GREEN);
    p1.getChildren().addAll(title, accts, intbtn);
    return p1;
  }
}
```

The view displays the list of accounts in a text box. The problem with this design decision is that a single account value cannot be updated individually. The setAccounts method must therefore replace the entire list with a new one. The next two sections will examine other controls that will produce a better implementation.

The controller is called AllController. Its code appears in Listing 11-31. The controller is an observer of all four Bank events. Whenever an event of any type occurs, the controller refreshes the displayed accounts by calling the method refreshAccounts. This method iterates through the bank accounts and creates a string that appends their toString values. It then sends this string to the view.

Listing 11-31. The AllController Class

```
public class AllController implements BankObserver {
   private Bank bank;
   private AllView view;

   public AllController(Bank bank) {
      this.bank = bank;
      bank.addObserver(BankEvent.NEW, this);
      bank.addObserver(BankEvent.DEPOSIT, this);
      bank.addObserver(BankEvent.SETFOREIGN, this);
      bank.addObserver(BankEvent.INTEREST, this);
   }

   // methods called by the view
   public void setView(AllView view) {
      this.view = view;
      refreshAccounts(); // initially populate the text area
   }
   public void interestButton() {
      bank.addInterest();
   }

   // method called by the model
   public void update(BankEvent e, BankAccount ba, int amt) {
      refreshAccounts();
   }

   private void refreshAccounts() {
      StringBuffer result = new StringBuffer();
      for (BankAccount ba : bank)
         result.append(ba + "\n");
      view.setAccounts(result.toString());
   }
}
```

Observable List Views

Using a text area to implement the list of all accounts is unsatisfying: it looks bad, and it needs to be completely refreshed even if a single account changes. JavaFX has a control, ListView, that is more satisfactory. Figure 11-8 shows a screenshot of it in the "All Accounts" view.

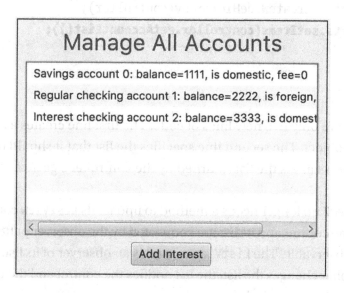

Figure 11-8. The Manage All Accounts screen

The difference between a list view and a text area is that the list view displays the contents of a Java List object. Each line of the list view corresponds to an element of the list, and displays the result of calling the toString method of that element.

The classes AllView2 and AllController2 rewrite AllView and AllController to use the ListView control. Listing 11-32 gives the code for *AllView2*, with new code in bold.

435

Listing 11-32. The AllView2 Class

```
public class AllView2 {
   private Pane root;
   ListView<BankAccount> accts = new ListView<>();

   public AllView2(AllController2 controller) {
      root = createNodeHierarchy(controller);
      accts.setItems(controller.getAccountList());
   }
   ...
}
```

There are only two new lines of code. The first line creates a new
ListView object. The second line specifies the list that it should display,
which in this case is the list returned by the controller's getAccountList
method.

AllView2 no longer needs a method to update its ListView control.
Instead, the control and its list are connected by the observer pattern. The
list is an observable. The ListView control is an observer of its list. When
the controller changes the list, the list notifies the control and the control
updates itself automatically.

This feature simplifies the view–controller interaction. The controller
no longer needs to explicitly manage the view updating. When the model
notifies the controller that the accounts have changed, the controller only
needs to modify its list. The view figures out the rest.

The code for the controller is named AllController2, and appears
in Listing 11-33. The variable accounts holds the observable list
of BankAccount objects. The JavaFX class FXCollections contains
several static factory methods for creating observable objects; the
method observableArrayList creates an observable list that wraps an
ArrayList object.

Listing 11-33. The AllController2 Class

```
public class AllController2 implements BankObserver {
   private Bank bank;
   private ObservableList<BankAccount> accounts
                 = FXCollections.observableArrayList();

   public AllController2(Bank bank) {
      this.bank = bank;
      bank.addObserver(BankEvent.NEW, this);
      bank.addObserver(BankEvent.DEPOSIT, this);
      bank.addObserver(BankEvent.SETFOREIGN, this);
      bank.addObserver(BankEvent.INTEREST, this);
      for (BankAccount ba : bank)
        accounts.add(ba); // initially populate the list
   }

   public ObservableList<BankAccount> getAccountList() {
      return accounts;
   }

   public void interestButton() {
      bank.addInterest();
   }

   public void update(BankEvent e, BankAccount ba, int amt) {
      if (e == BankEvent.INTEREST)
         refreshAllAccounts();
      else if (e == BankEvent.NEW)
         accounts.add(ba);
      else {
        int i = accounts.indexOf(ba);
        refreshAccount(i);
      }
   }
```

```
private void refreshAccount(int i) {
    // a no-op, to force the list to notify its observer
    accounts.set(i, accounts.get(i));
}

private void refreshAllAccounts() {
    for (int i=0; i<accounts.size(); i++)
        refreshAccount(i);
}
}
```

The controller observes four kinds of event, and its update method performs a different action based on the event. For an INTEREST event, the controller calls refreshAllAccounts, so that the view will redisplay each element of the list. For a NEW event, the controller adds the new bank account to the list. For DEPOSIT and SETFOREIGN events, the controller refreshes the list element having the specified account number.

Note that a DEPOSIT or SETFOREIGN event changes the state of a list element, but does not actually change the list. This is a problem, because the list will not notify the view unless it changes. The refreshAccount method solves the problem by setting the new value of a list element to be the same as the old value. Although that operation has no effect on the list element, the list recognizes it as a change to the list, and notifies the view to redisplay the element.

Observable Table Views

The ListView control displays the information about each BankAccount object in a single cell. It would be more visually pleasing if the account information could be displayed as a table, with each value in its own cell. This is the purpose of the TableView control. Figure 11-9 shows a screenshot of the view revised to use a TableView control.

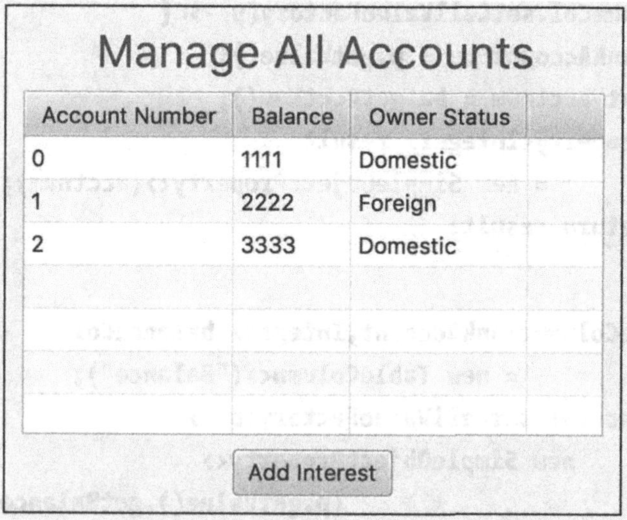

Figure 11-9. *Manage All Accounts as a table view*

This view is named *AllView3*, and its code appears in Listing 11-34. The variable accts is now of type TableView. A TableView control observes a list, the same as ListView. Its method setItems connects the control with that list. Because the mechanism is exactly the same as with the ListView control, AllView3 can use the controller AllController2 the same as AllView2.

Listing 11-34. The AllView3 Class

```
public class AllView3 {
   private Pane root;
   TableView<BankAccount> accts = new TableView<>();

   public AllView3(AllController2 controller) {
      root = createNodeHierarchy(controller);

      TableColumn<BankAccount,Integer> acctnumCol
            = new TableColumn<>("Account Number");
```

```
acctnumCol.setCellValueFactory(p -> {
   BankAccount ba = p.getValue();
   int acctnum = ba.getAcctNum();
   Property<Integer> result
         = new SimpleObjectProperty<>(acctnum);
   return result;
});

TableColumn<BankAccount,Integer> balanceCol
         = new TableColumn<>("Balance");
balanceCol.setCellValueFactory(p ->
      new SimpleObjectProperty<>
                        (p.getValue().getBalance())));

TableColumn<BankAccount,String> foreignCol
         = new TableColumn<>("Owner Status");
foreignCol.setCellValueFactory(p -> {
   boolean isforeign = p.getValue().isForeign();
   String owner = isforeign ? "Foreign" : "Domestic";
   return new SimpleObjectProperty<>(owner);
});

accts.getColumns().addAll(acctnumCol, balanceCol,
                        foreignCol);
accts.setItems(controller.getAccountList());
accts.setPrefSize(300, 200);
}
...
}
```

The difference between TableView and ListView is that a TableView control has a collection of TableColumn objects. The method getColumns returns this collection.

A TableColumn object has a header string, which is passed into its constructor. A TableColumn object also has a "cell value factory." The argument to this object is a method that computes the display value of the cell for a given list element. The argument p to the method denotes an element of the observable list, which here is an object that wraps BankAccount. Its method getValue returns the wrapped BankAccount object. The SimpleObjectProperty class creates a property from its argument object.

For example, consider the first lambda expression in Listing 11-34, which computes the value of the column acctnumCol.

```
p -> {
    BankAccount ba = p.getValue();
    int acctnum = ba.getAcctNum();
    Property<Integer> result =
                new SimpleObjectProperty<>(acctnum);
    return result;
}
```

This lambda expression unwraps p, extracts the account number from the unwrapped bank account, wraps the value as a property, and returns it. The lambda expression can be expressed more succinctly as follows:

```
p -> new SimpleObjectProperty<>(p.getValue().getAcctNum())
```

Summary

The *MVC design rule* states that each class in a program should have either model, view, or controller responsibilities. Designing programs in this way can require discipline. Instead of writing a single class to perform a task you might need to write three classes, so as to separate the model, view, and controller aspects of the task. Although creating these classes will undoubtedly require more effort, they come with significant benefits. The separated concerns make the program more modular and more easily modifiable, and therefore more in line with the fundamental design principle.

The *MVC pattern* describes an effective way to organize the model, view, and controller classes. According to the pattern, a program will have one model and possibly several views. Each view has its own controller, and uses the controller as a mediator to help it communicate with the model. Each controller has a reference to its view and to the model, so that it can send view requests to the model and model updates to the view. The model, however, knows nothing about the controllers and views. Instead, it communicates with them via the observer pattern.

The MVC pattern choreographs an intricate dance between the model, controllers, and views. The purpose of this dance is to support flexibility and modifiability of the program. In particular, the views are independent of each other; you can add and remove a view from an MVC program without impacting the other views.

This flexibility has enormous value. This chapter gave several examples of commercial MVC-based software—such as Excel, pdf viewers, and file managers—and describes features they have that are possible because of their MVC architecture.

Although this chapter has given enthusiastic support for the MVC pattern, the reality is that the pattern has no single agreed-upon definition. The definition given in this chapter is just one of several ways that have been used to organize models, views, and controllers. Regardless of their differences, however, the central feature of all MVC definitions is their following use of the observer pattern: *Controllers make update requests to the model, and the model notifies its observers of the resulting state changes.* I prefer using the controllers as model observers, but it is also possible to use the views, or even a combination of views and controllers. There are also different approaches for how a view can be connected to its controller.

As with all the design patterns in this book, there are always tradeoffs to be made. A good designer will adjust the connections among the MVC components to fit the needs of a given program. In general, the more deeply you understand how and why the MVC pattern works, the more freedom you will have to make the adjustments that will lead you to the best possible design.

Index

A

Abstract classes
  AbstractBankAccount
    class, 94, 96
  bank account classes,
    version 7, 98–101
  banking demo, 100
  CheckingAccount class, 101–102
  deposit methods, 93
  method of BankClient, 97–98
  RegularChecking class, 102–103
  SavingsAccount class, 96–97

Abstraction rule
  DataManager1 *vs.* DataManager2
    classes, 78–79
  DataManager2 class, 77–78
  DataManager3 class, 79–80

AccountCreationWindow class,
  325–326, 376, 380–381

Adapter classes, 237

Adapter pattern
  analogous situation, 241
  ArrayAsList class, 243–244
  asList method, 242
  class diagram, 241
  stack class, 242
  wrapper classes, 240

addInterest method, 58, 91–93, 119
addObserver method, 362
addRecipes method, 341
Agile methodology, 2
AllController class, 433–434
AllView class, 432–433
AndPredicate class, 317, 319, 321
Anonymous inner classes, 140–141
Application Program
    Interface (API), 4

B

Bank class, 354
Banking demo
  adapters
    BankAccountAdapter
      class, 266
    FBIAcctInfo interface,
      264–265
    FBIClient class, 267–268
    LoanAdapter class, 266–267
    Loan class, 264–265
  JavaFX interface, 423
    AllController class, 434
    AllView class, 432–433
    CreationController
      class, 427–428

E. Sciore, *Java Program Design*, https://doi.org/10.1007/978-1-4842-4143-1

P, Q

R

Printed in the United States
By Bookmasters